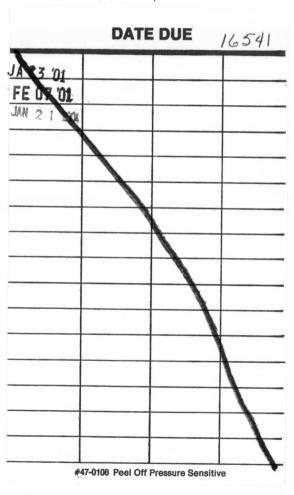

DIVIDED GOVERNMENT

Studies in American Political Institutions and Public Policy
General Editor: James W. Ceaser, University of Virginia

Presenting works on contemporary American politics that address the question of how institutions and policies can best function to sustain a healthy liberal democratic government in the United States.

Congress's Permanent Minority? Republicans in the U.S. House
     by William F. Connelly, Jr., and John J. Pitney, Jr.
Hostile Takeover: The House Republican Party, 1980–1995
     by Douglas L. Koopman
Divided Government: Change, Uncertainty, and the Constitutional Order
     edited by Peter F. Galderisi, with Roberta Q. Herzberg and Peter McNamara

DIVIDED GOVERNMENT

Change, Uncertainty, and the Constitutional Order

Edited by
PETER F. GALDERISI
with
Roberta Q. Herzberg
and
Peter McNamara

ROWMAN & LITTLEFIELD PUBLISHERS, INC.
Lanham • Boulder • New York • London

ROWMAN & LITTLEFIELD PUBLISHERS, INC.

Published in the United States of America
by Rowman & Littlefield Publishers, Inc.
4720 Boston Way, Lanham, Maryland 20706

3 Henrietta Street
London WC2E 8LU, England

British Cataloging in Publication Information Available

Library of Congress Cataloging-in-Publication Data

Divided government : change, uncertainty, and the constitutional
order / edited by Peter F. Galderisi, with Roberta Q. Herzberg and Peter
McNamara.
p.   cm. — (Studies in American political institutions and
public policy)
Includes bibliographical references and index.
1. Party affiliation—United States.   2. Political parties—United
States.   3. United States—Politics and government—1993–
I. Galderisi, Peter F.   II. Herzberg, Roberta Q.   III. McNamara, Peter.
IV. Series.
JK2261.G35   1996   324.273—dc20   96-22602   CIP

ISBN 0-8476-8295-1 (cloth : alk. paper)
ISBN 0-8476-8296-X (pbk. : alk. paper)

Printed in the United States of America

∞ ™ The paper used in this publication meets the minimum requirements of
American National Standard for Information Sciences—Permanence of Paper
for Printed Library Materials, ANSI Z39.48-1984.

To the memory of
H. Preston Thomas—
colleague, mentor, and friend

Contents

List of Illustrations   ix

Preface   *Peter F. Galderisi*   xi

Introduction: Divided Government Past and Present   1
    Peter F. Galderisi

1   Divided Government in Historical Perspective, 1789–1996   9
    Joel H. Silbey

2   The Causes and Consequences of Divided Government:
    Lessons of 1992–1994   35
    Morris P. Fiorina

3   Divided Government and the 1994 Elections   61
    Gary C. Jacobson

4   The Road to Divided Government: Paved without Intention   85
    John R. Petrocik and Joseph Doherty

5   It's the Constitution, Stupid! Congress, the President,
    Divided Government, and Policymaking   109
    Leroy N. Rieselbach

6   The New Deal, the Modern Presidency, and Divided
    Government   135
    Sidney M. Milkis

7   Unity versus Division: The Effect of Divided Government
    on Policy Development   173
    Roberta Q. Herzberg

8 Doing One's Job: A Constitutional Principle and a Political
  Strategy for an Uncertain Future 191
    Peter McNamara

Bibliography 213

Index 229

About the Contributors 239

Illustrations

Tables

1.1. Episodes of Divided Government, 1825–1957   12
2.1. Patterns of Party Control in the States, 1992–1994   39
2.2. Partisan Control of State Legislatures, 1990–1994   40
2.3. Americans' Opinions on Federal Power   56
3.1. Percentage of Districts Voting Republican in 1994 House Elections   73
4.1. Support for Divided Government, 1972–1994   87
4.2. Ticket-Splitting and Attitudes toward Divided Government   94
4.3. Issues Recalled from the 1992 House Campaigns   99
4.4. Voting for Republican Congressmembers as a Function of Campaign Issues   99
4.5. Ticket-Splitting as a Function of House Campaign Issues and Voters' Party Identification   101
4.6. Ticket-Splitting as a Function of House Campaign Issues and Most Important National Issue   102
4.7. Support for Divided Government and Issue Agendas in House Campaigns and the Nation Generally   103
4.8. Support for Divided Government as a Function of House Campaign Issues and Voters' Party Identification   104
5.1. Presidential Success in Congress, under Unified and Divided Government, 1953–1994   115
5.2. Clinton Victories in the House in the 103rd Congress   116
5.3. Clinton Victories in the Senate in the 103rd Congress   117
5.4. Clinton Losses in the 103rd Congress   118

Figures

1. Presidential Vote and Number of House Seats Won, 1960–1992   92

ix

2.   Off-Year Changes in House Seats as a Function of
      On-Year Deviations from the Party Average, 1960–1992   93
3.   Support for Divided Government and Perceived
      Interparty Policy Distance   97
4.   Policy Differences and Divided Government: Moderates
      and Nonmoderates   98

Preface

Peter F. Galderisi

In the fall of 1994, Professor Roberta Herzberg and I, with the help of our colleagues at Utah State University, and with the support of a grant from the Milton R. Merrill fund, organized a panel originally slated to study the 1994 midterm congressional elections (which, at the time, most assumed would maintain unified Democratic control of Congress and the presidency). As we discussed potential participants and topics, we quickly realized that our focus on the electoral process and outcomes of 1994 would be too theoretically limited. Moreover, it would not serve our students well. We instead decided to use this forum to discuss the congressional election process within the broader context of the causes and effects of divided (and unified) government. Even assuming a Democratic victory in the fall (an assumption that would, of course, prove false), we felt that our students would gain a better understanding of electoral processes and policy outcomes by focusing on this broader theoretical context. Thus, the choice of the title of the workshop and this volume, and the selection of participants and topics.

I wish to thank James Ceaser, Stephen Wrinn, Julie Kuzneski, and the editorial staff at Rowman & Littlefield for their guidance in completing this project. Rachel Hurst and Stephanie White deserve special thanks for their assistance in the production of the manuscript, as do J. Todd Thorpe and Jeannie Lyn Johnson for their invaluable and timely research support. My most personal thanks go to Holly Gottschalk, whose patience and moral support carried me through the long hours and deadline anxieties associated with editing this volume.

Introduction:
Divided Government Past and Present

Peter F. Galderisi

In 1992, Morris Fiorina published a volume on the subject of divided government.[1] Given the political realities of the times, a national government hopelessly divided between a Republican president and a Democratic Congress, interest in the subject of divided government was high, and sales of Fiorina's volume flourished. The post–Persian Gulf War popularity of George Bush, coupled with the seeming invincibility of congressional incumbents (which, among other factors, would help to sustain Democratic control), heightened this sense of inevitability. Divided partisan control of the elective branches of government was more than just an academic curiosity. The policy effects of division were evident to even the most casual observer of the political scene. Gridlock was a central subject of debate in the 1992 elections. President Bush, after all, had vetoed over forty legislative acts and was overturned only once. And evidence suggests that his veto threats often stopped legislation from reaching the House and Senate floors unaltered.

Then, the unthinkable happened. Republican control of the presidency ended; Democratic control of Congress was maintained (although with the highest House membership turnover in over four decades). The national government was unified for the first time in twelve years—and sales of Fiorina's book tumbled. More than just a turn of events for one author, this drop in sales indicates a much greater conceptual problem. Many academics, journalists, and other surveyors of the political scene have had too limited a view of divided government. We have concentrated unduly on *divided partisan control* of elective institutions and have assumed that control by one party would end the political stalemate between the executive and the legislative branches. Unified party control, in effect, lessened our academic curiosity in the fall of 1992 because the original problem seemed to disappear. Academic curiosity, unfortunately, was the victim of both causal and historical tunnel vision—the former because divided government is more than just the outcome of divided party control and, in fact, can operate even when partisan unity exists; the latter because divided government, even in its limited partisan sense, is not unique to the Reagan-Bush era. Different parties had controlled the presidency and Congress in the past, and there was no reason to believe that divided control of these institutions would not recur in the future. Of course, most predictions of a return to divided control were based on the expectation of a 1996 Republican recapture of the White House which, after all, Bill Clinton had won with only 43 percent of the 1992 popular vote. The surprising Republican capture of both the House and the Senate in 1994 moved up the time line. It quickly resurrected the interest of academics and journalists in the subject of divided government—and boosted Fiorina's sales.

Prior to the 1994 elections, however, the limitations of our views on divided government were already becoming clear. If divided partisan control caused gridlock, then, it could be assumed, unified control would produce a steady flow of legislation. Presidential proposals would meet with legislative favor, and legislative actions would not be subject to presidential veto. The latter was certainly true during the first two years of Bill Clinton's presidency, although we can probably attribute that more to the president's lack of confrontational style, and his concentrated concern on a few major policy issues, allowing Congress unhindered control of most legislative debate. The success of his policy initiatives, from executive orders on the treatment of gays in the military to legislative proposals for a massive overhaul of the nation's health care, was, however, in question from the first day of his administration. And his only early major policy victory—the enactment of the North American Free Trade Agreement (NAFTA)— was helped by the support of many (and mostly Republican) former presidents and administrative officials, and by the votes of a majority of Republican, not Democratic, congressmembers. Granted, George Bush, a Republican president, may not have been able to muster enough support among otherwise recalcitrant congressional Democrats to secure NAFTA's victory.[2] But the very vision of a Democratic majority in Congress in direct, and often vocal, opposition to a president of their own party certainly cast doubt on the traditional views of the positive effects of unified party control and may have actually helped the Republicans capture Congress in 1994.

Obviously, partisan differences and similarities may be relevant to an understanding of divided (or unified) government. But party may in itself be neither a sufficient nor even a necessary condition to that understanding. *Divided governmental institutions* originated in the U.S. Constitution, a document that, until the ratification of the Twelfth Amendment, did not even formally consider partisan divisions. The executive, legislative, and judicial branches were separated from each other in more than functionality. Differing constituencies and terms of office created the institutional prerequisites for conflict. Even the legislative branch was separated into two chambers. House members would represent, in temperament and geographic proximity, a public that would directly evaluate their performance every two years. Senators would represent the broader interests of the states; they would be given six years to deliberate on which policies best suited those interests and, it was hoped, the interests of the nation at large. Both chambers would be necessary for legislative action. Only presidents and judges would by elective or appointive procedure represent a truly national constituency. Even with the expansion of the franchise and more direct public participation in the selection of senators and the president, the constitutional scheme of separation of powers and checks and balances continues each institution's ability to check or temper the excesses of the others.

The latter point is worth developing. Separate governing institutions, separately formed and subject to evaluation at separate times, can make quick and deliberate policy change difficult. Separate partisan control of each institution can certainly increase that difficulty. But the process is not necessarily a confrontational one; the outcome not necessarily gridlock. An elaborate system of checks and balances, although cumbersome and slow, can also lead to compromise and the development of policy outcomes built on consensus. The politics of consensus is not ruled out by the original constitutional design. Many would argue that it was, in fact, a conscious part of that plan.[3] Nor is consensus politics ruled out by partisan division. As David Mayhew has pointed out, the ability of presidents and congresses to reach agreement seems little different in periods of divided party control than in periods of unified party control.[4]

Certainly, rigid adherence to partisan divisions can at times exacerbate the difficulties inherent in the original constitutional design, particularly when realigning forces increase the polarization between the parties, which, in turn, may increase each party's refusal to compromise with the other (particularly during election cycles). Certainly, the partisan unification of the executive and legislative (and eventually judicial) branches that follows the completion of a realignment can usher in a period of rapid policy change. But lest we assume that such *partisan* unification of necessity leads to the same level of *institutional* unification, we should be reminded of the fact that Franklin Roosevelt vetoed more legislation per year than any other twentieth-century president, and may have done more to place limits on the Democratic Congress's activity than did the decisions of a Supreme Court defined by previous Republican administrations.[5] Similarly, there are no guarantees that a Republican presidential victory in 1996, even by a recent Senate majority leader, coupled with the continuation of Republican congressional control, will move the GOP congressional agenda along as far as some may wish.

*   *   *

The authors included in this volume represent the full spectrum of expertise on the subject of divided government. Morris Fiorina, Gary Jacobson, and John Petrocik were chosen for their expertise on electoral and partisan processes, and because they have written widely on the causes and consequences of divided partisan control. In his essay, Morris Fiorina argues that, in spite of seemingly major electoral upheavals in 1992 and 1994, incumbency advantage, the dynamics of policy deliberations (under either divided or unified partisan control), and public perceptions of government maintain a remarkable continuity with the past. Divided partisan control at the state level continues unabated. He suggests that "those who yearn for energetic, effective government probably should shift their focus away from the simple question of party control to the more complicated question of how to build majorities for the ends they espouse." Gary Jacobson discusses the reasons for the long-term Democratic control of the House of Representatives, and how the tide against incumbency, coupled with the Republicans' successful attempt to nationalize the election, reversed that control in 1994.[6] He also suggests why our thinking about future congressional elections may have to change. On a similar note, John Petrocik, along with Joseph Doherty, examines the conventional wisdom that voters choose to create institutions with divided partisan control. In their detailed analysis, Petrocik and Doherty argue that the voters' split-party preferences may have more to do with the issues most relevant to the different campaigns than with a conscious attempt to moderate the potential excesses of each party.

Leroy Rieselbach and Sidney Milkis are well known for their analyses of the institutional factors influencing the decision-making processes of the legislative and executive branches of government and the changing nature of the relationship between those branches. Rieselbach asserts that policy gridlock is a function of the constitutional scheme of separation of powers and that gridlock can be exacerbated by a host of factors, including, but not limited to, divided partisan control. Had it not been for the extraconstitutional peculiarities of Senate procedures, President Clinton's agenda might have actually met with a reasonable level of success. Sidney Milkis discusses how changes in the partisan nature of presidential politics since the New Deal created the conditions for gridlock regardless of which parties control the separate governmental institutions. The institutionalization of the presidency effectively divorces its officeholders from the rigors of partisan unity. Roberta Herzberg is a policy specialist who has researched in detail the failure of Clinton's main policy initiative, health care reform, in spite of unified partisan control. In her essay, she explores the differing dynamics of presidential, senatorial, House, and electoral politics which have contributed to the major gridlock story of 1995–1996—the battle over the budget. The difficulties of policymaking may extend well beyond those inherent in the separation of powers. Real answers to policy gridlock need to take into account the disaggregated and complex nature of congressional lawmaking, including the influence of committees, subcommittees, and interest groups.

Peter McNamara is a theorist who understands the similarities and differences between our presidential democracy and more traditional parliamentary democracies. In his concluding essay, he returns us to our beginnings, discussing the constitutional origins of divided government, particularly the framers' views of separation of powers and partisanship. He then uses these views to reflect on the future of American politics, concluding that the best way to deal with divided government is for "officials to do their constitutionally assigned jobs."

I invited our first essayist, Joel Silbey, to help keep us political scientists historically honest. Eons ago, as I sat through his lectures on political history, I developed an interest in the politics of the past, which brought me to my interest in the politics of the present and future. Although I cannot fault him for my often unorthodox (and sometimes incorrect) views of the political world, I credit him for whatever sense of historical context I bring to my teaching and research. While the popular press was comparing 1994 to 1946, thereby warning the new and eager Republican majority against premature celebration,[7] I was instead lecturing about 1994's similarities to the midterm election of 1894, when the Democratic Party, left with its more populist and radical base, began its slide to long-term minority status.[8] Of course, as Silbey argues in the opening essay, the nature and relevance of partisanship at the end of the twentieth century are not quite what they once were. He argues that the study of divided partisan control of national governing institutions is more relevant to an understanding of electoral and policy politics during an era of strong partisanship characteristic of the end of the nineteenth century, than to an understanding of the dealigning politics of the late twentieth century.

Parties may have lost much (although not all) of their ability to control and unite office seekers, office winners, and voters with any degree of depth or consistency. And if the contests for the 1996 Republican presidential nomination are any indication, the exigencies of modern electoral politics can heighten division even among fellow institutional travelers. Republican policy deliberation in the Senate in 1995 and early 1996 was conditioned as much by the necessity of individual senators to score points against each other (and thereby attract primary and caucus participants) as by their reaction to a Democratic president's agenda. The ability of partisan unity or division to alter the natural tendencies of a divided governmental system may indeed be weakened. Divided government, in its broader institutional context, however, will continue as a fundamental part of our political landscape, regardless of the victors in 1996.

Notes

1. Morris Fiorina, *Divided Government* (New York: MacMillan, 1992).
2. Ronald Reagan, however, accomplished this seemingly impossible task with major tax reform in spite of a Democratic House majority.
3. See, for example, Forrest McDonald, *Novus Ordo Seclorum: The Intellectual Origins of the Constitution* (Lawrence: University Press of Kansas, 1985).
4. David R. Mayhew, *Divided We Govern: Party Control, Lawmaking, and Investigations, 1946–1990* (New Haven: Yale University Press, 1991).
5. Grover Cleveland vetoed 584 legislative acts in his two disjointed terms, a higher yearly average than FDR's.

6. As part of his discussion, Jacobson argues that for years the Republican Party seemed better suited to national constituencies and concerns (and the presidency), while the Democrats were viewed more favorably as the party of local needs (and the Congress). Interestingly, this division of partisan power may have unintentionally reinforced the original constitutional logic of those separate institutions (although the framers would certainly not have predicted or desired the modern level of congressional parochialism).

7. For example, see the analysis in the *Wall Street Journal*, 4 January 1995, A12.

8. Of course, Patrick Buchanan's fairly successful 1996 Republican nomination campaign demonstrates that both parties can appeal to a floating, populist core. A permanent alignment of these voters with either party seems rather unlikely.

Chapter One

Divided Government in Historical Perspective, 1789–1996

Joel H. Silbey

Research into America's experience with divided government has deservedly become both a preoccupation and a growth industry among scholars—an industry that is driven by the phenomenon's recent centrality to our political situation and our expectation that it will, more likely than not, continue to be important in the immediate future. The fascination with the topic is further heightened, I suggest, by the frequent comparisons that are made between the present political situation and past patterns of government control, which seem to underscore sharply the unique qualities of the current age so far as the extent and intractability of the divisions between Congress and the presidency are concerned. As Morris Fiorina has pointed out in his book, *Divided Government*, in forty-four of sixty elections between 1832 and 1952, that is, 73 percent of the time, the same political party controlled both the presidency and both houses of Congress. Since the second election of Dwight Eisenhower in 1956, in contrast, we have had such a unified partisan situation seven out of twenty times, in only 35 percent of the time.[1] And Eisenhower, as James Sundquist notes, was the first newly elected president in seventy-two years, that is, since Grover Cleveland's inauguration in 1885, to confront a Congress in which even one house was in the hands of the opposition.[2] It seems clear, as we contemplate that long record, that the political uniqueness of the period since the mid-1950s stands out in bold relief.

Nevertheless, divided government did not begin in the United States when Harry Truman faced off against the Republican-controlled Eight-

9

ieth Congress at his midterm State of the Union address in 1947, or when Dwight Eisenhower met a Congress controlled by the Democratic opposition ten years later.[3] There were a great many earlier instances of such divided moments in our history. Some occurred when both houses of Congress were in the hands of a party other than the one that controlled the presidency; others, when the presidency and only one house were in different partisan hands. Some happened at the outset of a presidential administration; others resulted from midterm elections to Congress. In their number and variety, they provide a rich resource of comparative cases to examine.

There has been little scholarly description of this chronologically broader range of cases nor much systematic analysis of any similarities, differences, meanings, or comparative situations rising out of them, particularly those that go much further back in time than most analysts of divided government have ventured. I suggest that it is time to extend our range and bring the insights of American political historians into the discussion about the nature and importance of divided government. Widening our knowledge longitudinally in this way is a useful exercise for a number of reasons: it helps fill in and deepen our understanding by providing more data than we have been used to working with; it allows us to assess more extensively than we have the similarities and differences between earlier episodes and those in the present; and it can lead to a more general, less time-bound, understanding of the phenomenon of divided government and its role in American political life.

The Historical Pattern

After the sweeping claim, made at the beginning of these remarks, about the interpretive relevance of the past, what follows is, at best, only a beginning, and perhaps a skimpy one at that, toward organizing what is in the record, and toward thinking about divided government during the many years before Dwight Eisenhower had to deal with those two indomitable Democrats, Senate leader Lyndon Johnson and Speaker Sam Rayburn in the mid-1950s.[4] What were these earlier cases? What was the particular and more general situation in each? What happened, and what data and generalizations can we draw from them?

The first instinct when we dip into the past is to broaden even further our definitions of divided government to incorporate some of the numerous other conflicts that dot the historical record. Quite obviously, divided government appears to be an inevitable consequence of American political realities from the very beginning of our history as a nation. The Constitution established an institutional framework of division between the separate branches of government. But that truism is only the beginning. From the outset, factionalism, sectionalism, and frequent internal conflict within political groups all created prime additional resources for subsequent divisiveness in the nation's governmental affairs.

Certainly, such realities and conflicts were sometimes as important as partisan differences in shaping and determining political events. The essence of governing in the United States has always been to find means to overcome these powerful institutional and political elements and to find ways of effectively managing complexity and potential fragmentation so as to accomplish, therefore, a lessening of the potential for one kind of divided government. Out of that need came the eventual formation of political parties and, as a result of their appearance and sweep, the beginning of the intellectual problem that we are exploring here. This allows us to ignore these other possibilities and focus only on the situations where the presidency and at least one house of Congress were controlled by different parties.

Before Eisenhower and the onset of our current understanding of divided government, I count twenty instances of such circumstances in what I will refer to as the premodern era, that is, from the beginnings of the development of a comprehensive national two-party system in the mid-1820s until the Second World War more than a century later[5] (table 1.1). In eight of these twenty instances, both houses of Congress were in the hands of the president's opponents, while in twelve, one house was so controlled. Eight occurred before the Civil War, in the administrations of Presidents John Quincy Adams, Andrew Jackson, John Tyler, James K. Polk, Zachary Taylor, Millard Fillmore, Franklin Pierce, and James Buchanan, that is, in sixteen of the thirty-six years between 1825 and 1861. In five of these eight instances, the other party controlled one house of Congress (usually the more volatile House of Representatives); in the other three—in the Adams, Taylor, and Fillmore years—the opposition Democrats controlled both houses. (The Adams instance, of course, occurred just as parties were emerging and clarifying what they were about; the Taylor and Fillmore instances, in the aftermath of the Democratic presidential split and three-party race of 1848, which cost the Democrats the victory they had expected given what was then the normal distribution of the nation's popular vote.)[6]

Joel H. Silbey

TABLE 1.1
Episodes of Divided Government, 1825–1957

President	Years	Congress	Controlling party	
			House	Senate
Phase I				
Adams	1827-1829	20th	Jackson	Jackson
Jackson	1833-1835	23rd	D	Opposition
Tyler	1843-1845	28th	D	W
Phase II				
Polk	1847-1849	30th	W	D
Taylor	1849-1851	31st	D	D
Fillmore	1851-1853	32nd	D	D
Pierce	1855-1857	34th	R	D
Buchanan	1859-1861	36th	R	D
Grant	1875-1877	44th	D	R
Hayes	1877-1879	45th	D	D
Hayes	1879-1881	46th	D	D
Arthur	1883-1885	48th	D	R
Cleveland	1885-1887	49th	D	R
Cleveland	1887-1889	50th	D	R
Harrison	1891-1893	52nd	D	R
Cleveland	1895-1897	54th	R	R
Phase III				
Taft	1911-1913	62nd	D	R
Wilson	1919-1921	66th	R	R
Hoover	1931-1933	72nd	D	D
Truman	1947-1949	80th	R	R

In the post-Civil War years until the end of the century, there were eight instances of divided government, in the administrations of Ulysses S. Grant, Rutherford B. Hayes, Chester A. Arthur, Grover Cleveland, Benjamin Harrison, and Cleveland again (that is, in sixteen of the twenty years between 1875 and 1895). Twice, under Hayes and Cleveland, the opposition controlled both houses. And Cleveland found the Senate under Republican control throughout the whole of his first term from 1885 to 1889.

Of the sixteen cases identified thus far, some divisions were quite decisive numerically; others involved either narrow partisan control of Congress or a very close presidential election. Several occurred during periods of electoral realignment; others not. Finally, in three of the administrations referred to, those of Zachary Taylor and his vice presidential successor, Millard Fillmore, from 1849 to 1853, and that of Rutherford B. Hayes, from 1877 to 1881, the incumbent presidents spent their whole administration with both houses of Congress controlled by the other party.

As can be gathered from this listing, in the nineteenth century, midterm congressional elections were usually the occasion for the creation of divided government. Of the sixteen instances, three occurred in the first years of an administration; all of the others, in the latter half of a president's term. Also, in the twentieth century, we find that in the more than half century before Eisenhower's second election in 1956, instances of divided government occurred (under William Howard Taft, Woodrow Wilson, Herbert Hoover, and Harry Truman) only in the last half of a president's term, a moment when the president's honeymoon had ended and some of his determination and energy had flagged as well.

Six of the presidents who lived with divided government in the years prior to 1950—John Quincy Adams in 1828, Grover Cleveland in 1888, Benjamin Harrison in 1892, William Howard Taft in 1912, Herbert Hoover in 1932, and Harry Truman in 1948—ran again at the end of their divided term. (And all but Truman lost).[7] Among those presidents who did not run again, some retired from politics, and others were denied renomination by their party. All of which suggests some sort of relationship, in these instances, between, on the one hand, divided government and, on the other, a changing electoral situation, presidential reputation, and subsequent electoral attractiveness. Such a relationship is quite different from our own time, and makes the Truman case analytically interesting as a mark of perhaps something new and different emerging on the American political landscape. But more on that in a moment.

I could explore these data even more. But let us turn to the crucial matter that has so concerned contemporary students of the divided government phenomenon. What was the impact of all of these potentially hostile political situations on the policy process and the activities of the federal government? To be sure, we begin by reaffirming the conventional wisdom that most of the cases I have listed belonged to an era when not much policy energy was expected, or to be had, from the federal government—certainly what was done in Washington never approached the most recent standards. There was, of course, much less congressional business in this premodern era. The number of bills considered and laws passed were far fewer than in the present, although there were significant increases from the beginning of the twentieth century. The length of congressional sessions was also significantly shorter than it is now.[8]

Nevertheless, the participants in the earlier moments of governmental division all believed that they had much to do in their everyday official activities, much to fight about, and much to achieve—or to prevent—in the policy area. And they were always conscious of how deeply divided they were from each other along partisan lines, in their policy commitments, and in their outlooks about the role of government, the nature of society, and what the nation's future looked like or should be. In short, the conventional wisdom about limits and expectations in this earlier period is, I suggest, only a partial truth. Premodern political confrontations had more substance to them than that of mere electoral calculation.

Mapping the Terrain

For analytic purposes, the premodern cases of divided government can be separated into three groups, or phases. Phase I, involving the cases of Adams, Jackson, and Tyler, occurred at the dawn of America's party system when the primitive and undeveloped state of the political parties resulted in a great deal of disarray on the political landscape. The party identification of congressmen was volatile, often quite unpredictable, and much less important than it was to become later on. Each of these early cases played itself out in terms of our classic expectations about divided government: constant battles between the president and Congress, accompanied by much tactical maneuvering to outwit each other, the growing use of the presidential veto, and an enormous and vicious acrimony in which each side cast what was at stake in the most polarized terms and brutally demonized all of the players on the other side.

In the 1820s, under President John Quincy Adams, the president's supporters lost control of both houses of the Twentieth Congress, "a state of things," Adams gloomily noted in his diary, which had "never before occurred under the Government of the United States."[9] The results were dire so far as the president was concerned. The Jacksonians in control on Capitol Hill proved to be "as bitter as wormwood in their opposition" to him.[10] The antiadministration forces, led by Senator Martin Van Buren of New York, as divided as they often were among themselves, made life hell for President Adams. They successfully hamstrung implementation of his ambitious program of nationalist development so well expressed in both his first annual message in 1825 and his extensive foreign policy initiatives. His policies were either not passed or not funded. His appointments to important international meetings were not confirmed. Just before the end of his single term in office, the Democrat-controlled Senate rejected the president's nominee for the Supreme Court.[11]

Under Adams's successor, Andrew Jackson, the political environment continued to contain an unstable congressional coalition even when the president's supporters allegedly controlled matters on the Hill. These years were dominated electorally by the continued shaking down of various political groups into different party homes and the clarifying of everybody's political identification. The results of the persistent political uncertainty were clear to see. The historian Alvin Lynn refers to "the frequent and galling legislative defeats suffered by Jackson and the Jacksonians" even when they ostensibly controlled Congress.[12] The leaders of the hostile groups that faced the president worked overtime to forestall Jackson's expansion of presidential power and his determination to get his way in executive appointments, in Indian affairs, over the Bank of the United States, and in the confrontation with South Carolina over the tariff and nullification. The conflict wound up amid the opposition's cries against the executive usurpation practiced by "King Andrew," with the Senate's refusal to confirm many of his nominees for office, and with its unprecedented and stinging formal censure of the president by roll call vote in 1834.[13]

In the Tyler administration, from 1841 onward, the congressional Whigs, led by Henry Clay, aggressively pushed a wide-ranging economic program against the president's opposition to much of it. This culminated in Tyler's extensive use of the presidential veto, a number of bitter personal confrontations in the White House between the president and the Whig leadership, and the Whig congressional caucus's formal reading of "His Accidency" out of the party of which he had always been, at best, a nominal member. Tyler then allied himself with various Democratic factions for the rest of his angry stay in office.[14] Congressmen, under the leadership of Senator Clay, never let up in their sniping, or in making frequent insistent, intrusive, and combative requests for information as a means of embarrassing the president. The Whig Congress climaxed their opposition by considering two crippling resolutions against the president: one a constitutional amendment to allow presidential vetoes to be overridden by a majority congressional vote, the other a proposal to impeach the president. The whole period was one of the most disruptive moments in all of the history of executive-legislative relations, including the first overriding of a presidential veto in 1845.[15]

In all of this, there were always serious policy initiatives at stake. As those involved in the battles saw it, most of these initiatives sought to establish a critical role for the central government in shaping and directing the national economy. In two cases, the party with the more aggressive policy agenda failed to get its way. In the third, under Jackson, the power of the presidential office was expanded into unprecedented channels, but at the cost of a most poisonous set of relations with the Senate. In all of this as well, the president's veto power came into its own, although Adams vetoed no bills because the hostile congressional coalition allowed few contentious matters to reach him. Jackson, in contrast, vetoed twelve and Tyler ten. Both of these figures were the highest by far since the ratification of the Constitution and, further, the highest until twelve years after the Civil War.[16]

These three Phase I episodes suggest, in their divisiveness and failure to find much common ground, an intense policy deadlock (so far as the more aggressive party in the two-sided contest believed) and, in the extraordinary bitterness and undercutting that occurred, the kind of image of divided government that has been presented in much of the scholarly literature. But these early instances involved much more. First, as a number of historians have demonstrated, the notion of legitimate opposition had not yet been internalized in American political culture in these years.[17] One did not recognize opponents, negotiate with them, learn how to work with them, or accept their being part of the process of governing. One sought, rather, to destroy one's opponents as illegitimate, threatening dangers to the republic. Second, Congress was always quite assertive against any claims to presidential power, phrasing its opposition in terms that went rhetorically well beyond the partisan situation. As a result, these early battles were cast in constitutional, not political, terms and always had much of that more far-reaching quality about them, a quality that went to the depths of the meaning of the American political experience and that seemed to justify trying to destroy the other side when one could.

Divided government in the American experience began, obviously, with the way people voted, the structure of electoral outcomes, and the reach and influence of political parties. Did the bitter, destructive quality of Phase I cases remain as, in the early 1840s, the American political nation matured and settled into a stronger institutional framework, more patterned popular voting, and an understanding that two-party sharing of government in some kind of cyclical pattern had become the nation's norm? In fact, after Tyler left office in 1845, we move into Phase II of the divided government experience, which includes the eleven cases in the rest of the nineteenth century, from Polk to the second Cleveland administration. This second phase was all completely bounded by the power of the partisan structure that had emerged to dominate American politics. It was characterized by the full formation and acceptance of national political parties with quite marked policy differences between them. The ideas of legitimate opposition, compromise, and the working out of matters through negotiation all became accepted political norms.

Each of these Phase II episodes, from James K. Polk's presidency onward, contained a familiar variety of experiences associated with divided government: much conflict between Congress and the president over policy matters and personnel, the failure of legislative initiatives, and, in most cases, the ultimate wearing down of an already tired administration in the latter half of its life course. Each contained, as well, a range of situations unique to its particular moment in time. Finally, in each case, the party holding the presidency lost the next election.[18]

James K. Polk, in the first half of his only term in office, had accomplished much with the assistance of a supportive Democratic congressional majority.[19] By the summer of 1846, he had successfully masterminded the passage of a range of economic and diplomatic legislation. His last two years in office, however, were quite different. From 1847 onward, he faced the backlash against an increasingly unpopular war with Mexico, the concomitant rise of the issue of slavery extension into the new territories acquired as a result of the war, and the maneuverings of a hostile House of Representatives led by a Whig speaker, Robert Winthrop of Massachusetts. These were years of particularly fierce partisanship, and it showed in Polk's relationships with Congress, exacerbated by his following Jackson's example and forcefully asserting himself as an unusually powerful chief executive. But this brief period of divided government occurred after Polk's main policy agenda had already been passed. Before the Whigs took command of the House, his legislative accomplishments were all in, and he had already faced stinging attacks on the floor of Congress, including Illinois Representative Abraham Lincoln's "Spot Resolutions" of 1847 against the war with Mexico.[20]

Nevertheless, the partisan division had important consequences. While the Whigs led the House, Polk faced difficulties working out the peace treaty with Mexico, and, in the most startling episode of all, he endured a Whig-sponsored resolution that passed the House 85 to 81, declaring that the Mexican War had been "unnecessarily and unconstitutionally begun by the President of the United States"—all of which reflected the intense bitterness between the parties that had become characteristic by the mid-1840s.[21]

In the Whig administrations of Taylor and Fillmore that followed Polk's presidency, with the Democrats in control on Capitol Hill, the political emphasis was somewhat different, focusing on the need to build cross-party coalitions in order to deal with the growing sectional crisis.[22] Both presidents were preoccupied with an increasingly intractable issue concerning slavery expansion which was beginning to break down party lines somewhat in favor of sectional factions. Congress was extremely divided in these years as the Mexican Cession problems led to the longest congressional sittings to that time. President Taylor pushed forward a set of proposals about the sectional issue that Congress would not accept, and leading congressmen offered proposals that the president rejected. At the same time, partisanship remained strong. As one historian has written, there was "a vigorous effort by the Democrats to split the Whigs into warring factions."[23] But this was mitigated by the fact that Taylor had little in the way of a partisan legislative program to push and usually indicated his willingness that Congress should take the legislative lead in areas of traditional policy-making.

Taylor's successor, Fillmore, largely contributed to the settling of the territorial crisis via a series of proposals worked out along nonpartisan lines in 1850. Although a strong sense of partisanship remained in the political atmosphere during the New Yorker's brief time in the White House, the events of the moment reduced the opportunity for divided government to have great effect on the political process despite its continued presence and well-established bitter history. Due to the sectional crisis, these were years of some cross-party cooperation amid the usual range of partisan rancor.

In the following decade, partisan divisions took a different turn as they continued to divide president from Congress. Presidents Pierce and Buchanan both maintained their policy commitments despite the hostility of congressional majorities seeking other legislative pathways.[24] Both wielded the veto to preserve traditional Democratic notions of limited government. (Pierce, for example, in a short period in 1856, vetoed five internal improvements bills, all of which would have, in his view, unconstitutionally expanded the authority of the federal government. Four of the vetoes were overridden.)

Both Pierce and Buchanan also had to deal with a new situation that was beyond the immediate and customary political rituals of Whig-Democratic partisanship. They were caught up in a powerful realigning process involving a major shift of voter support in the 1850s, a new policy agenda, and the rise of the new Republican Party, coupled with the renewal and expansion of the issue of slavery in the territories. The result was more partisanly instigated confrontation and bitterness, many unfriendly congressional investigations directed against the chief executive, and a few moments of successful legislation. But, as the slavery issue grew increasingly divisive, neither Congress nor the president could handle it, and the reality of divided government exacerbated the issue with great intensity.[25]

Divided government was, therefore, a constant reality to the Americans living in the partisan era before 1861. It became even more commonplace in America after the Civil War.[26] No president between 1875 and 1895 enjoyed having his own party in control of both houses of Congress for his full term in office. These repetitive incidents of divided government were the product of the most competitive electoral situation in our political history. Between 1876 and 1888, for example, Republicans won the presidency three out of four times but had a popular electoral majority only once. They controlled both houses of Congress only between 1881 and 1883 and again between 1889 and 1891. (And this was an era in which it was very difficult, actually almost impossible, to split one's ticket given the nature of the ballot and the existing procedures for casting it).[27]

Such conditions reinforced the need, already established, to learn

how to live and work with divided government as an American political norm. This was not always easy for the participants to do. Ideological fervor cooled somewhat as the Civil War's influence on policy matters faded, but in the participants' view, the policy distance between the parties remained very wide along the traditional lines concerning the reach and power of the federal government. Further, Congress had come out of the Civil War more aggressive than ever about its authority while, after Abraham Lincoln and Andrew Johnson, the presidents generally accepted a more restricted role for themselves. (What was said about one president served for most in this era: presidents had "a feeling of total legislative supremacy."[28])

When divided government occurred, therefore, the situation was somewhat less, I suggest, than meets our eyes. Politics as usual seemed to be the dominant situation. Certainly the political surface remained contentious. There was a range of confrontations, clashes, and vetoes, to be sure. No one liked divided government very much, and partisan point-scoring was constant. But these episodes lacked the searing, threatening intensity of the earlier cases, those that either had been imbued by constitutional considerations or had occurred during the years of intense partisanship and electoral realignment in the 1840s and 1850s.

The closeness of the electoral margins between the parties put a premium on building coalitions and, in particular, holding them together. Some bills were passed; some programmatic advances made. New issues were emerging all of the time in the economic realm, in civil rights, and in foreign policy.[29] The curve indicating the number of presidential vetoes continued to go up. (The three Democrats of the pre–Civil War era—Polk, Pierce, and Buchanan—averaged six each. After the war, from Grant's administration to Cleveland's second term, the average expanded to almost 125 per president.) These figures were magnified by Cleveland's extraordinary number, 414 in his first term, and 170 in his second.[30] The number of vetoes overridden at times of divided government went down, and most vetoes continued to be sustained.

Only Grover Cleveland behaved somewhat differently from his contemporaries. The first Democratic president in twenty-five years, coming into office after an era of Republican reform and government expansionism, he wielded presidential power more vigorously than had his immediate predecessors. He set a new veto record against Congress's private-pension-bill profligacy, and vetoed a number of more substantive bills dealing with monetary and tariff policies.[31] His situation reflected not only the reinvigorated Democratic Party, but also the end of an era in which sharp, well-organized policy polarization remained the crucial element in American political life, while a sense of the legitimacy of opposition and the cyclical nature of politics was acknowledged. To repeat, Americans lived with divided government as a norm.

Phase II incidents, therefore, were contextually different from those of both earlier and later eras. The whole period was dominated by political players who had strong and quite polarized policy views but who, unlike those in Phase I, acknowledged and accommodated their differences. While they did not seek common ground, the Phase II players realized that they were all bound together in a governing process. Their battles were no longer constitutional but clearly political. There was no apocalyptic sense of Armageddon in most of what went on, as once had been the case. Finally, in contrast to the contemporary era, divided government was never considered to be a permanent condition, one that dictated, therefore, a need for new political understandings and theories; but, rather, it was viewed as a situation all but sure to right itself in the next election when political unity at the top of the government would return. When I suggest, therefore, that there is less here than meets the eye, I mean that divided government was perceived as a frequent occurrence, yet as a temporary problem that was likely to be corrected in the next election, a problem that was always well handled, in the meantime, by the widespread expectation of a return to unified normality.

Phase III, which includes the final four incidents of divided government in the premodern period of the American political experience, is distinguished from Phase II in a number of important ways. In Phase III, the first half of the twentieth century, political parties were beginning, albeit slowly at first, to lose their command of the nation's political process (a matter I will return to), but they still retained much of their sting. This changing partisan condition was coupled with the great expansion of the functions and powers of the federal government, and of the potential for sharp policy differences, that we associate with Progressivism and the New Deal. The authority of the president expanded as the issues of industrialization and economic adjustment moved beyond the capacity of existing institutions, formal and partisan, to handle them. In Phase III, elections were much less competitive than they had been earlier. One or the other major party dominated the races in successive blocs of years. All of these factors made the possibility of divided government much rarer than it had been in Phase

II. In fact, in Phase III, divided government did become much less common than it had ever been on the American scene and, therefore, more noticeable when it did occur.[32]

Is there something different in the cases in Phase III from the earlier ones? In general, there does not seem to be. While there are variants among the cases, the main points look the same. Each of the four presidents in Phase III was a policy activist. Each enjoyed success in getting desired legislation through Congress in the first half of his term.[33] William Howard Taft's divided situation from 1911 to 1913 was at a moment of extreme party factionalism, as was Harry Truman's thirty-five years later. Under the Republican Taft, Democrats took much legislative initiative, working with his Progressive Republican enemies to introduce a number of bills that foreshadowed Woodrow Wilson's policy agenda in the next administration. Wilson's last two years in office, after the Democratic disaster in the congressional elections of 1918, were dominated by Republican blockage of the last gasps of the president's legislative hopes, especially in foreign affairs. Under Herbert Hoover from 1931 to 1933, and under Truman, there were no incentives for the opposition to work with the president (and they did not), again given the expectation that a major political shift in the presidential office was imminent, a shift that would make the sitting president irrelevant. What Congress did, therefore, was to act aggressively against the president's plans and policies, as the opposition always had done.

In all of these cases, as in Phase II, Congress sat and waited for the imminent political change to occur. To the Phase III congressmembers, therefore, divided government was a nuisance but not a massive problem. They continued to look to the next presidential election as certain to restore the nation to its customary united situation, a hope that was more often realized than not.[34] These men, therefore, did not focus on divided government in the same way that we have done recently. They regarded it, most likely, as a cue to the outcome of the next presidential election. Posturing, bickering, and gridlock accompanied divided government but, in all but the Truman instance, lasted only for the short term until the system, as expected, righted itself again, away from division. That expectation, and its usual achievement, is, of course, remarkably different from our recent experiences with divided government, in the now quite long era since Truman left office.

The Contribution of the Historical Record

What has this exploration of our past political history contributed, if anything, to our understanding of the phenomenon of divided government? I believe that there are a number of things in the record, some obvious, others more elusive, that are worth mentioning at the end of this review. First, a certain depth and texture has been added to the story of divided government—something that is always analytically useful. As a result, we can see that the phenomenon has a more extensive presence throughout the American political experience than has been fully appreciated. From the 1820s onward, certainly into the 1890s, the fact of divided government stands out in the record for its persistent quality, its importance in our political affairs, and its acceptance as a fact of political life, rather than an unusual situation to brood about constantly. Second, the incidents of divided government that I have discussed vary significantly in their nature and situation. They occurred on different political terrains with different defining and shaping elements at play in each phase. There was, in fact, a highly contextual element present in the cases cited, contexts that I have tried to underscore in my discussion of the different historical phases. In the years from 1875 to 1895, for example, as we have seen, divided government occurred with a frequency comparable to that of our own time, a frequency that immediately challenges claims to the current period's uniqueness. These earlier cases, however, occurred in a time of fervent and persistent party loyalty, and of the most closely competitive national elections in our entire history. This is quite different from our own time, when party loyalty in the electorate has sagged precipitously, all but to the point of disappearance, and when most of our current elections are nowhere near as closely contested as they once were.[35] Those differences, I suggest, shed important light on what we identify as the phenomenon of divided government in our own time.

Such contextual differences in the various cases under review bring up what seems to me to be the most interesting analytic possibility to be drawn from this probe of past political episodes. (I am afraid that, like many historians turned loose on social science generalizations, in what follows I may be seen as needlessly complicating matters. In this case, I am, in fact, complicating things, but not, I believe, needlessly). Viewing divided government through a contextual lens significantly changes our understanding of the phenomenon in one macrocosmic

way. I agree with the current conventional wisdom that the contemporary political era is unique. But my reasons for believing that do not
hinge on the number of cases of divided government that we have had
since 1957. Although some numerical differences exist, the uniqueness
of our era grows, rather, out of the importance of its contextual
configuration. In fact, the more one considers the whole of American
history, the clearer it becomes that much about the current situation
that we call divided government is mislabeled because divided government has been, essentially, a time-bound phenomenon, limited in reach
and applicability, and not a particularly appropriate description of the
situation we have in our own time.

Of course, divided government nominally exists in the present—at
least in formal (and often dramatic) fashion. Once again, after a brief
interlude of unity, Democrats and Republicans, as the result of the
congressional elections of 1994, have organized the different branches
of the federal government as they had done for some time before the
Democratic victories in 1992. But what does that really mean? Since
the advent of Newt Gingrich and his allies in January 1995, partisanship at the top of the government apparently has been much revived
and extraordinarily reenergized beyond anything seen for a very long
time. Divided government, as a clearly marked political phenomenon,
however, only makes descriptive and analytic sense in the presence of
a strong two-party system organizing and dominating the American
political world with national parties that are disciplined enough to
frame and articulate different policy agendas at their cores, and unified
enough to carry their proposals through (or that have some other
strategic reason to do so in the pursuit of party advantage). Divided
government does not make descriptive or analytic sense in any other way.

At first glance, it may appear as if we have returned to that condition.
Speaker Gingrich and his Republican allies have underscored their
differences with Democratic perspectives and policies both in Congress and in the White House. Nevertheless, despite current events,
the descriptive situation that defines divided political realities simply
does not exist in our current political world *in any sustained manner*,
as it did in the past. The notion of the persistence of parties and party
conflict in our political culture is, of course, rooted not only in the
existence of parties and party labels identifying the contestants. It is
based also on the general scholarly acceptance of the party system
model of American political development, a model originally elabo-

rated by V. O. Key, William N. Chambers and Walter Dean Burnham, and the Michigan Survey Research Center group thirty years and more ago.[36] This model, which has widely penetrated our scholarly understanding, has to assume that parties in combat with each other always exist—first, Federalists versus Republicans; then, Democrats versus Whigs; and finally, Republicans versus Democrats—in a number of permutations and combinations, in successive periods of our history. Without believing in such organization and combat, how could we define either united party government or its divided opposite? But, along with a number of other scholars, I have argued elsewhere that to organize our political history through the party system paradigm is not always analytically helpful—that our nation's political development has reflected something else for much of its history.[37]

The story of American politics has not been shaped by a pattern of cyclical formation and reformation of party systems through electoral realignments involving similar combat between the two dominant political parties at different moments. Such realignment patterns did exist for part of our past, and the role that parties played did follow the party system paradigm in some large part of that past as well. But at different times that role varied enormously in its extent, reach, authority, and command of the political landscape and thus in its importance. Not every past political situation has been basically constructed, and primarily influenced, by two-party competition even when the national parties have been nominally present and apparently operational. Most of all, in our own time, the sweeping changes in the role parties play have been particularly noticeable, but not in ways supportive of the party system paradigm. Quite the opposite, in fact.

Since the 1890s, we have witnessed, in this country's politics, the steady, all but irreversible decline of partisan command of the political landscape.[38] Attacks on the parties and on the partisan manner of governing have been nearly unremitting and always intense. Legal and cultural changes have critically reduced partisan resources and significantly weakened the parties' ability to direct the political world as they had been able to do in previous moments of our history. As a result, we have not had an electoral realignment for some time (since the 1930s), and the phenomenon of closely competitive, two-party-dominated elections has disappeared as well. Popular voting behavior has shifted away from the all but automatic party loyalty of earlier years, and that unprecedented shift has contributed to the extensive decline of the influence of parties more generally.[39]

Remapping the Terrain

American political history is better served, I have argued, if we jettison
the party system paradigm as a universal organizing notion in favor of
one that frames our political history through the interpretive lens of
what I label political eras. In seeking to describe and assess the
nature and quality of divided government over the course of American
history, we must begin by noting that what seems to have been the
same political playing field has, in fact, not been. As I have defined the
concept of political eras in earlier work, its elements include the kind
of society that predominated in different moments, and the kinds of
political institutions, norms, and behavior that were predominant in
each, predominances that changed the playing field several times.[40]

In different contexts and circumstances, Americans have engaged in
politics differently, the institutions that they have utilized have varied
in nature, and the importance of these institutions has been significantly different. My earlier work has divided American history into
four political eras that roughly correspond with Phases I to III outlined
above, together with the current era. Each era has had a different
configuration of its constituent elements. Each has had a distinct
consensus about what was at stake, what proper behavior was, and
which political resources and institutions were important. Each has
been demarcated by a unique complex of distinctive elements. There
were specific foci that shaped each, constrained each, gave each a
different central core, and thus limited the possibility of universal
definitions and behavior across time. The most prominent of these
elements and foci for our purposes have been the role played by, and
the importance of, national political parties at different times.[41]

Parties have been present, off and on, for most of the years since
the 1790s, but never with the same degree of authority and centrality.
That is the crucial fact in trying to understand an apparently universal
political phenomenon such as divided government. In analyzing the
first political era, from the 1780s through the 1830s, divided government is a meaningless concept, given the absence for much of the
period of effective political parties shaping the political landscape.
With the exception of part of the 1790s, the political system was almost
always fractured and splintered, not framed in terms of bipolar partisan
conflict.[42] The Republicans and Federalists were certainly there in
Congress and elsewhere, but they were, most of the time, more
ephemeral than not. They did not dig into the political soil very deeply
and could not count on consistent voter support from one election to

the next. One of them eventually disappeared from the scene and, unlike the Whigs in the next era, left hardly a trace behind.

Given the nominal presence but limited reach of the two national parties, this era appears to be quite similar to our own time. If the presidents of the first political era wished to engage in some policy initiative in Congress, they usually had to build coalitions across a wide spectrum of factions, interests, and groups, with only occasional, and quite unsustained, party adherence to guide, or to divide, the groups in their outlook and behavior. Parties did not take much root in the electorate. Some congressional factions did wear party labels, but often briefly and uncomfortably. In such a situation, no sure patterns of divided government, as we have understood that term, were possible. Who, after all, was divided from whom?

In contrast, from the late 1830s, during the nation's second political era, parties permeated American life in thoroughgoing and intrusive ways. They defined the American political nation—among the voters and among officeholders in both national and state governments. The intensity of partisan commitment was profound at every level of politics. Most critically, there was a chasm between the Whigs and Democrats and, later, between the Democrats and the Republicans. The ideological, policy, and cultural differences between parties were wide enough to encourage persistent confrontation and to discourage attempts to build coalitions across partisan lines.[43] In this era, the possibility and importance of divided government as an organizing principle makes a great deal of sense. Where the previous era had been dominated by limited partisan consciousness and organization, by a great number of quirky independents, and by various regional and interest blocs, each with its own agenda, all of which made governing difficult, this second political era was clearly shaped in a very different manner and acted quite differently as two powerful national parties grappled for control of the political nation.

This intensely partisan era passed, however, to be replaced by very different political configurations. The third political era, from the mid-1890s to the 1940s, was marked by the assault on parties referred to earlier, and by the beginning of their fall from their previous heights as the major force on the nation's political landscape. Their loss of sovereignty was not immediate but spread over the whole of the twentieth century, moving in fits and starts but particularly intensifying from the 1960s onward. Parties remained intermittently powerful throughout the era and were somewhat reinvigorated, for a time, by the last electoral realignment in the 1930s.[44] In this era, divided government, while rare, was, as noted, still possible. More critically, this political era was qualitatively different from the one that succeeded it, America's fourth, which began after the Second World War.

The continuing decline of political parties, apparently toward near oblivion, is the central political characteristic of the current era. Since the mid-1940s, national parties have lost most of their authority and ability to influence politics powerfully and determinedly. Unlike in the two political eras immediately preceding it, in the fourth political era political parties have become pale imitations of what they once had been, their influence, at best, occasional, unsustained, and limited in reach. There has been a massive erosion of party presence and party effectiveness over time, which has now become both steep and breathtaking. By the 1970s and 1980s, while parties still operated throughout the political world, their ability to forge effective discipline across the governing system had become very limited indeed, particularly in comparison to what it once had been. (This is, of course, not surprising, given that a major shift in how the American people vote has occurred, a shift from an essentially party-oriented behavior to a more quirky selectivity, in which party identification is an occasional label but rarely an influence.)[45] Parties now penetrate ever more shallowly throughout the system, and their demise, to repeat, seems far advanced.

Given these facts, the current order that has emerged since midcentury cannot be viewed as simply the recurrence of conditions growing out of a periodic political disruption that always challenges, but does not overthrow, the country's basic political situation. In the mid-1990s, we live in a political world dominated, not by parties and their power, but by "rough and tumble, nihilistic politics . . . in which party loyalty counts for almost nothing," in which "the two major parties are," according to Gordon and Benjamin Black, "a little like the Soviet Union before it began to break up."[46]

To be sure, we still readily fall into the language of partisan confrontation, and, of course, some imposing shards of such party-directed conflict remain on the scene. The current intense polarization between the parties in Congress is, as noted, quite marked, as are the apparently severe policy differences between President Clinton and his Republican enemies. The activist spasms of the House Republicans in 1995 and their startling unity suggest what looks like an ideologically partisan power unknown in recent American history. But such partisan power clearly does not extend much beyond Congress, except in a few instances, and does not have the importance and systemic meaning or,

I would argue, the sustainability that it would have had at another time in our history. The long-term trend against parties and their organizing and directing power continues and remains clear-cut. In such a situation, it is not always clear, except during brief episodes, as exciting as they seem, how the nation can have divided government, or what divided government means, even in the presence of a Republican-labeled president and a Democratic-labeled Congress, or vice versa. Or, as Calvin Jillson asks in relation to President Clinton, reversing the usual interpretive question, "what good is unified government in the absence of strong parties?"[47]

In light of this powerful contextual transformation of our political landscape, the recent remarks of Paul Frymar about the futility of developing better theories of divided government seem apt: "Future arguments on this subject need first to ask why the concept of divided government remains important as an analytical category." Writing before the Republican congressional resurgence of 1994, he noted that "as President Clinton continues to search for consensus during a period of unified party government, it is apparent that numerical party majorities are an insufficient way of explaining existing political orders."[48]

I agree. In the fourth political era, as in the first, there is an enormous amount of fragmentation in our political system. Most of the time now (and very likely in the future as well) both presidents and congressional leaders have to build support as they can, when they can, from among who and what is present on the political landscape, whatever the putative party labels happen to be. Both Democratic and Republican presidents have to work with a range of groups in Congress, whatever the formalities of partisan nomenclature. Even presidents with a theoretically secure majority of their own party members in Congress increasingly, more often than not, must use other than party division notions to build coalitions from the fragments that litter Capitol Hill. That situation—with some legislators more committed and polarized than are the mass of voters in general, and with demonized confrontations in which there is no expectation of the other side winning, followed, therefore, by very difficult searches for policy consensus—is reminiscent of the pre-party period of our history.[49]

Not Divided, but Fragmented, Government

In conclusion, I reiterate my original point—that divided government, at first glance, seems to have been more of a pervasive reality throughout American history than we have usually acknowledged. But, as I have also tried to argue, the real descriptive and analytic meaning of the phenomenon is much more complicated than its mere presence, particularly as we consider the current era in light of the past. What we really have now is not divided but *fragmented* government. To repeat the essential point, divided government can exist only when there is a clear and dominant pattern of national two-party competition and when each party stands for different policies, so that when the government becomes divided along party lines, there will be a predictable, clear-cut policy conflict. Fragmented government, in contrast, exists when the parties are weak and voters and legislators do not receive or welcome sustained and meaningful partisan cues and are extremely volatile in their behavior most of the time, whatever their occasional deviations from that anarchic norm.

The latter situation seems likely to continue. There is, at present, a widespread antipolitical mood and a greater hostility toward political parties in our culture than at any time since the early years of the republic. The outcome of elections, therefore, is more likely to lead to largely independent, and extremely volatile, legislative behavior, no matter who holds the presidency, than to discernible, clear-cut, sustained, partisanly-driven policy conflict. This condition has developed over the course of the twentieth century and continues and grows stronger as the century nears its end. And there are only a few signs, at best, anywhere on the political landscape that the conditions that encourage such persistent and dominating volatility are likely to change soon—or permanently. As a result, if scholars want to discuss divided government and use it as an analytic category, they are going to have to take into account the realities of a world without strong and meaningful political parties. Or they are going to have to modify their definitions and strikingly change their focus and understanding, as students of electoral realignment and party systems theory have been forced to do by the intractability of current political behavior as regards the analytic usefulness of their favorite paradigm.

Notes

1. Morris Fiorina, *Divided Government* (New York: Macmillan, 1992).
2. James L. Sundquist, "Needed: A Political Theory for the New Era of Coalition Government in the United States," *Political Science Quarterly* 103 (winter 1988–89): 613.

3. In addition to Fiorina and Sundquist, the best and most interesting work on the divided government phenomenon includes Gary W. Cox and Samuel Kernell, eds., *The Politics of Divided Government* (Boulder, Colo.: Westview, 1991); and David R. Mayhew, *Divided We Govern: Party Control, Lawmaking and Investigations, 1946–1990* (New Haven: Yale University Press, 1991).

4. On Eisenhower, see Fred Greenstein, *The Hidden-Hand Presidency: Eisenhower as Leader* (Baltimore: Johns Hopkins University Press, 1982); Chester J. Pach, Jr., and Elmo Richardson, *The Presidency of Dwight D. Eisenhower* (Lawrence: University Press of Kansas, 1991). The latter is part of the University Press of Kansas's multivolume history covering each presidential administration since that of George Washington. Other volumes in the series are referred to as appropriate below.

5. On dating the emergence of party conflict in American politics, see Joel H. Silbey, *The American Political Nation, 1838–1893* (Stanford: Stanford University Press, 1991); Richard P. McCormick, *The Presidential Game: The Origins of American Presidential Politics* (New York: Oxford University Press, 1982); Ronald P. Formisano, "Deferential-Participant Politics: The Early Republic's Political Culture," *American Political Science Review* 68 (June 1974): 473–87.

6. On the distribution of congressional seats between the parties, see Kenneth Martis, *The Historical Atlas of Political Parties in the United States Congress, 1789–1989* (New York: Macmillan, 1989).

7. See Arthur M. Schlesinger, ed., *History of American Presidential Elections, 1789–1968*, 4 vols. (New York: Chelsea House, 1971).

8. These data are drawn from *Historical Statistics of the United States from Colonial Times to 1970* (Washington, D.C.: U.S. Government Printing Office, 1975); and *The Biographical Directory of the American Congress, 1774–1989* (Washington, D.C.: U.S. Government Printing Office, 1989).

9. Quoted in Mary W. M. Hargreaves, *The Presidency of John Quincy Adams* (Lawrence: University Press of Kansas, 1985), 280.

10. Quoted in ibid., 282.

11. All of this is drawn from ibid. See also Robert Remini, *Martin Van Buren and the Making of the Democratic Party* (New York: Columbia University Press, 1959).

12. Alvin Lynn, "Party Formation and Operation in the House of Representatives, 1824–1837" (Ph.D. diss., Rutgers University, 1972), 467.

13. Donald B. Cole, *The Presidency of Andrew Jackson* (Lawrence: University Press of Kansas, 1993).

14. Norma L. Peterson, *The Presidencies of William Henry Harrison and John Tyler* (Lawrence: University Press of Kansas, 1989).

15. As John Quincy Adams, a member of the House of Representatives in the early 1840s, characterized Tyler's vetoes: "The power to enact laws essential to the welfare of the people has been struck with apoplexy by the Executive hand." Quoted in ibid., 104.

16. Carlton Jackson, *Presidential Vetoes, 1792–1945* (Athens: University of Georgia Press, 1967). The number of vetoes by each president is listed in *Historical Statistics of the United States*, II, 1082.

17. Richard Hofstadter, *The Idea of a Party System: The Rise of Legitimate Opposition in the United States, 1780–1840* (Berkeley: University of California Press, 1969); Silbey, *American Political Nation*.

18. Schlesinger, *History of American Presidential Elections*.

19. Paul Bergeron, *The Presidency of James K. Polk* (Lawrence: University Press of Kansas, 1987).

20. Don Riddle, *Congressman Abraham Lincoln* (Urbana, Ill.: University of Illinois Press, 1987); John H. Schroeder, *Mr. Polk's War: American Opposition and Dissent, 1846–1848* (Madison: University of Wisconsin Press, 1973).

21. Bergeron, *Presidency of James K. Polk*, passim.

22. Elbert B. Smith, *The Presidencies of Zachary Taylor and Millard Fillmore* (Lawrence: University Press of Kansas, 1988); Holman Hamilton, *Prologue to Conflict: The Crisis and Compromise of 1850* (Lexington: University Press of Kentucky, 1964).

23. Smith, *Presidencies of Zachary Taylor and Millard Fillmore*, 122.

24. Larry Gara, *The Presidency of Franklin Pierce* (Lawrence: University Press of Kansas, 1991); Elbert B. Smith, *The Presidency of James Buchanan* (Lawrence: University Press of Kansas, 1975).

25. Michael Holt, *The Political Crisis of the 1850s* (New York: Norton, 1978); William E. Gienapp, *The Origins of the Republican Party, 1852–1856* (New York: Oxford University Press, 1987).

26. I have omitted the Andrew Johnson administration from this discussion because it was never, technically, an example of divided government (Johnson, a lifelong Democrat had, of course, been elected on the Lincoln ticket with an overwhelmingly Republican Congress), although Johnson's experience bears a great deal of comparison to that of John Tyler twenty-five years before.

27. Michael McGerr, *The Decline of Popular Politics: The American North, 1865–1928* (New York: Oxford University Press, 1986); Morton Keller, *Affairs of State: Public Life in Late Nineteenth-Century America* (Cambridge: Belknap Press of Harvard University Press, 1977); Silbey, *American Political Nation*.

28. Homer E. Socolofsky and Allan B. Spetter, *The Presidency of Benjamin Harrison* (Lawrence: University Press of Kansas, 1987), 47.

29. Ari Hoogenboom, *The Presidency of Rutherford B. Hayes* (Lawrence: University Press of Kansas, 1988); Justus D. Doenecke, *The Presidencies of James A. Garfield and Chester Alan Arthur* (Lawrence: University Press of Kansas, 1981).

30. *Historical Statistics of the United States*.

31. Richard E. Welch, Jr., *The Presidencies of Grover Cleveland* (Lawrence: University Press of Kansas, 1988).

32. Silbey, *American Political Nation*, 237ff.

33. Paolo E. Coletta, *The Presidency of William Howard Taft* (Lawrence: University Press of Kansas, 1973); Kendrick A. Klements, *The Presidency of Woodrow Wilson* (Lawrence: University Press of Kansas, 1992); Martin L. Fausold, *The Presidency of Herbert C. Hoover* (Lawrence: University Press of Kansas, 1985); Donald R. McCoy, *The Presidency of Harry Truman* (Lawrence: University Press of Kansas, 1984).

34. Schlesinger, *History of American Presidential Elections, 1789–1968*.

35. Walter Dean Burnham, *The Current Crisis in American Politics* (New York: Oxford University Press, 1982); Norman H. Nie, Sidney Verba, and John Petrocik, *The Changing American Voter* (Cambridge: Harvard University Press, 1976).

36. V. O. Key, Jr., "A Theory of Critical Elections," *Journal of Politics* 17 (February 1955): 3–18; idem, "Secular Realignment and the Party System," *Journal of Politics* 21 (May 1959): 198–210; William N. Chambers and Walter Dean Burnham, eds., *The American Party Systems: Stages of Political Development*, 2d ed. (New York, Oxford University Press, 1975); Angus Campbell et al., *The American Voter* (New York: Wiley, 1960); Angus Campbell et al., *Elections and the Political Order* (New York: Wiley, 1966).

37. Byron Shafer, ed., *The End of Realignment?: Interpreting American Electoral Eras* (Madison: University of Wisconsin Press, 1991).

38. Burnham, *Current Crisis in American Politics*.

39. This is not a universally held position. For a different view, in addition to Burnham's essay, "Critical Realignment: Dead or Alive?" in *End of Realignment?*, ed. Shafer, 101–40, see, most recently, William G. Mayer, "Changes in Elections and the Party System: 1992 in Historical Perspective," in *The New American Politics: Reflections on Political Change and the Clinton Administration*, ed. Bryan D. Jones (Boulder, Colo.: Westview, 1995), 19–50.

40. Joel H. Silbey, "Beyond Realignment and Realignment Theory: American Political Eras, 1789–1989," in *End of Realignment?*, ed. Shafer, passim.

41. Ibid., 16–17.

42. Ronald P. Formisano, *The Transformation of American Political Culture: Massachusetts Parties, 1790s–1840s* (New York: Oxford University Press, 1983); Silbey, *American Political Nation*, 5ff.

43. This is the main point of Silbey, *American Political Nation*.

44. Ibid.; Burnham, *Current Crisis in American Politics*.

45. Nie, Verba, and Petrocik, *Changing American Voter*.

46. *Wall Street Journal*, 15 August 1994, A12. See Gordon and Benjamin Black, *The Politics of American Discontent: How a New Party Can Make Democracy Work* (New York: Wiley, 1994).

47. Calvin Jillson, "Patterns and Periodicity in American National Politics," in *The Dynamics of American Politics: Approaches and Interpretations*, ed. Lawrence C. Dodd and Calvin Jillson (Boulder, Colo.: Westview, 1994), 54.

48. Paul Frymar, "Ideological Consensus within Divided Party Government," *Political Science Quarterly* 109 (summer 1994): 310–11.

Joel H. Silbey

49. The ability of presidents and congressional leaders to find effective means of building policy coalitions across what passes for partisan lines is also greatly affected by the presence, in the Republican-controlled 104th Congress, of an important congressional coterie apparently uninterested in compromise in the formation of policy, unwilling to make deals, and stridently intractable in its members' refusal to regard what David Mayhew has called "a reason of state" as important enough to cause them to move the policy process forward whatever the state of government division. As David Broder has written, "the 90s so far look to be a time when the disruptive devices—the tools for stopping government—are far more effective than the mechanisms of consolidation and compromise." See David R. Mayhew, "The Return to Unified Party Control under Clinton: How Much of a Difference in Lawmaking?" in *New American Politics*, ed. Jones, 111–21. The reference is at 118. Broder's comment appeared in the *Boston Globe*, 20 December 1995, 15. See also Adam Clymer, "Politics and the Dead Arts of Compromise," *New York Times*, 22 October 1995, *News of The Week in Review*, 1.

Chapter Two

The Causes and Consequences of Divided Government: Lessons of 1992–1994[1]

Morris P. Fiorina

In the spring of 1992, I published a small book entitled *Divided Government*.[2] The timing proved somewhat awkward. When the writing was completed—in the spring of 1991—the evening newscasts were filled with pictures of jubilant Kuwaitis marching around with arms upraised chanting "Bush! Bush! Bush!" In the aftermath of the war, Bush's approval ratings soared to historic heights, nearing 90 percent, and heavyweight contenders for the Democratic presidential nomination took themselves out of contention. With Bush looking unbeatable and the Democratic base in the House of Representatives appearing as unshakable as ever, divided government looked to be a permanent part of the national political landscape.

Even in the spring of 1992, when the book appeared, the timeliness of the topic seemed reasonably assured. Bill Clinton was fighting for his political life in the wake of Gennifer Flowers' revelations, and additional salacious rumors abounded. And if not Clinton, who? President Paul Tsongas? Not likely. President Jerry Brown? Even less likely. Although Clinton survived the spring, the odds on divided government still looked pretty high in the summer of 1992. For a time, Clinton was running third in the polls, and pundits mused that Perot was the real alternative to Bush. Then came a series of strange Perot stories, the happy Democratic convention, the unhappy Republican convention, and the reversal of Bush's and Clinton's political stocks.

After what is generally viewed as one of the poorer Republican campaigns in memory, the voters supposedly expressed their frustration with "gridlock" and put an end to twelve consecutive years of divided national government by electing Bill Clinton.

From a scholarly standpoint this development, however awkwardly timed, did not trouble me. After all, the election of a Democrat by a 43 percent plurality hardly signaled an end to the national dissensus that I had discussed in the book. Counting Perot voters, presidential-congressional ticket-splitting was at an all-time high in 1992, and even not counting them, ticket-splitting was at a level comparable to that in elections of the 1980s. Many observers felt that the Republicans could very well capture the Senate in 1994, given the competitiveness of Senate elections and the fact that Democrats would be defending two-thirds of the seats at risk with the inexorable off-year tide running against them. Moreover, most observers overlooked the fact that the 1992 elections did not diminish the frequency of divided government in the states. Quite on the contrary, the elections left state governments arguably more divided than they had been going in. All in all, the 1992 elections indicated little or nothing in the way of fundamental change.

Popular political commentary saw things differently, at least for a while. After being a major campaign issue, "gridlock" disappeared from political discussions, and divided government became yesterday's news, a subject of historical interest only. As far as many observers were concerned, Democratic capture of the presidency put an end to gridlock, although as time passed, more than a few began to notice that the reemergence of unified national government had not worked any miracles.

And then came the 1994 elections. Just as 1992 had ended the era of divided national government by breaking the Republican lock on the presidency, so 1994 restored divided national government by breaking the Democratic lock on Congress, the House of Representatives in particular. In the states, the Republicans made enormous gains in 1994, but divided government remains at 1980s levels.

So, two years after some thought it had ended, the era of divided government is back. Even if the Republicans capture the presidency in 1996 while retaining control of Congress, or if Bill Clinton is reelected and the Democrats recapture Congress, the recent swings in party fortunes will make most analysts cautious about assuming that divided national government has ended, as some of them assumed too quickly in 1992. As for the states, the era of divided government continues uninterrupted.

This essay updates the discussion in my 1992 book. First, it looks at the election results that unified control in 1992, then redivided it in 1994. Not surprisingly, I conclude that the era of divided government is still very much with us. Second, this essay considers the implications of the 1992–1994 performance of the Clinton administration for arguments about the consequences of divided government. Little in this two-year performance suggests that divided control is to blame for the various perceived ills that beset the nation.

The 1992 and 1994 Elections

The 1992 National Elections

For the media and for many popular commentators on American politics, the main story of the 1992 elections was a story of change. Bill Clinton broke the supposed Republican "lock" on the presidency, only the second time since 1964 that a Democrat had been able to poll more votes than a Republican at the presidential level. Certainly that was a noteworthy change from recent electoral history, and understandably it became the focus of a news establishment that defines news largely in terms of things that change.

To those who looked closely at the underlying reality, however, the story was as much a story of continuity as of change. Like his regional predecessor in 1976, Clinton won under exceptional conditions.[3] Although his popular vote margin over Bush was a comfortable 5.6 percent, and his electoral vote margin overwhelming, the presence of Ross Perot in the race clouded matters considerably. Clinton won a majority of the popular vote only in his home state of Arkansas. The most detailed analyses that have been done conclude that Perot took about as many votes from Clinton as from Bush, suggesting that Clinton's popular vote margin over Bush in a two-way race would have been about the same as Bush's 1988 margin over Dukakis, but there is no denying the relative unpopularity of both major party candidates in 1992.[4]

Whatever the uncertainties and ambiguities, Clinton won, and given that the Democratic "lock" on Congress continued, unified government was restored to the national level. There had been much speculation in the media about 1992 being the "year of the outsider." Congress had been buffeted by a series of scandals—the Keating Five, the House Post Office, the House Bank, Danny Rostenkowski—and popular esteem for the institution was at historic lows. Approval of the performance of Congress, for instance, was below 20 percent, in contrast to more normal (albeit still low) levels of about 35 percent.[5] Disgust with the campaign finance system was widespread. Term limit proposals passed wherever they got on the ballot.

Despite such a generally negative view of Congress, constituents continued to view their own representatives and senators much more favorably than they viewed the collective Congress, although 1992 approval levels in the 50 to 60 percent range for individual members of Congress were lower than the 60 to 70 range that was normal in the 1970s and 1980s.[6] As a consequence of this continued differentiation between individuals and the collectivity, the year of the outsider was much less apparent than feared by some Democrats and hoped for by some Republicans. In the House, many of the more tainted incumbents either retired or were defeated in primaries, leading to a relatively quiet general election.[7] Eighty-eight percent of all incumbents were reelected, clearly lower than the 1980s average of 95 percent, but a figure not suggestive of any wholesale rejection of Washington.[8] Republicans had put much effort into the redistricting process after the 1990 census, and hoped to make significant gains, but in the end they gained only ten seats.

The Senate results were even more disappointing for the Republicans. Twenty of the thirty-five contested seats were held by Democrats. Given that Senate elections in this era are highly competitive, and that incumbency counts for less in the Senate than in the House, on statistical grounds alone the Republicans expected to make gains.[9] When all the votes were counted, however, the Republicans actually lost one seat, leaving them on the short side of a 57 to 43 division.

In sum, in 1992 the voting decisions made by millions of Americans brought back unified government, a significant change from the recent past. But a look at the voting decisions that accomplished that result does not reveal major shifts in the way Americans were making their choices. Counting Perot voters, a record 36 percent of those voting split their tickets between the parties' candidates for the presidency and the House. Not counting Perot voters, 22 percent of those voting split their tickets, a figure just three points below the 1972–1988 average.[10]

The 1992 Elections in the States

Arguably, then, if one looked only at the national returns, indications that the era of divided government had ended in 1992 were weak and unclear. In contrast, the picture presented by election returns in the American states was crystal clear: there the era of divided government continued uninterrupted. The 1990 elections had left only twenty-one states under unified party control; the 1992 elections left twenty states in that condition. The number of unified Democratic states barely changed in 1992, and the Republicans continued their abysmal showing of the 1980s by capturing full control in only three states (Arizona, New Hampshire, and Utah). This summary figure, however, hides what might well be considered a further increase in divided control in the states, for a more detailed examination of patterns of divided control indicates that party control of state legislatures underwent an interesting decline in 1992 (table 2.1).

The big story of state elections was the upsurge in split legislatures.[11] Prior to 1992, split legislatures generally numbered 12 to 18 percent of the total, that is, about eight legislatures, give or take a couple. The 1992 elections raised that number to 35 percent of the total—seventeen

TABLE 2.1
Patterns of Party Control in the States, 1992–1994

Governor	Legislature	1992	1994
Democrat	Democrat	16	8
Republican	Republican	4	15
Democrat	Republican	4	4
Republican	Democrat	7	10
Democrat	Split	8	6
Republican	Split	8	5
Independent	Split	1	1
Independent	Democrat	1	0

Source: Emily Van Dunk and Thomas M. Holbrook, "The 1994 State Legislative Elections," *Extension of Remarks, APSA Legislative Studies Section Newsletter* 18 (1994): 8–11.
Note: Nebraska has a nonpartisan legislature and is therefore not counted in this analysis.

legislatures—far and away the high point of the post–Second World War period, and in all probability the highest proportion of split legislatures in American history. Moreover, although there did not appear to be any clear trend in this indicator prior to 1992, with the addition of the striking 1992 figure, there is a clear suggestion of a jump to a new, higher level of split legislatures beginning in 1984 when the number rose to twelve. It has not fallen below that level since. Given that the Supreme Court's one-person one-vote decisions imposed strict population equality in constructing both senate and house districts, the increase in split legislatures since the mid-1980s suggests an increased rate of ticket-splitting in state legislative elections. I am not aware of any research that addresses this question, but it is one that bears investigation.

The split in state legislative control came at the expense of Democratic control (table 2.2). Before the 1992 elections, the Democrats controlled both chambers in twenty-eight states; the Republicans, in only six states. After the elections, the Democrats controlled both in twenty-four states; the Republicans, in eight. This modest gain in Republican legislative strength in 1992 is noteworthy given that their presidential candidate was going down to defeat. Whether it foreshad-

TABLE 2.2
Partisan Control of State Legislatures, 1990–1994

	1990	1992	1994
Democratic chambers	69	64	47
Republican chambers	25	31	49
Democratic legislatures	28	24	18
Republican legislatures	6	8	19

Source: For 1990 and 1992, data were calculated from *Book of the States* (Lexington: The Council of State Governments). For 1994, from Karl Kurtz, "The Tide's In for Southern Republicans," *APSA Legislative Studies Section Newsletter* 18 (1994): 9–11.

ows in any way their major legislative victories in 1994 is impossible to say, but the development probably deserved more attention than it received.

The 1994 National Elections

Political conditions changed as much between 1992 and 1994 as they had between 1990 and 1992. According to the polls, the electorate that had wavered in its preference for divided over unified national government in the fall of 1992 decided after two years of experience with unified government that it really preferred divided government after all.[12] Whether out of an actual preference for divided government or for a host of other reasons, the electorate restored divided national government with the only means at its disposal: electing Republican majorities to Congress.

If the main story of 1992—electoral change—was something of an exaggeration, few will make a similar claim about the main story of 1994—electoral change in the form of the Republican capture of the House of Representatives. Not since 1952 had the Republicans won a majority of House seats, the longest period of one-party control in American history. And not since 1952 had the Republicans received a majority of the nationwide popular vote cast for House candidates. The gain in the party's national popular vote between 1992 and 1994 was 7 percent, not large in absolute terms, but relatively speaking, very large—the largest shift in either party's House vote since 1948.[13] With a loss of fifty-four House seats and eight Senate seats, the "earthquake," "tsunami," and other geological and meteorological metaphors that filled the media were understandable. The House figure, in particular, was a throwback to the first half of the twentieth century: not since 1946 had a party lost so many seats in one election.

Despite the common tendency to paint the Republican victory as a "tsunami" that washed away all the Democrats in its path, in reality the voting patterns were more complex and their causes more differentiated than such metaphors suggest. The House results had at least four significant components, although as yet there is little research on how important they were and how they interacted with one another: the normal midterm loss, the secular realignment in the South, unpopular issue stands, and reapportionment and redistricting.

First, in every midterm election since the Civil War, save one (1934), the party of the president has lost seats. Given the state of the economy in 1992 (according to the traditional indicators, it was pretty good), most statistical forecasting models predicted these "normal" losses to be relatively small. But given Clinton's low approval ratings and the fiasco in Congress created by his health care plan, most analysts expected losses somewhat larger than the historical norm.

Second, the Republicans made their first breakthroughs in the South in the 1960s. During the intervening thirty years, many southern states had become downright Republican at the presidential level and at least competitive statewide, but the Democrats had been hanging on at the congressional level and holding firm at the state legislative level. The 1994 elections showed significant breakthroughs at these levels.

Third, national Democrats continue to get burned by a variety of symbolic issues on which they are at odds with constituencies who have traditionally supported the Democrats on economic grounds.[14] Such issues contribute to a popular impression that the Democrats are out of step with the values and aspirations of ordinary middle Americans, an impression the Republicans have been happily exploiting for nearly a generation.

In the fourth component of the House results, reapportionment and redistricting, two distinct factors are at work. One is that following the past two decennial censuses, there has been a reallocation of congressional districts from the Frost Belt to the Sun Belt—from areas more heavily Democratic to areas less so. In the 1990 reapportionment, Sun Belt states gained eighteen seats. The other factor is majority-minority redistricting. In recent years, Republicans have joined civil rights groups to press for redistricting plans that create the maximum number of seats with African-American and Hispanic majorities. This practice increases the likelihood of electing minority members to Congress but marginally weakens adjacent Democratic districts that lose minority voters. David Lublin estimates that majority-minority redistricting cost the Democrats twelve seats in 1992 and 1994, an estimate he calls "conservative."[15]

The important point to notice is that losses from these two distinct sources probably should have occurred entirely in 1992, the first election after the census, but the poor showing of George Bush may have enabled some Democratic incumbents to hang on in weakened districts and some Democratic challengers to win in others where they were not expected to. When such districts belatedly fell to the Republicans in 1994, they added to the impression of a national Republican tide.

A close look at the congressional voting reveals some important elements of continuity, as well as the major instances of change that we have noted. In particular, 90 percent of all running House incumbents were reelected, a slight increase over 1992, but 5 percent below the average of the previous decade. Still, the incumbent reelection rate in 1994 was higher than the *average* for the elections between 1946 and 1966, suggesting that even in 1994, incumbency was of a different order of importance than a generation ago. To be sure, with the electoral tide running in the Republican direction, not a single Republican incumbent lost, while thirty-five Democratic incumbents did. The latter is an unusually large number but one that still left the Democrats with an 85 percent success rate. Using one widely accepted method of calculation, the incumbency advantage in 1994 was something over 12 percent for Republicans and something over 8 percent for Democrats; the advantage of incumbency certainly did not disappear in 1994.[16]

In the Senate, the Republicans also enjoyed great success, although their takeover there was much less of a surprise. For the second election in a row, the Democrats were heavily exposed in Senate races: twenty-two of the thirty-four seats up for election in 1994 were held by Democrats. Because Senate races have become highly competitive in recent years, few observers thought it was out of the question that the Republicans would gain enough seats to win control, despite their failure to do so when the Democrats were similarly exposed in 1992. The Republicans needed a net gain of seven seats and got eight (plus Richard Shelby of Alabama, who defected from the Democrats shortly after the election). Only two Democratic incumbents lost, but every single open seat was captured by the Republicans.

Whatever the policy consequences of the Republican victories (at the time of this writing, there has been much sound and fury in the House, but not much has made it into law, or even through the Senate), the 1994 election results make it clear that the Democratic "lock" on the House of Representatives has been broken. Taken in combination with the 1992 results wherein the Democrats at least picked the Republican lock on the presidency, the 1994 elections indicate that either party can capture any one of the three elected branches of the national government, given circumstances that we have seen transpire in a three- or four-year span of time. This suggests that divided government at the national level will be common in years to come, although it may take patterns different from the Republican president/ Democratic Congress that had been the norm between 1954 and 1992. In particular, the present division of Democratic president/Republican Congress is the first instance of such a pattern since 1948.

Morris P. Fiorina

The 1994 Elections in the States

And what of the states in 1994? There, too, the Republicans made great gains. About three-quarters of the states elect their governors in the midterm elections, so this office was highly exposed to the Republican tide. The Republicans did very well, winning twenty-four of thirty-six races, giving them control of a majority of the governorships for the first time since the halcyon days of 1966 to 1968, although there had been other, more recent elections (1980 and 1986) where they had also done relatively well.

However one characterizes the Republican gubernatorial gains, Republican gains at the state legislative level were striking (table 2.2). They gained a total of eighteen chambers, taking full control of nineteen legislatures to the Democrats' eighteen. This is the largest number of legislatures the Republicans have controlled since 1968 and the first time since 1954 that they have controlled more legislatures than the Democrats.

Despite the great Republican gains, there was little or no increase in unified control in the states (table 2.1). The number of unified states rose from twenty to twenty-three after the 1994 elections. The parties flopped positions, of course; the Republicans controlled only four states before the election and fifteen after, whereas the Democrats dropped from sixteen to eight, so the changes largely offset each other. The level of divided government in the states today is basically unchanged from the historic low point reached in the late 1980s. Republican governor/Democratic legislature continues to be the single most common divided pattern, but it has declined in frequency in recent years as the number of split legislatures has increased. In 1994, the number of split legislatures dropped back from its record 1992 level to twelve, a figure still high by historical standards.

The other noteworthy development in 1994 was the Republican state legislative breakthrough in the South. Between 1946 and 1990, the Republicans had never won control of either chamber of a state legislature in any southern or border state. In 1992, the Republicans achieved a tie in the Florida senate, and in 1994, they broke through with majorities in the Florida and North Carolina senates, and in the South Carolina house.

All in all, a Republican tide rolled across the states in 1994. That tide produced major changes in party control of governorships and state legislative chambers. Somewhat surprisingly however, the Republican surge did little to alter the overall distribution of party control in the states. Some unified Democratic states were pushed into the various divided categories, and some divided states were pushed into the unified Republican category, but on net the divided category stayed about the same size. Thus, in the states, the era of divided government continues uninterrupted.

The Era of Divided Government Continues

Indisputably, 1992 and 1994 were interesting elections. Change in control of the presidency for the first time in twelve years is news; change in control of the House of Representatives for the first time in forty years is big news. But the major lesson of these elections is that the era of divided government continues. At the national level, a quasi-stable pattern of Republican presidents/Democratic congresses may have broken down, but it is now clear that 1992 did not herald a return to an era of unified Democratic government, and it is far too early to tell whether 1994 foreshadows a new era of unified Republican government. My suspicion is that recent national developments indicate that we have now entered a period where divided government will continue to be frequent, but it will occur in a richer variety of patterns of control than the Republican president/Democratic Congress pattern of the past generation.

As for the states, a look at patterns of control in these forty-nine separate political systems reveals no indication that the 1992 and 1994 elections broke the tendency toward divided control that had become apparent during the past generation. The Republicans certainly are stronger now than at any time since 1968, and the decline of Republican fortunes in state legislative elections has at least been arrested. But Republican gains have not been matched by increases in unified control, for they have been offset by declines in Democratic unified control.

Indeed, in the states too, we are seeing not only as much divided control as in recent years, but a richer variety of patterns as well. In particular, the increase in split state legislatures indicates that the common divided pattern of Republican governor/Democratic legislature has given way to more complicated patterns where the legislature too is split.

The Consequences of Divided Government Revisited

During the 1992 presidential campaign, a new issue came to the fore. It was not a policy issue like reducing the deficit, "ending welfare as we know it," or admitting gays into the military. Nor was it an issue of personal or institutional performance like Bush's handling of the economy or the apparent venality of Congress. The issue was broader than either policy or performance and was blamed for shortcomings in both. The issue was *gridlock*. According to many commentators—by no means all of them Democrats—the United States had taken a long look at Sundquist's "new era of coalition government" and, like him, they found it wanting.[17] Years of Republican presidents cohabiting with Democratic congresses had generated an indictment that charged divided government with "bitter partisanship, poor governmental performance, policy incoherence, nondecisions, showdowns, standoffs, checkmate, stalemate, deadlock, and in the most recent nomenclature, *gridlock*."[18]

In *Divided Government*, I noted that there was little empirical support for the strong claims that have been made about the negative effects of divided control. Whether one looked closely at deficits, at legislative productivity, at interbranch conflict, or at presidents' ability to conduct foreign affairs or staff their administrations, there was little in the empirical record that pointed to significant differences between years of unified government and years of split control.[19] That may have been the case as of 1988, but had the picture changed during the Bush Administration? Had the divided government chickens finally come home to roost? Many Democrats suggested as much, many pundits agreed with them, and even voters became less supportive of divided government than they had been earlier.[20]

Efficiency and Effectiveness under Unified Government in 1993–1994

When Bill Clinton was elected, advocates of activist government breathed a sigh of relief. With unified government restored, the country could once again expect innovative programs, decisive government action, and efficient institutional performance. Such expectations were not just the exaggerated expectations of naive observers. Experienced congressional leaders convinced President-elect Clinton that he should ignore moderate Republicans and adopt a legislative strategy that relied exclusively on the Democratic majorities in Congress. For his own part, Clinton indiscreetly suggested that his first hundred days would be the most productive period since Franklin Roosevelt.

Things do not seem to have worked out that way. Almost immediately, President Clinton was slapped down by Congress when he attempted to end discrimination against gays by the military. Not only did his own party not stand behind him, but Democrats made it clear that they would provide enough votes to override his veto if he sought to block a joint resolution overturning his proposed executive order. This was hardly an auspicious beginning. The finale of his first two years was far worse. Health care reform, the planned centerpiece of the Clinton administration, died a long, noisy, and messy death in Congress, some months after the congressional Democrats rejected the president's plan and attempted to substitute various ones of their own.

In between, there was considerably more of the same. Many of the president's victories recalled the "perils of Pauline" stories of the silent movie era. His budget passed by a single vote in the House, as conservative Democrats abandoned ship. The president won on the North American Free Trade Agreement (NAFTA) only because Republican Speaker-to-be Newt Gingrich delivered the Republican votes to make up for Democratic defections. Dissident Democrats joined with Republicans to hold up the crime bill, forcing the president to make concessions on spending. A Democratic senator, Fritz Hollings, held up a vote on the General Agreement on Tariffs and Trade (GATT) until after the 1994 elections, at which time President Clinton was forced into embarrassing negotiations with the newly empowered Republican minority. But on these matters, at least Clinton won in the end, however difficult and damaging the process.

Other policymaking episodes did not have happy endings. The president's economic stimulus package died in the Senate as the strategy of relying exclusively on Democratic votes in Congress encouraged Republicans to adopt a "take no prisoners" approach to the president's program. The campaign finance reform package also died in the Senate, but not before complacent House Democrats had delayed it for a year. Congress rejected the president's proposal to reform grazing rights in the West, and Superfund died as well. Environmental spokespersons labeled the 103rd Congress a disappointment.[21]

Faced with such developments, the high hopes expressed only two years earlier now turned to disappointment. Rank-and-file House Democrats rushed to adjourn, suggesting a desire to get out of Washington before they did any further political damage.[22] Polls found that voters once again overwhelmingly saw the virtues of divided control. Some in the media could scarcely contain their disgust:

> This will go down in the record books as perhaps the worst Congress— least effective, most destructive, nastiest—in 50 years. The wisdom

of the moment is that the dismal record represents a victory for the Republicans. . . . But it's also a myth to claim that they bear the entire responsibility for the failure that has occurred. The Democrats brought a major part of the wreckage on themselves. . . . The only good news as this mud fight finally winds down is that it's hard to imagine much worse.[23]

Certainly things were not as bad as that. The disappointment and disillusion expressed in late 1994 were no more justified than the hope and anticipation expressed in late 1992. Unified government should not have been expected to work miracles, and a fair review of the record suggests that unified control in 1993 and 1994 was by no means the disaster suggested by some.

After updating the research reviewed in his earlier book, David Mayhew judged the 103rd Congress as "relatively productive . . . good . . . respectable. . . . I think with five year's perspective we'll say this is an average first Congress for a president. . . . It's like Truman's first Congress, or Carter's first, maybe a little bigger than Kennedy's first."[24] To be sure, Mayhew by no means was retreating from his earlier conclusion that divided government was as productive as unified government. He went on to say, "Once you step back and look, you wonder whether it adds up to more than Bush's first Congress. . . . I don't think it's in a class with Ronald Reagan's first Congress."[25]

Contrary to much of what has been written in the media, most academic observers of Congress judge that the two years of unified government under Clinton were reasonably productive. In addition to deficit reduction, NAFTA, and GATT, one finds amidst the various defeats and embarrassments significant policy initiatives such as the Family and Medical Leave Act, the National Service Corps, the Brady (handgun control) Bill, and the Anticrime Bill, as well as procedural reforms such as "motor voter" registration, Hatch Act revisions, and reform of government procurement. Moreover, Charles O. Jones, James Thurber, and other scholars point out "negative" accomplishments, including termination of giant pork-barrel projects such as the superconducting super collider.[26]

All in all, the lessons to be drawn from the 1993–1994 episode of unified national control appear quite consistent with those drawn from previous episodes. There were plenty of instances of gridlock and stalemate, but also instances of legislative accomplishment. Despite hyperbolic newspaper editorials and bitter partisan commentary, the experience of the 103rd Congress suggests no need to revise the earlier conclusions regarding the relative unimportance of divided control.

This episode of unified government seems well within the historical range of what one could expect from either a unified or a divided government.

Recent research supports that verdict about the relative unimportance of split versus unified control. Although their approaches and methodologies could not be more different, important studies by Charles Jones and Keith Krehbiel reach very similar general conclusions.[27] Based on an extensive empirical study of post–Second World War presidents, Jones finds that divided government is only one of many factors that determine legislative productivity and other measures of presidential success. Indeed, split-party control may not even be a major factor in many cases; only when it occurs in combination with other considerations does divided control have the popularly assumed negative effects.

Jones identifies four patterns of presidential-congressional relations.[28] In the first, *partisanship*, split control can indeed lead to gridlock, as in the final two years of the Bush administration. But Jones concludes that gridlock was not inevitable; the perceived weakness of both sides led them to eschew compromise in favor of an all-out attack on the opposing party/institutional actor. In contrast, when both parties have acknowledged strengths, a pattern of *copartisanship* may develop, in which parties compromise their positions—even very different positions. Jones points to the 1990 budget deal as a prime example. Democrats swallowed budget cuts and accepted restraints they swore they would never accept, and Bush abandoned his "read my lips, no new taxes" pledge.[29]

An even kinder, gentler form of executive-legislative relations is *bipartisanship*, by which Jones means that parties cooperate and compromise, not just at the final-passage stage of the legislative process, but in the development of legislative proposals. Foreign relations, especially the Marshall Plan under Truman and congressional Republicans, is the classic example. Finally, *crosspartisanship* occurs when a segment of one congressional party joins with the other party to form a majority. Thus, although formally divided, was the government practically unified when the southern "boll weevils" gave Reagan "ideological control" of the House in 1981 and enabled him to win passage of far-reaching budget and tax proposals? Although formally unified, was the government practically divided when defections by southern Democrats blocked some parts of the agendas of Democratic presidents such as Roosevelt and Kennedy?

All in all, in his major extension of Mayhew's work, Jones finds little merit in the traditional argument that American government functions best when a strong president actively leads a Congress controlled by his party. Reading Jones's account, any disinterested observer will find examples of ineffective and effective government, successful and unsuccessful presidents, and good and bad legislation, under both unified and divided governments.

Krehbiel arrives at strikingly similar conclusions via an entirely different route. He sets up a sequential game-theoretic model of the national policymaking process, then solves the game for the equilibria that exist under different configurations of the institutional actors. The elements of the configurations in Krehbiel's formal model are three: the position of the president, the position of the median voter in the legislature, and the positions of legislators empowered by extramajoritarian features of the national policymaking process, that is, the one whose vote, when added to those of one-third of a chamber, makes a veto override impossible and the one whose vote, when added to those of two-fifths, makes a filibuster succeed. Krehbiel finds that divided or unified control makes little difference. Under a wide range of parameter values, both unified and divided configurations have gridlock equilibria. Even when Krehbiel assumes, contrary to fact, that the majority party is perfectly cohesive, gridlock still characterizes the equilibria of the unified government game. Krehbiel does identify one important factor that determines legislative movement: the position of the status quo ante. Where the status quo is far from the preferences of all the important actors—president, party or legislature median, and filibuster and veto pivots—the legislature passes and the president signs legislation. But this happens with either divided or unified control!

Divided Government and Executive-Legislative Conflict

The studies reviewed thus far examine the impact of divided government on legislative productivity: does divided control result in a lower level of legislative output? Such a clear, direct effect is not the only logically possible one, of course; divided control might have other, more subtle, more indirect effects on the political process, such as raising the level of executive-legislative conflict. For example, the historical record clearly indicates that presidents veto more legislation when government is divided than when unified. Consistent with that record, President Clinton vetoed no bills during his first two years in office, whereas President Bush vetoed twenty-five during the preceding two years.

Sean Kelly recently has shown that interbranch conflict on roll call votes is greater during periods of divided government. Policy agreement between the president and congressional majorities is more than 20 percent lower when the institutions are controlled by different parties.[30] Significantly, the effect seems to be a step function reflecting the presence or absence of control, not a linear function of the number of seats controlled by the president's party. These findings support Sundquist's argument that under divided control congressional majorities are loath to do anything that would enhance the president's standing; on the contrary, they will bring matters the president opposes to a vote precisely to demonstrate their disagreement.[31]

On the other hand, examination of another congressional arena—committee hearings—reveals no difference between unified and divided control. Paul Peterson and Jay Greene find that hostile questioning of executive branch witnesses has declined in the postwar period even as divided control has become more common.[32] Congressional members of the president's party have become friendlier over time, whereas congressional members of the opposition are no more hostile now than in earlier decades. Peterson and Greene suggest that the common perception of increased interbranch conflict is a misperception. One way of reconciling Kelly's findings based on roll call votes and Peterson and Greene's based on committee hearings is to suggest that partisan conflict will be more likely to emerge in more public arenas such as the floor of the House and Senate than in more private arenas such as the committee rooms. This would also help to reconcile findings of greater conflict with findings of little or no difference in legislative productivity. Legislators might posture when the cameras are on but continue to do the work of government when out of the spotlight.

Divided Government and Budget Deficits

Many observers have attributed the huge deficits of the 1980s to divided government. More systematic research over a longer period of time has raised doubts. What is the current state of opinion? The national experience of recent years does little to settle the question. President Bush and the Democratic Congress negotiated a budget package/tax increase in 1990 that significantly lowered the growth of the deficit. And in 1992, the Democratic congressional leadership rammed through President Clinton's budget package/tax increase without a single Republican vote in either chamber. Whatever the electoral cost to Bush of violating his "no new taxes" pledge and to Clinton of appearing to be an "old Democrat," most analysts judged both Bush's and Clinton's tax increase to have been among the significant accomplishments of their respective administrations. The former is an example of what Jones calls crosspartisanship; the latter, of partisanship. One was produced by divided government; one by unified government. At the national level, the relationship between divided government and budget deficits is as unclear as before.

At the state level, there is new evidence, and the picture is somewhat clearer. Two ambitious empirical studies conclude that divided government—at least a particular form of it—has generally negative effects on budget deficits. Alt and Lowry examine state budgets between 1968 and 1987.[33] Based on a combination of formal models of party and institutional interaction, they test three hypotheses about patterns of control and deficits: first, that states with unified control will react to budget shocks by adjusting revenues; second, that states with split-branch control (one party controls the legislature; one the executive) will react with a mixture of revenue and spending adjustments; and third, that states with split legislative control will be slower to react than states with other patterns of control. The findings for split-branch control are inconclusive, but the others are not. Although Alt and Lowry find no general tendency for any pattern of control to produce chronic deficits, unified governments respond more quickly and more effectively to shocks, especially where they are subject to balanced budget constraints. States with split legislatures are slower to react, whether constitutionally constrained or not.

A similar but independent study by Poterba examines state budgeting in the deficit-ridden years of 1988 to 1992.[34] Whereas Alt and Lowry examine year-to-year changes, Poterba examines within-year adjustments. His conclusions are very similar. Unified governments react more quickly, generally on the tax side, and balanced budget requirements enhance the speed of reactions.

These complex empirical studies yield an intuitively plausible picture. Unified state governments (typically Democratic in the era studied) respond to deficits by raising taxes. Split-branch governments (typically Republican governor/Democratic legislature) respond with a mixture of tax increases and spending cuts; neither branch can go it alone, and the inevitability of compromise is obvious to both branches. Split legislatures, however, are more likely to become gridlocked, as each chamber is tempted to try to outlast the other in a "war of attrition," as in the California budget battle of 1991 to 1992. Such findings suggest that the 1990s rise in split state legislatures is not a positive development. And on a more retrospective note, such findings add credence to McCubbins's account of the deficit politics of the Reagan era, even if the national data are not statistically conclusive.[35]

Divided Control and Government Performance

The literature continues to suggest that the stronger claims for the negative effects of divided government have little empirical support. Four years of additional experience and research does not markedly change that earlier conclusion. At the national level, in particular, there is little evidence that divided government alone can account for the perceived failings of the federal government.

At the state level, there is less research, but it is more suggestive. When the experiences of the fifty states are pooled, there are sufficient data to generate statistically significant differences, which point in the direction predicted by critics of divided government: divided control, at least of the legislature, appears to exacerbate budgetary difficulties. Still, many factors other than divided control play a role, and there is no evidence that split-branch government (one party controls both legislative chambers but not the governor's office) performs any worse than unified government.

Accountability under Unified Control: The Lessons of 1993–1994

Beyond questions of governmental efficiency and effectiveness, critics of divided government have charged that divided control confuses the lines of responsibility in American politics. With different institutions controlled by different parties, how can voters hold parties collectively responsible for their performance? Moreover, knowing that it is hard for voters to assess responsibility, elected officials have less reason to worry about their performance; even if they have nothing to show by way of tangible accomplishments, they can resort to the "blame game," posturing about what they support and blaming the other party for their inability to deliver.

Certainly, the 1994 congressional elections are consistent with the notion that unified control enhances electoral accountability. For two decades, election observers had marveled at the ability of congressional incumbents to insulate themselves from larger issues of national policy and performance, but many of these incumbents evidently found their insulation insufficient in 1994. Speaker of the House Tom Foley, Judiciary Chair Jack Brooks, Senate Majority Leader heir-apparent Jim Sasser—these and many others found themselves too closely tied to the policies and performance of the Clinton administration for a majority of their constituents. As usual, they ran, but this time they couldn't hide. Unified Democratic control may well have been the difference.

Still, it is easy to exaggerate the extent to which the election was dominated by an angry electorate exacting its revenge on the Democrats. That image takes too literally the earthquake, tidal wave, and tsunami metaphors that dominated postelection commentary. As noted above, a variety of important considerations underlay the election results. Certainly, I will not be surprised if subsequent research shows that national issues and presidential performance affected the congressional voting in 1994 to a greater extent than in other recent elections. But that still leaves open the question of why? Why were the Republicans able to "nationalize" the 1994 elections? Was the answer simply "unified Democratic control"? If so, why were they not able to nationalize the 1978 elections against a floundering Carter administration? Do the 1994 results indicate that collective account-ability was there all along, just lying dormant and waiting for unified control to revive it—despite the Republicans' inability to capitalize in 1978—or was 1994 an aberration? If unified control has revived collective responsibility, then we might see an older pattern of politics reassert itself, a pattern wherein one party or the other expects to gain unified control in the presidential elections, and divided government occurs as a consequence of losing one or both houses at the midterm. If this were to happen, proponents of unified government would have the chance to test their beliefs against contemporary reality. As citizens, we can only hope that in such an eventuality, the optimism of the advocates of unified government would be justified. But as ana-lysts, it is far too early to conclude either that the era of candidate-centered elections has reverted to an older party-centered era or that if it has, conditions will necessarily improve.

Conclusion: Divided Government or Divided Citizenry?

All in all, there is little in the record of the mid-1990s to support the stronger claims of the critics of divided government. To the extent that the effects of divided government can be identified at all, they appear quite limited. Critics and commentators have been too quick to lay the blame for the perceived failings of governments on political-institutional processes, while ignoring other, more important factors.

Prominent among those other factors are the preferences of the voters. If citizens condemn budget deficits while overwhelmingly opposing cuts in entitlements and/or increases in taxes, there is not much that even a unified government can do to reduce the deficit. If citizens want a zero-risk society but resent bureaucratic intrusion and red tape, they are unlikely to be satisfied with the regulatory process. If citizens want guaranteed health care for all, choice of doctors and facilities, and cheaper insurance premiums for health care than they currently pay, they are unlikely to be happy with any conceivable national health care plan. Does it make sense to blame political-institutional processes for failing to satisfy incompatible wants?

Of course, the fault may lie with our leaders. After all, if we had inspiring, charismatic leaders who could educate the voters, inform their preferences, and dispel the illusions and contradictions, then the political process would work better. Perhaps, but I will not hold my breath waiting for such leaders, and I suspect that there have been few of them in the past. Such demigods are created after the fact in the panegyrics of palace historians. The times make the leader more than the leader makes the times.[36]

Even more than before, I believe that the prevailing dissatisfaction of Americans with their governments largely reflects their lack of agreement on what, if anything, should be done. If almost no one likes the status quo but different groups strongly disagree over what direction policy should move in, no one is going to be very happy. Consider the suggestive data in table 2.3. Over the course of the past generation, Americans' views of the power of the federal government have polarized. When Lyndon Johnson and the Eighty-ninth Congress were adopting Great Society initiatives, a plurality of the electorate expressed satisfaction with the level of activity of the federal government, and a significant minority favored additional activity. In contrast, when Bill Clinton and the 103rd Congress were trying to pass a national health care program, only a tiny minority were satisfied with the federal government as is, while large and equal-sized pluralities wanted to go in opposite directions. In both cases, government was unified, but it acted in the former case and gridlocked in the latter. The difference was the size of the center relative to the opposed extremes in the 1960s versus the 1990s.

TABLE 2.3
Americans' Opinions on Federal Power

	1964	1992
Too much federal power	26%	39%
About right	36%	12%
Not enough federal power	31%	40%

Source: American National Election Studies.
Note: Respondents were asked: "Which one of these statements comes clos-est to your own views about governmental power today? (1) The federal government has too much power. (2) The federal government is using about the right amount of power for meeting today's needs. (3) The federal govern-ment should use its powers more vigorously to promote the well-being of all segments of the people."

Those who yearn for energetic, effective government probably should shift their focus away from the simple question of party control to the more complicated question of how to build majorities for the ends they espouse. If both divided control and government inaction reflect the absence of popular consensus, attention should shift toward explaining the lack of consensus. Does this lack result from the decline of consensus-building actors such as parties and the rise of consensus-destroying actors such as single-issue groups, conflict-obsessed media, and ideologically rigid political elites? Or are these developments, too, just symptoms, not causes? Or both? In the final analysis, we are talking about the ability of a nation to govern itself democratically, and no single factor operating in simple, straightforward fashion will determine how well or poorly we do. It would have been nice if political scientists could have shown to everyone's satisfaction that unified control is the answer to most of our problems. Unfortunately, the world is not so simple.

Notes

1. The discussion in this paper is drawn from my *Divided Government*, 2d ed. (Boston: Allyn & Bacon, 1996).

2. Morris Fiorina, *Divided Government* (New York: Macmillan, 1992).

3. In 1976, Carter was running against the *appointed* vice-president of a president who had resigned in disgrace, in the aftermath of a serious recession. Under such conditions, it was less noteworthy that a Democrat won than that he won by such a narrow margin—less than 1 percent.

4. Paul R. Abramson, John H. Aldrich, and David W. Rohde, *Change and Continuity in the 1992 Elections* (Washington, D.C.: Congressional Quarterly Press, 1994); Herbert F. Weisberg and David C. Kimball, "Attitudinal Correlates of the 1992 Presidential Vote: Party Identification and Beyond," in, *Democracy's Feast: Elections in America*, ed. Herbert F. Weisberg (Chatham, N.J.: Chatham House, 1995), 72–111.

5. David Magleby and Kelly Patterson, "The Polls—Poll Trends: Congressional Reform," *Public Opinion Quarterly* 58 (1994): 419–27.

6. Compare Magleby and Patterson, 423, with Kelly Patterson and David Magleby, "Public Support for Congress," *Public Opinion Quarterly* 56 (1992): 549.

7. Gary C. Jacobson and Michael Dimock, "Checking Out: The Effects of Bank Overdrafts on the 1992 House Elections," *American Journal of Political Science* 38 (1994): 601–24.

8. Norman Ornstein, Thomas Mann and Michael Malbin, *Vital Statistics on Congress, 1993–1994* (Washington, DC: Congressional Quarterly Inc., 1994): table 2–7.

9. If every race were a toss-up, then the Republicans would have expected to win seventeen or eighteen of the thirty-five seats. Incumbency would have dampened such expectations somewhat, but the situation still looked highly promising for the Republicans. On statewide competitiveness, see Alan Abramowitz and Jeffrey Segal, *Senate Elections* (Ann Arbor: University of Michigan Press, 1995): chapter 8.

10. Calculated from the 1994 American National Election Study. These data were made available through the Interuniversity Consortium for Political and Social Research.

11. Karl Kurtz of the National Conference on State Legislatures called this to my attention before I had done my own tabulations. Personal communication, 18 March 1993.

12. In the autumn of 1992, support for divided government in the *Wall Street Journal*/ABC poll dropped below a majority for the first time since the question was asked in 1984. By the autumn of 1994, a comfortable majority supported divided government once again.

13. Everett Carll Ladd, ed., *America at the Polls: 1994* (Storrs, Conn.: The Roper Institute, 1995), 2.

14. For example, gun control is an issue that is political poison in southern and western states and even in states like Pennsylvania where the National Rifle Association has a large membership. While I have no systematic evidence on this point, my reading of campaign reports and my conversations with

various local observers suggest that gun control may have made the difference in at least a half-dozen seats in 1994, including the defeats of longtime incumbents like Jack Brooks of Texas and Dan Glickman of Kansas. For a comprehensive treatment of the gun control issue, see Robert Spitzer, *The Politics of Gun Control* (Chatham, N.J.: Chatham House, 1995).

15. David Lublin, "Costs of Gerrymandering," *New York Times*, 13 December 1994, letter to the editor. Lublin's estimates are based on analyses described in "Gerrymander for Justice? Racial Redistricting and Black and Latino Representation" (Ph.D. diss., Harvard University, 1994). At a panel held during the 1991 American Political Science Association meetings in Washington, D.C., Gary C. Jacobson, a leading expert on House elections, predicted a loss of between twenty and twenty-five seats, based in large part on the delayed impact of the 1991 redistricting. This was well before Congress took up health care, and a year before Clinton's approval ratings hit bottom.

16. The method is set forth in Andrew Gelman and Gary King, "Estimating the Incumbency Advantage without Bias," *American Journal of Political Science* 34 (1994): 1142–64. Thanks to Gary King for the 1994 figures.

17. James L. Sundquist, "Needed: A Political Theory for the New Era of Coalition Government in the United States," *Political Science Quarterly* 103 (winter 1988–89): 613–35.

18. This pithy summation of the bill of particulars aimed at divided government is due to Keith Krehbiel, "Institutional and Partisan Sources of Gridlock: A Theory of Divided and Unified Government," *Journal of Theoretical Politics* (forthcoming).

19. The exception to this summation is vetoes: presidents were significantly more likely to veto bills and resolutions when Congress was controlled by the other party. Consistent with this finding, President Clinton cast no vetoes during his first two years.

20. See note 12 above.

21. David S. Cloud, "Health Care's Painful Demise Cast Pall on Clinton Agenda," *Congressional Quarterly Weekly Report*, 5 November 1994, 3144.

22. David S. Cloud, "End of Session Marked by Partisan Stalemate," *Congressional Quarterly Weekly Report*, 8 October 1994, 2849.

23. "Perhaps the Worst Congress," *Washington Post National Weekly Edition*, 17–23 October 1994, 27.

24. David R. Mayhew, *Divided We Govern: Party Control, Lawmaking, and Investigations, 1946–1990* (New Haven: Yale University Press, 1991). For Mayhew's update see Stephen Gettinger, "View from the Ivory Tower More Rosy than Media's," *Congressional Quarterly Weekly Report*, 8 October 1994, 2850–51.

25. Gettinger, "View from the Ivory Tower," 2850.

26. Ibid., 2851.

27. Charles O. Jones, *The Presidency in a Separated System* (Washington, D.C.: Brookings Institution, 1994); Krehbiel, "Sources of Gridlock."

28. Jones, *The Presidency*, 19–23.

29. See also Weatherford's analysis of an earlier budget deal, the national response to the 1958 recession. M. Stephen Weatherford, "Responsiveness and Deliberation in Divided Government: Presidential Leadership in Tax Policy Making," *British Journal of Political Science* 24 (1994): 1–31.

30. Policy agreement is calculated from a subset of important votes included in *Congressional Quarterly's* presidential success scores. See Sean Q Kelly, "The Institutional Foundations of Inter-Branch Conflict in the Era of Divided Government," *Southeastern Political Review* (forthcoming).

31. Sundquist, "Needed: A Political Theory."

32. Paul E. Peterson and Jay P. Greene, "Why Executive-Legislative Conflict in the United States Is Dwindling," *British Journal of Political Science* 24 (1994): 33–55.

33. James E. Alt and Robert C. Lowry, "Divided Government, Fiscal Institutions, and Budget Deficits: Evidence from the States," *American Political Science Review* 88 (1994): 811–28.

34. James Poterba, "State Responses to Fiscal Crisis: The Effects of Budgetary Institutions and Politics," *Journal of Political Economy* 102 (1994): 799–821.

35. Mathew D. McCubbins, "Party Governance and U.S. Budget Deficits: Divided Government and Fiscal Stalemate," in *Politics and Economics in the 1980s*, ed. Alberto Alesina and Geoffrey Carliner (Chicago: University of Chicago Press, 1991): 83–111.

36. Stephen Skowronek, *The Politics Presidents Make: Leadership from John Adams to George Bush* (Cambridge: Harvard University Press, 1993).

Chapter Three

Divided Government and the 1994 Elections

Gary C. Jacobson

The 1994 elections gave the Republican Party its greatest congressional triumph in more than four decades. Republicans picked up fifty-two House seats and eight Senate seats to win controlling majorities in both bodies for the first time since 1952. After a two-year hiatus, the United States again had divided government—one party controlling the presidency, the other party controlling Congress. But in a startling reversal, this time the White House belonged to the Democrats, while Congress belonged to the Republicans.

The Republican victory thrust its chief architect, Newt Gingrich, to the forefront of American politics, elevating him to Speaker of the House and *Time*'s 1995 "Man of the Year." Although Gingrich deserves plenty of credit for helping Republican candidates to make the most of their opportunities in 1994, the Republican most responsible for Gingrich's ascension was not Gingrich but George Bush. It was Bush's failure to win reelection that gave Republicans the opportunity that Gingrich and other Republican leaders exploited so effectively. The termination of divided government in 1992 was essential to its return, transposed, in 1994.

Divided and unified government are the creators as well as the creatures of electoral politics. Elections naturally determine whether control of Congress and the presidency is monopolized or shared between the parties, and scholars have devoted a great deal of attention to the electoral foundations of divided (or unified) government.[1] The question of how divided government (or its absence) shapes elections has attracted considerably less attention. The upheavals of 1994 should change all that, for neither their occurrence nor their timing can be explained without understanding the electoral politics of divided and unified government. My purpose in this essay is thus to examine how divided government during the Reagan-Bush years shaped the congressional elections of the 1990s, most particularly that of 1994, and to consider how the post-1994 form of divided government will shape electoral politics in 1996 and beyond.

The Roots of Divided Government

In the four decades prior to 1994, the federal government was divided in only one way: a Republican president faced a Democratic House and, except for the period from 1981 to 1987, Senate. Republicans won seven of the eleven presidential contests held between 1952 and 1992 but, except for the Eighty-third Congress (1953–1954), never won a majority in the House. The twelve years of the Reagan and Bush administrations (1981–1993) were the longest period of divided government in U.S. history. As I argued at length in *The Electoral Origins of Divided Government*, divided government during the Reagan-Bush era faithfully mirrored the public's own divided and self-contradictory preferences.[2] Polling data make it abundantly clear that most voters want a balanced federal budget, low inflation, less intrusive government, greater economic efficiency, and a strong national defense. But the same polls make it equally clear that voters object to paying the necessary price for these collective goods. They object to cuts in middle-class entitlements and other popular programs, higher unemployment, greater exposure to market forces, and greater environmental risk. These costs are more narrowly focused than the broader collective goods, and for those who get stuck with them, they certainly outweigh the benefits of those goods. People naturally prefer a job to lower inflation, a larger Social Security check or lower Medicare premium to an imperceptibly smaller deficit or tax bill.

During the 1980s, the parties took positions that allowed voters to express both sets of preferences at the polls. They could elect Republican presidents committed to low taxes, economic efficiency, and a strong national defense, and Democratic congressmembers who promised to minimize the price voters would have to pay for these goods in forgone benefits and higher economic and environmental risks. The ground for this sort of ticket-splitting was evident in the way the public viewed the strengths of the two parties. While Republicans were judged better than Democrats at ensuring prosperity, handling inflation, reducing the deficit, and maintaining a strong defense, Democrats were thought better at dealing with issues of social welfare, economic security, education, and the environment. Democrats were also considered more likely to make fair fiscal decisions and be more attuned to the groups paying the bill for the collective benefits of greater economic efficiency and growth: women, union members, farmers, African-Americans, and "people like you." Republicans were thought to be more solicitous only of "big business" and "the rich."[3]

Democrats also thrived on a candidate-centered election system in which, as Tip O'Neill famously put it, "all politics is local." As the party believing in the value of government and thus of governmental service, they fielded a higher proportion of ambitious, experienced, talented candidates who were willing to do the hard work it took to build and maintain a personal constituency back in the district. House Democrats became adept at building local majority coalitions out of whatever material was at hand. The party's fractious diversity, which frustrated its presidential candidates' efforts to construct majority coalitions, allowed Democrats to adapt to a wide variety of political environments. They wooed organized labor, or civil rights activists, or feminists, or environmentalists when doing so added votes, and found other allies when it did not. Southern Democrats, for example, had little difficulty portraying themselves as military hawks, social conservatives, and friends of the National Rifle Association despite their national party's image. By keeping the electoral focus local in districts where the national party's liberal reputation was a millstone, Democrats were able to capture and retain House seats that otherwise had a distinctly Republican coloration.

The ticket-splitting that produced divided government thus required neither cynicism nor even conscious calculation on the part of voters. Offered two presidential candidates, majorities chose the one they expected to reduce spending, resist tax hikes, and keep defense strong. Offered two House candidates, majorities chose the one they trusted to defend local interests, deliver local benefits, and protect their favorite programs.[4]

The Consequences of Divided Government

Divided government, reflecting the public's incompatible and unreconciled preferences (as well as the Democrats' superior skill at retail politics), set up a dynamic that was guaranteed to leave the public frustrated and angry at Congress and the president. Conflicts that were not resolved on election day had to be resolved in Washington. Resolution did not come easy; indeed, often it did not come at all. Whenever Republican presidents and Democratic congresses faced major policy decisions, divided government encouraged the kind of partisan posturing, haggling, delay, and confusion that voters hate. In effect, divided government forced policymaking out into the open, and as John Hibbing and Elizabeth Theiss-Morse have shown, leaders' images always suffer when intense political disagreements are thrashed out in public. "Just as people want governmental services without the pain of taxes, they also want democratic procedures without the pain of witnessing what comes along with those procedures"—wrangling, finger-pointing, and compromise.[5] The politics of divided government also guaranteed that voters would wind up feeling betrayed by the inevitable compromises that made agreement possible.

The principal nexus of partisan conflict was the federal budget. Budget politics was certainly not the only area where the incompatible promises that elected Republican presidents and Democratic congresses collided, but it was the most consequential. During the Reagan-Bush years, budget politics was virtually guaranteed to alienate large segments of the public. Republicans had taken the White House and Senate in 1980 while promising the political equivalent of a free lunch: tax cuts without spending cuts or larger deficits because, according to the happy theory of supply-side economics, lower taxes would stimulate so much economic growth that total revenues would not fall. It was faulty economics but irresistibly good electoral politics. Supply-side tax cuts, combined with increases in total spending and the sharp 1982 recession, soon put the budget deeply in the red. Only steep tax increases, sharp spending cuts, or some combination of the two could put the budget back in balance.

Congress, by indexing entitlement spending and tax brackets to inflation, had unwittingly intensified the political threat posed by the budget squeeze after 1981. Before entitlements and tax rates were indexed, inflation steadily, quietly, and automatically reduced spending and increased revenues. Inflation eroded the real value of pension and welfare checks; it also increased tax revenues through "bracket creep," as inflated incomes pushed more taxpayers into higher-paying tax brackets. With steady inflation, Congress could allow entitlements to shrink and taxes to rise simply by doing nothing. Better yet, members could please voters by raising entitlements and lowering taxes to counteract (partially) the effects of inflation. By the end of the 1970s, however, Congress had indexed all the major entitlements so that they would grow with inflation, and a provision in the 1981 tax bill did the same with tax brackets. Since then, members of Congress have had to act explicitly to cut entitlement spending or boost taxes, exposing them to sharply greater electoral risk when trying to make the federal budget balance.[6]

Not only indexing, but also the politics of budgeting under divided government, tilted against any serious attack on the deficit. The Reagan administration's early experiments with supply-side economics taught Republicans that opposition to taxes was good politics but attacking middle-class entitlements and other popular programs was not. Democrats learned that most large domestic programs were indeed popular but people did not like to pay for them. Subsequent election campaigns, built on these insights, gave voters the opportunity to declare themselves for both low taxes and generous domestic spending, electing Republican presidents who promised "no new taxes" and Democratic majorities in Congress committed to maintaining or enlarging middle-class entitlements.

Because Congress and the president could not amend the laws of arithmetic, budget compromises faithful to these electoral stances meant large deficits. The public, however, also wants a balanced budget. Large majorities tell pollsters that they favor amending the Constitution to force the government to match spending with income. The American people are divided, however, on whether reducing the deficit is more important than avoiding tax increases or spending cuts. The bad things attributed to deficits—higher long-term interest rates, lower private investment, and slower economic growth—are diffuse and distant in time, while the costs of reducing the deficit are more immediate and palpable. The economically vulnerable—people with less education, lower incomes, and more precarious employment—would rather put up with deficits than cut social spending *or* increase taxes. The deficit hawks willing to cut spending *and* raise taxes to reduce the deficit are found mainly among the better off, better educated, and economically secure.[7] Preoccupation with reducing the deficit at all costs is an elite, not a mass, phenomenon.

Elites, however, shape fiscal policy. Leaders of both parties, advised by Wall Street as well as by the experts in the Congressional Budget Office and Office of Management and Budget, eventually decided that the growing mountain of national debt was a serious threat to the long-term vitality of the American economy. When that happened, ordinary citizens, having been led to believe that the budget could be balanced by economic growth or by eliminating "waste, fraud, and abuse," were not at all prepared for the sacrifices it would take to make a serious assault on red ink. Thus, when political leaders on both sides became sufficiently alarmed about the deficit to do something about it, they confronted an electorate they had left unprepared to face fiscal reality and unconvinced that the benefits of deficit reduction outweighed the costs.

Under divided government, any feasible outcome had to be a compromise, and any compromise had to include both spending cuts and tax increases, each of which smacked of betrayal to core constituencies of one party or the other. Both parties' incumbents thus felt the heat when, just before the 1990 midterm, Bush and Democratic leaders in Congress cut a deal to reduce the deficit through a combination of tax increases and program cuts. The public hated both the process and the result, heaping disdain on both parties and both branches, though Republicans took the harder hit because Bush's betrayal of his "read my lips, no new taxes" pledge stood out so starkly.

Public anger at the 1990 budget deal, though unmistakable in opinion surveys, registered only slightly in the 1990 congressional elections, for the action had come too late to stimulate the vigorous challenges that could have exploited it. Besides, divided government diffused responsibility for unpopular policies, leaving voters bereft of partisan cues for assigning blame and conferring punishment. The simplest alternative was to turn on incumbents as a class. Few incumbents lost, but the electorate sent a strong signal when, for the first time in any postwar election, the average vote for incumbents of *both* parties fell.[8] Voters also vented their anger by enthusiastically supporting congressional term limits in polls and referenda.

Both sides hoped that the 1990 budget deal would take the deficit issue off the agenda for a while, and it did for the brief time that public attention turned to the Gulf War. But the deal also put a straitjacket on budgeting. One of its features was "pay as you go": any spending increase had to be paid for by a specific tax increase or a spending cut elsewhere; any tax cut had to be matched by a spending cut or a tax increase elsewhere. This made it politically impossible for the Bush administration to stimulate a weak economy by cutting taxes (or by boosting spending) in time for the 1992 elections, for it would have required him to reopen budget negotiations with the Democrats, who were not disposed to help him out.[9] Divided government thus kept Bush from doing anything to allay the greatest threat to his reelection.

1992: Unified Government Again

The Bush administration's failure to deliver on the economy or hold the line on taxes nullified the usual Republican presidential advantage on these issues, giving Bill Clinton his victory and the United States its first unified government in twelve years. It was by no means a general Democratic triumph, however. Republicans actually picked up ten House seats while breaking even in the Senate. The electorate was, if anything, even more angry with Congress in 1992 than it had been in 1990, with the House Bank scandal and Anita Hill's treatment by the Senate Judiciary Committee adding to the outrage. Largely because of a postwar record number of retirements and primary election defeats, 1992 produced the greatest turnover of House seats in fifty years, with 110 new members taking office in 1993. But as in 1990, the forces behind the turnover were bipartisan in their effect; with both parties sharing responsibility for governing, neither party could turn public anger to partisan advantage.[10] The 1992 elections resurrected unified government, but not because of any great popular swing to the Democrats.

Bill Clinton and the 103rd Congress

Bill Clinton had campaigned promising to "put people first"—to cut taxes on the middle class, reform the health care system, enact an economic stimulus package, and invest in education and the national infrastructure. His mantra was "change." It was a compelling theme in 1992, and it enabled him to win election despite serious doubts among voters about his personal character. Clinton thus entered the White House with high expectations but without a strong base of personal or political support (he had, after all, won only 43 percent of the popular vote).

Clinton had also promised to cut the deficit in half during his first term. Ross Perot's independent candidacy had elevated the deficit to a major issue and served as a beacon to those voters who put deficit reduction ahead of both lower taxes and generous middle-class entitlements. With both parties pursuing the Perot constituency after the election, attention to the deficit took on new political urgency; deficit hawks among the elite now had some allies. Very early, the Clinton administration had to choose between, on the one hand, its more populist promises of new investment, tax cuts for middle-income families, and greater spending on health and education and, on the other, attacking the deficit. Like Bush before him, Clinton found that sound economic management, as conceived by most economic experts in both parties as well as by Wall Street bond traders, required attacking the deficit. And like Bush before him, he found that doing so alienated some of his core supporters, exposed him as yet another untrustworthy politician, and opened him to full-throated attacks from the other party. Both Bush and Clinton won elections on popular economic themes but found that to govern, they had to reject economic populism in favor of policies catering to Wall Street and official Washington. Both were urged not to give in—Bush by House Republicans and others for whom "no new taxes" was holy writ, Clinton by his populist campaign staffers and congressional liberals—but governing makes different demands than campaigning.[11]

Unlike Bush, however, Clinton undertook the thankless task of deficit reduction without the cover provided by divided government. Republicans, liberated by the 1992 elections from any responsibility for governing, were free to attack the Democrats' plans without defending any alternative. Senate Minority Leader Bob Dole berated Clinton for proposing "the largest tax increase in world history" as part of his deficit reduction package, but declined to offer a Republican alternative on the ground that "well, we're not the government."[12] Another Republican senator, Trent Lott, claimed at a committee hearing to have a list of $216 billion in "basically painless budget cuts" that could be made immediately. When Clinton's budget director asked to see the list, Lott demurred, "I'm going to keep it right here," indicating his breast pocket, "until I see yours."[13]

In both the House and the Senate, every Republican member voted against the 1993 reconciliation bill that embodied Clinton's deficit reduction plan. Democrats thus had to take total responsibility for both the tax increases ($241 billion) and the spending cuts ($255 billion) designed to reduce the deficit by nearly $500 billion over the ensuing five years.[14] The tax increases resurrected the Republicans' favorite issue for the 1994 campaigns, while the spending cuts (in Medicare, Medicaid, student loans, and federal pensions, among other things) sapped enthusiasm for Democrats among their own core constituents.

The tax increases and spending restraint required to reduce the deficit were all the more painful because so many Americans had not shared in the economic growth of the 1980s. Most studies indicate that the Reagan prosperity, bought on credit, benefited only the top quintile of income groups.[15] The middle three quintiles have made little, if any economic progress for a quarter century. Moreover, some evidence suggests that middle-class incomes have become more volatile from one year to the next, so that even if middle-income people have not done worse on average, their level of uncertainty about the economic future is appreciably greater. It is a matter of debate how much government policy has had to do with this. Most observers attribute the growing inequality of incomes and greater economic uncertainty to increased competition in world markets, which has forced corporations to cut costs by employing fewer workers and paying them less. Middle-management positions have disappeared along with the well-paying production jobs that were once available to people with only high school educations. Many families have maintained middle-class life-styles only by adding a second income from a working wife or by working longer hours.

Although the economy grew during the Clinton administration, the fruits of growth again went largely to families at the upper end of the economic scale.[16] Economic prosperity, moreover, is not the only measure of the quality of life. The public institutions that serve ordinary people—public schools, police, and courts—seemed to be in trouble. The issues of crime, illegal immigration, and unmarried teen-age mothers on welfare that dominated the 1994 campaigns in many places were not new, but they had gained new urgency. For millions of Americans, government had delivered neither physical nor economic security, failing conspicuously to reverse what they saw as moral and cultural decline.

The federal government's sorry reputation helped doom the Clinton administration's most ambitious legislative effort, health care reform. The public supported Clinton's goals (universal coverage, portability, and even, by a small plurality, having employers pay 80 percent of the cost) but did not support the means his task force proposed, at least as those means were successfully depicted by opponents of health care reform: elaborate federal regulation, fewer choices, and higher costs.[17] In the end, Republicans were able to portray the Clinton plan as another expensive big government program that would make most people's lives worse rather than better, which succeeded in killing it.

Stagnant incomes, declining public services, more work, and more hectic schedules left large segments of the population with poorer lives and diminished prospects. It is in this context that congressional malfeasance—scandals involving senior leaders in the House and the Keating Five in the Senate, bank overdrafts, unpaid restaurant bills, post office frauds, and pay raise subterfuges—was so damaging to members of Congress. The image of representatives as self-serving, easily corrupted, and out of touch with the lives of ordinary Americans pervaded the 1992 elections and helped produce that year's huge turnover. Members were unable to shake that image in the 103rd Congress, and now that Democrats were ostensibly in full control of the federal government, they took the full brunt of the public's disgust with career politicians and politics as usual.

A final problem for the Democrats was that ending divided government in the formal sense did not end legislative gridlock. Like health care reform, many of the Clinton administration's most ambitions plans died in an agony of conflict and partisan recrimination. The truth, revealed early in the 103rd Congress when Bob Dole led a successful Republican filibuster against Clinton's economic stimulus package, is that, as Keith Krehbiel's insightful analysis has demonstrated, divided government had not ended at all. Divided partisan control of policymaking persists as long as the minority party holds at least forty seats in the Senate and can therefore kill any bill it wants to kill.[18]

The illusion of unified government put the onus of failure on the Democrats; the reality of divided government let Senate Republicans make sure that the administration would fail. Clinton was elected on a promise of change. Senate Republicans could prevent change, and they did. It was not difficult, for while everyone may agree that change is desirable, rarely is there a consensus on what to change *to*. The health care issue is exhibit A. If voters did not get change with Clinton—or if they did not like the changes he proposed—the alternative was to elect Republicans.

In sum, budgetary and other national problems left unresolved by years of partisan stalemate did not go away after 1992. The public was no more prepared for the sacrifices needed to match programs with resources than it was before the election. Any move in that direction by the Democrats was bound to disappoint their own supporters or open them up to the Republicans' favorite lines of attack or, as the case turned out, both.

To compound his party's problems, Clinton had also alienated important groups of swing voters: the so-called Reagan Democrats and much of the largely male Perot constituency. The cultural symbolism conveyed by many of the administration's actions offended socially conservative white men, especially in the South. The conspicuous attention to race and gender diversity in making appointments called to mind detested affirmative action programs. Support for gays in the military, restrictions on gun ownership, and the role and style of Hillary Rodham Clinton reminded these swing voters of the cultural liberalism that was at the core of what they did *not* like about the Democratic Party. Clinton's reputation with this segment of the population was worsened by one of his most notable successes: the passage of the North American Free Trade Agreement, which put him at odds with traditional blue-collar Democrats.

With the end of divided government in 1992, and with the Clinton administration's problems, political forces lined up uniformly against the Democrats for 1994. Disgust with government had a partisan focus. Issues that Republicans had used to win the presidency could now be used against Clinton's Democratic allies in Congress. Republican leaders, notably Newt Gingrich, recognized their opportunity and did their utmost to exploit it. They sought, with considerable success, to nationalize the campaign, undercutting the Democrats' usual advantage when "all politics is local."[19] Republican candidates offered themselves as vehicles for antigovernment rage by taking up the banner of popular structural panaceas—term limits, a constitutional amendment mandating a balanced budget, and cuts in congressional staffs and perks. They hammered on policy issues that resonated with voters' fears for the future direction of the country—crime, illegal immigration, welfare dependency, taxes, and big government. Recognizing Clinton's unpopularity, especially in the South, Republican candidates sought to portray their opponents as Clinton clones, using television ads showing their opponents' faces digitally "morphing" into Clinton's.

Ironically, the Contract with America, which became the ironclad blueprint for House Republican action after the election, had, by itself, little impact on voters. In signing the contract on the steps of the Capitol in late September, some three hundred Republican candidates pledged themselves to act swiftly on a grab bag of proposals for structural and legislative change, including major cuts in income taxes, cutbacks in spending on welfare programs for poor families, and amendments mandating term limits and a balanced budget. Although the contract got some attention from the news media and attracted Democratic counterattacks, only a small minority of voters were aware of its existence, and it had no discernable effect on the vote.[20] Still, individual parts of the contract were used effectively by Republican campaigners. Fed a constant stream of advice and encouragement from Gingrich and his allies, Republican candidates all over the country followed a common script designed to squeeze maximum advantage from the public's discontents.

The party's effort to nationalize the campaign also benefited enormously from the efforts of conservative talk-show hosts and Christian activists across the country. Conservatives in general and evangelical Christians in particular turned out at notably higher rates than other voters and constituted a significantly larger proportion of the electorate than in 1992.[21]

Nationalizing the Vote

Although the contract had little to do with it, Republicans did succeed in nationalizing the elections to a much greater degree than in other recent elections. The end of divided government in 1992, coupled with the Clinton administration's shortcomings, enabled the Republicans to run a set of midterm congressional campaigns that mirrored their successful presidential campaigns of the 1980s. As a result, their showing in House elections echoed their showing in recent presidential elections far more accurately than at any time during the last forty years.

Most of the seats Republicans took from Democrats were in districts that leaned Republican in presidential elections. A serviceable measure of a district's presidential leanings can be computed by taking the average division of its two-party vote between the presidential candidates in 1988 and 1992.[22] The national mean for this measure of district presidential voting habits is 49.9 percent Democratic; its median is 48.3 percent Democratic. As table 3.1 shows, Republican gains in 1994 were heavily concentrated in districts where the Democratic vote, averaged over the two elections, fell below 50 percent. For example, 31 open seats formerly held by Democrats were at stake. Republicans won all 16 open Democratic seats in districts where George Bush's share of the two-party vote, averaged together for 1988 and 1992, exceeded 50 percent; they won only 6 of the 15 where the Democratic presidential average exceeded 50 percent. Republican challengers defeated 29 percent (21 of 73) of the incumbent Democrats in districts where Bush's average exceeded 50 percent, but only 9 percent (13 of 152) in districts where Bush's average fell short of this mark.

The handful of switches to the Democrats followed the same pattern: Democrats took 4 of 5 open Republican seats where the Democrats' average share of the presidential vote exceeded 50 percent; they won

TABLE 3.1
Percentage of Districts Voting Republican in 1994 House Elections

	Republican-leaning districts	Democratic-leaning districts
Seats held by Democrats		
Incumbents	28.8%	8.6%
	(73)	(152)
Open seats	100.0%	40.0%
	(16)	(15)
Seats held by Republicans		
Incumbents	100.0%	100.0%
	(141)	(16)
Open seats	100.0%	20.0%
	(16)	(5)
Total	78.9%	19.1%
	(246)	(188)

Note: Republican-leaning districts are defined as those in which the two-party vote for George Bush, averaged across 1988 and 1992, was greater than 50 percent; Democratic-leaning districts are those in which this average fell below 50 percent. The number of districts from which the percentages were computed are in parentheses. Except for seats held by Republican incumbents, all differences in results between the two types of districts are significant at $p < .001$.

none of the other sixteen open Republican seats and defeated no Republican incumbents. The net effect of seats changing party hands in 1994 is a closer alignment of district-level presidential and House results than we have seen in any election since 1952—all the more remarkable because no presidential candidates were on the 1994 ballot.

As always, strategic behavior both reflected and magnified election-year trends in 1994.[23] Democrats behaved as if they expected it to be a bad year for their party, which helped to make it so. Strategic Democratic retirements clearly hurt their party's overall performance. Although about the same proportion of House Democrats and Republicans retired (11 percent), most of the Republicans left to run for higher office (13 of 20, or 65 percent), while most of the departing Democrats (20 of 27, or 71 percent) did not. The closer the margin in 1992 and the more Republican the district in presidential voting, the more likely a Democrat was to retire; 18 percent of the Democrats in districts that leaned Republican in presidential elections retired, compared with only 7 percent of the Democrats in districts that leaned Democratic in presidential elections. The retirements of the former group proved disastrous for the party, for, as we noted in table 3.1, Republicans took every one of the 16 seats thereby exposed. Another sign of the Democrats' strategic response to expectations was the unusual distribution of uncontested seats. For the first time in the entire postwar era, Democrats conceded more seats to Republicans (35) than Republicans conceded to Democrats (17) in the general election.

The quality of challengers also reflected rational career strategies, though as usual, potential Democratic challengers were much more sensitive to election-year expectations than were Republicans. Democrats have long enjoyed a stronger "farm system" to supply experienced House candidates because Democrats hold more of the lower-level offices that form the typical stepping stones to Congress (particularly in state legislatures). Normally, therefore, Democrats have a substantial advantage in experienced challengers. Prior to 1994, Republicans fielded the more experienced crop of challengers only twice: in 1966, when they picked up 47 seats, and 1992, when they picked up 10 seats while losing the White House. They did so again in 1994, but mainly because so few experienced Democrats were willing to take the field; only 14 percent of Republican incumbents faced experienced Democratic challengers, the second lowest proportion in any postwar election.[24]

The Republicans' proportion of experienced challengers (15 percent of all the Republicans running had had governmental experience) was merely average for them, but then many of their most highly touted challengers were unapologetic amateurs running as antigovernment outsiders. Despite all of the rhetoric condemning "career politicians," experienced Republican challengers greatly outperformed the novices, picking up significantly more votes and victories. Experienced Republican challengers won 44 percent (15 of 34) of the races they entered, compared with 11 percent (19 of 174) for inexperienced Republican challengers. Naturally, experienced challengers were more common in districts with Republican presidential leanings. But even controlling for local partisanship and other relevant variables, experienced challengers did significantly better on election day.[25]

One reason experienced Republican challengers did better than the amateurs is that, as always, they raised and spent much more money. The distribution of campaign funds in 1994 followed the expected pattern in a year when campaign activists expect a strong partisan tide. Republican challengers were significantly better funded than Democratic challengers. Not only was their average spending higher but many more of them were financed beyond the threshold usually required for a competitive campaign. Democrats, on the defensive, channeled relatively more money to incumbents; Republican incumbents had far less to worry about and could get away with lower spending.[26]

A New Structure of Electoral Competition

The 1994 election altered the fundamental distribution of partisan strength in the House, substantially reducing, though by no means eliminating, the chances that future elections will resurrect divided government in the form it took during most of the postwar era. For a number of reasons, Democrats have little prospect of taking back many of the seats lost to the Republicans in 1994, particularly in the South, and they are quite likely to lose more seats. First, the logic of electing conservative Democrats rather than Republicans to protect local (southern) interests no longer prevails now that Democrats have lost the special influence wielded by members of the majority party. These new realities were not lost on the conservative southern Democrats who remained in the House; by the end of 1995, five of them had switched to the Republican side. So had Senators Richard Shelby of Alabama and Ben Nighthorse Campbell of Colorado, the only nonsoutherner to make the switch.

Second, and equally important, the Democrats will no longer have their majority status and committee power to attract Political Action Committee (PAC) contributions from business interests. The pragmatic corporate and trade association PACs who were happy to make a marriage of convenience with Democrats as long as Democrats were running the show are now free to pursue a love match with the ideologically more compatible Republicans. Their fondness for Democrats has never extended to challengers, and now they have less incentive to contribute to incumbents as well. They also have less reason to worry about contributing *against* incumbent Democrats, whose ability to retaliate against PACs who fund their opponents has diminished. Because such groups supply about 60 percent of all PAC donations, Democrats face the prospect of a severely unfavorable imbalance of campaign resources in future elections. An early sign: As of June 1995, the National Republican Congressional Committee (NRCC) had raised $18.4 million, compared to the Democratic Congressional Campaign Committee's $5.2 million. Representative Bill Paxon, chair of the NRCC, claimed that PACs, which had been giving 65 percent of their money to the Democrats, were now giving 58 percent to the Republicans.[27]

Third, despite the Republican gains in 1994, Democrats still have more House seats at risk than do the Republicans. Although the parties won similar numbers of the most marginal seats (those won with less than 55 percent of the two-party vote) in 1994, thirty-six of the forty-four marginal Democrats were incumbents, whereas thirty-eight of the forty-one marginal Republicans were newly elected and so can expect the "sophomore surge" to raise their margins next time. Furthermore, only thirty-six Republicans represent districts that, on average, voted Democratic in 1988 and 1992, whereas fifty-two Democrats represent Republican presidential districts, twenty-six of them in the South. As the insults of minority status inspired an additional round of Democratic retirements, Republicans were poised to pick up even more seats. By April of 1996, twenty-nine Democrats (seventeen of them from the South) had officially announced that they would not run for reelection to the House, compared to only seventeen Republicans. Eight Democrats (four of them southerners) also planned to retire from the Senate, compared to only five Republicans.[28]

Finally, all of these developments come on top of the boost given to Republicans by the redistricting that followed the 1990 census. In my earlier writing on divided government, I took pains to show that, contrary to Republican allegations, gerrymandered districts were not to blame for their inability to make headway in the House.[29] Their problem was not the way Republican voters were distributed but that Republican candidates simply did not attract enough voters. In 1994, they finally did attract enough voters. For the first time since 1952, Republicans won more House votes than Democrats (53.6% of the two-party House vote went Republican), and for the first time since 1952, they won more House seats than the Democrats.

Still, there is no question that reapportionment and redistricting did contribute to the Republican victory. The states in the South and Southwest that gained seats after the 1990 census are notably more Republican than the states in the Northeast and Midwest that lost seats. The creation of minority majority districts also strengthened Republicans by packing African-American (that is, Democratic) votes into minority districts.[30] The effects of reapportionment were muted in 1992 because George Bush was a drag on the whole Republican ticket, but the potential was evident in the party's gain of ten House seats that year despite losing the White House. In 1994, Republicans more than fulfilled their potential.

Taken together, these circumstances suggest that the Democrats' postwar ascendancy in the House is history. Despite the Republicans' relatively narrow majority (narrower than any of the Democrats' majorities during their forty uninterrupted years of control), the Democrats face a steep uphill battle in trying to take the eighteen or more seats they would need to regain control of the House in 1996. And with the loss of so many incumbents through retirement, the Democrats' prospect of retaking the Senate is even dimmer. The Democrats' best hope for 1996 was that the Republicans in the 104th Congress would go too far in their zeal to dismantle federal programs and balance the budget. Working against that hope, however, was divided government.

Divided Government in the 104th Congress

After 1994, the parties divided control of Congress and the presidency again, though in a way not seen since Harry Truman's first term. In this transposed version of divided government, partisan roles remained the same, but the institutional roles were reversed. After 1994, it was the Republican Congress that sought lower spending, lower taxes, a smaller government, and a balanced budget. And it was the Democratic president who vowed to protect popular programs and middle-class entitlements.

The House Republicans' Contract with America may have had little electoral impact, but it provided a ready agenda for swift, focused action when the new Republican majority took power in January 1995. The House Republicans kept their promise to act on all of the items during the first hundred days of the 104th Congress. Yet by the end of 1995, most items had yet to become law. Internal House reforms were easy to implement, and bills applying antidiscrimination rules to

Congress and ending unfunded federal mandates also quickly became law. The rest of the Congress-bashing elements in the contract stalled or failed, however. No version of a constitutional amendment limiting House and Senate terms could get the required two-thirds vote in the House. The balanced budget amendment went down in the Senate. Legislation giving the president a line-item veto passed in 1996, but was not to apply until after the next election.

It is not difficult to understand why. These reforms were promoted by Republicans to weaken Congress and strengthen the president on the implicit assumption that the old pattern of divided government would continue indefinitely. Reforms designed to weaken a Democratic Congress facing a Republican president were obviously less urgent to a Republican majority confronting a Democrat in the White House. Why enhance Clinton's power with a line-item veto? Who needs term limits once Republicans have managed to take over the House the old-fashioned way? Similarly, Republicans no longer talked about repealing the War Powers Act or banning PACs.

On the budgetary front, the contract had recapitulated the kind of promises that have been so effective in winning votes but so troublesome when it comes to governing: billions of dollars in tax cuts, higher defense spending, and a balanced budget, but little detail as to how and where the budget would be cut to make the arithmetic work. It was plain, however, that balancing the budget while cutting taxes and raising military spending would require drastic cuts in domestic spending. Well aware that balancing the budget is a popular idea but that the sacrifices it will take are not, Republicans proposed a budget that would impose as much of the cost as possible on people who usually vote for Democrats (if, indeed, they vote at all), most notably beneficiaries of welfare, housing, and job training programs. According to a report by Democratic staffers of Congress's Joint Economic Committee, fully half of the spending cuts in the Republican plan to balance the budget by 2002 were to be borne by families in the poorest fifth of the population, with 75 percent coming from the lowest two-fifths.[31]

The difficulty, from the Republicans' perspective, is that not nearly enough savings can be squeezed out of programs for poor people and other Democratic constituencies to balance the budget, even without a tax cut. The Republicans have to take on middle-class entitlements as well. (Clinton and the Democrats faced a kindred dilemma, of course: feasible taxes on corporations and the rich could not provide enough revenue to balance the budget, so they had to cut middle-class entitlements and raise middle-class taxes). Medicare for the elderly, the fastest-growing middle-class entitlement program, was an obvious target. It was also a dangerous target—Medicare recipients are numerous and vote—and Republicans strove to justify their proposed changes by pointing out that they sought only to reduce the rate of growth in Medicare spending and that doing so was necessary to save the program from bankruptcy. This rhetorical frame came up against the hard reality that, for recipients, costs would go up and services would be curtailed.

At the strong urging of congressional Democrats, who smelled potent political issues for their party's candidates in 1996, President Clinton promised to veto any Republican plan that went too far in cutting Medicare, Medicaid, student loans, or other social programs. The Republicans' counterstrategy was to use the pressure of a partial government shutdown to get the president to sign off on their general plan to balance the budget by 2002, forcing him to share the blame for the programmatic cuts this would inevitably require. They tried to frame the choice as one of whether to balance the budget in seven years or not, while Democrats sought to put the spotlight on the details of how the budget would be balanced.

As always, when it came down to particulars, public support for slashing domestic programs to balance the budget withered. By the fall of 1995, polls indicated that the public had lost much of its enthusiasm for Republican plans. Back in January, the *Wall Street Journal*/NBC poll had found 48 percent of respondents saying that they agreed with what the Republicans in Congress were trying to do, while only 22 percent disagreed; by September, only 32 percent were still on board, while 45 percent disagreed with Republican proposals.[32] Asked in November, "When it comes to dealing with the tough choices involved in both cutting programs to reduce the deficit and still maintaining needed federal programs, whose approach do you prefer?" 49 percent said the Democrats, 36 percent, the Republicans. Earlier, in July, the breakdown had favored Republicans, 44 percent to 43 percent. In November, far more people disapproved (64 percent) than approved (22 percent) of Speaker Newt Gingrich's handling of the budget, while a majority of those expressing an opinion approved of Clinton's budget performance (48 percent, compared with 43 percent disapproving).[33] Indeed, Gingrich had become so unpopular that Democrats running in local elections and by-elections in 1995 took a leaf from the Republicans' 1994 playbook and ran television ads "morphing" their Republican opponents' heads into Gingrich's.

All this brought a glimmer of hope to congressional Democrats, especially when it was revealed that public support for some elements in the Contract with America had been overstated from the start.[34] Democratic campaigners were planning to use Gingrich again as a foil in 1996 to symbolize Republican excesses. They had unwitting allies among junior House Republicans, many of whom seemed willing to risk House careers that were, in the words of Oklahoma freshman Steve Largent, "brilliant but brief" in order to shrink the government and balance the budget.[35] Less resolute House Republicans put on a brave front, arguing that the public would swing around to their side once they had delivered on their promises of a balanced budget and smaller federal government. John Boehner, an Ohio Republican, posed the key question for the more pragmatic Republicans: "How far can we push the revolution and bring back a majority of our members?"[36]

The best thing Republican pragmatists had going for them was divided government. The principal problem for congressional Democrats hoping to cash in on the unpopular aspects of the Republicans' legislative agenda was the reality that a Democrat, Bill Clinton, sat in the White House. The Democratic minority found itself in the same unhappy position as the Republican minority during the Reagan and Bush administrations. Whenever Reagan and Bush tried to reduce the deficit, they had to agree to tax increases and smaller domestic spending cuts than they wanted in order to win congressional support, undercutting the antitax, antigovernment themes congressional Republicans depended on to win elections. Similarly, Clinton could score political points by selectively wielding his veto, but having agreed to work with Congress to balance the budget in seven years, and needing a budget to continue governing, he could not avoid cutting a deal with the Republicans. Clinton's compromises made it much harder for Democrats to run all out against the Republican cuts in middle-class entitlements and other popular programs.

Just after the 1990 election, I offered this analysis of the way in which divided government, in the form it then took, affected electoral politics:

> Democratic congresses and Republican presidencies buttress one another. Democratic majorities in Congress make a Republican presidential candidate's promise (however ephemeral) of "no new taxes" more appealing. At the same time, people may feel more comfortable voting for a Republican president knowing that the Democrats on the Hill will keep him from gutting their favorite programs. A Democratic Congress whose

members are responsive but not responsible helps to elect Republican presidents; but it is also more difficult to persuade voters to toss Democrats out of Congress when there is a Republican in the White House to limit their collective irresponsibility.[37]

Although the parties have traded institutions, the same logic holds. Clinton's ability to temper the more extreme (and unpopular) Republican proposals protects Republicans, not only by keeping them from going too far, but also by reducing the threat they pose to Medicare, environmental protection, programs for schoolchildren, and so forth. By presenting himself as a force for reason and moderation limiting the damage congressional Republicans inflict on popular programs, Clinton improves his own reelection prospects. But in doing so, he also undercuts Democratic congressional challengers' most promising campaign theme. I finished my earlier argument this way:

> Credit for good times is shared, so incumbent Democrats are not threatened by successful Republican administrations. Indeed, the only serious threat to congressional Democrats in the past four decades has come from failed Democratic administrations (see table 3.1). In this light, the most plausible scenario for ending divided government is for a Democrat to win the presidency. All it takes is for a Republican administration to stumble badly and for the Democrats to nominate an acceptable alternative. A Democratic presidency is also the only scenario offering Republicans much hope of making substantial gains, let alone winning a majority, in the House during the remainder of the century.[38]

Again, the same logic holds now, although the shoe is on the other foot. If history is any guide, Democratic control of the White House makes it harder for Democrats to retake Congress in 1996. And if Bill Clinton wins reelection, the Democrats' prospects of taking over in 1998 are also greatly diminished. Their best opportunity will wait until a disgruntled electorate turns its wrath on a unified Republican regime. There is more than a grain of truth in Robert Erikson's tongue-in-cheek argument that losing the White House is the congressional Democrats' rational strategy for winning House and Senate majorities.[39]

Notes

1. Richard Born, "Split-Ticket Voters, Divided Government, and Fiorina's Policy-Balancing Model," *Legislative Studies Quarterly* 19 (1994): 95–115;

Gary W. Cox and Samuel Kernell, eds., *The Politics of Divided Government* (Boulder, Colo.: Westview, 1991); Morris Fiorina, *Divided Government* 2d ed. (Boston: Allyn & Bacon, 1996); Gary C. Jacobson, *The Electoral Origins of Divided Government: Competition in U.S. House Elections, 1946–1988* (Boulder, Colo.: Westview, 1990).

2. Jacobson, *Electoral Origins of Divided Government.*

3. Ibid., 113–15.

4. Ibid., 113–15.

5. John R. Hibbing and Elizabeth Theiss-Morse, *Congress as Public Enemy: Political Attitudes toward American Political Institutions* (New York: Cambridge University Press, 1995).

6. Paul E. Peterson, "Vulnerable Politicians and Deficit Politics" (paper presented at the annual meeting of the American Political Science Association, Chicago, 1995).

7. John Mark Hansen, "Public Constituencies for Deficit Financing" (paper presented at the annual meeting of the American Political Science Association, New York, 1993).

8. Gary C. Jacobson, "Deficit Cutting Politics and Congressional Elections," *Political Science Quarterly* 108 (1993): 375–402.

9. Gary C. Jacobson, "Congress: Unusual Year, Unusual Election," in *The Elections of 1992*, ed. Michael Nelson (Washington, D.C.: Congressional Quarterly Press, 1993).

10. Ibid.

11. Bob Woodward, *The Agenda: Inside the Clinton White House* (New York: Simon & Schuster, 1994).

12. As quoted in Paul J. Quirk and Joseph Hinchcliffe, "Domestic Policy: The Trials of a Centrist Democrat," in *The Clinton Presidency: First Appraisals*, ed. Colin Campbell and Bert A. Rockman (Chatham, N.J.: Chatham House, 1996), 270.

13. As quoted in ibid., 270.

14. Ibid., 273.

15. Frank S. Levy and Richard C. Michel, *The Economic Future of American Families: Income and Wealth Trends* (Washington, D.C.: Urban Institute Press, 1991).

16. Gary Burtless, "Worsening American Income Inequality," *Brookings Review* 14 (spring 1996): 29.

17. See the *New York Times*/CBS poll of March 1994 and the *Washington Post*/ABC poll of February 1994.

18. Keith Krehbiel, "A Theory of Divided and Unified Government" (Graduate School of Business, Stanford University 1994, photocopy.)

19. Gary C. Jacobson, "The 1994 House Elections in Perspective," in *Midterm: The Elections of 1994*, ed. Philip A. Klinkner (Boulder, Colo.: Westview, 1996).

20. Ibid.

21. Gary C. Jacobson, *The Politics of Congressional Elections*, 4th ed. (New York: Harper Collins, 1997).

22. Michael Barone and Grant Ujifusa, *The Almanac of American Politics, 1994* (Washington, D.C.: National Journal, 1993).

23. Gary C. Jacobson and Samuel Kernell, *Strategy and Choice in Congressional Elections*, 2d ed. (New Haven: Yale University Press, 1983).

24. Gary C. Jacobson, "1994 House Elections in Perspective," 11.

25. Ibid., 12.

26. Ibid., 15.

27. "GOP Says It Expects to Gain Up to 30 House Seats in '96," *San Diego Union*, 4 November 1995, A12.

28. "Congressional Departures," *Congressional Quarterly Weekly Report*, 13 April 1996, 1005.

29. Jacobson, *Electoral Origins of Divided Government*.

30. Kevin A. Hill, "Does the Creation of Majority Black Districts Aid Republicans? An Analysis of the 1992 Congressional Elections in Eight Southern States," *Journal of Politics* 57 (1995): 394–401.

31. As cited in Elizabeth Shogren, "GOP Budget Plans Would Put Burden on the Poor," *Los Angeles Times*, 29 October 1995, A1.

32. *The Hotline*, 26 September 1995.

33. *The Hotline*, 15 November 1995.

34. Frank Greve, "GOP Pollster Gauged Appeal of Slogans, Not of 'Contract,'" *San Diego Union*, 12 November 1995, A33.

35. As quoted in Jackie Koszczuk, "Freshmen: New, Powerful Voice," *Congressional Quarterly Weekly Report*, 28 October 1995, 3251.

36. As quoted in Richard T. Kooper, "GOP Changes Held in Check by Earlier Revolutionaries," *Los Angeles Times*, 31 December 1995, A13.

37. Gary C. Jacobson, *The Politics of Congressional Elections*, 3d ed. (New York: Harper Collins, 1992).

38. Ibid.

39. Robert S. Erikson, "Why the Democrats Lose Presidential Elections," *PS: Political Science & Politics* 22 (1989): 30–34.

Chapter Four

The Road to Divided Government: Paved without Intention

John R. Petrocik and Joseph Doherty

> There is a lot of evidence . . . that the American people . . . have believed for decades now that divided government may work better than united government.
>
> —President Clinton, postelection news conference,
> 9 November 1994, 3:43 P.M.

American government is based on majority-producing institutions that work to encourage and protect a system of two dominant parties. The electoral college virtually assures that a president will be selected with majority support from the Democratic or Republican party. Almost universal single member-simple plurality election rules present few opportunities for new parties to compete with the current major parties in legislative elections. Perversely enough, even our purportedly anti-party primary system may promote a two-partism by allowing dissidents to take control of one of the major parties in primary elections, thereby reducing incentives to form third parties that thwart majority outcomes.

But these majoritarian institutions have not guaranteed one of the benefits of majority government: unified government. There were many instances of divided government in the Second, Third, and Fourth party systems (fourteen of thirty-four by Fiorina's count).[1] The presence of significant third and fourth parties during the nineteenth century might easily have disrupted the translation of presidential tides into unified government. The twentieth century, however, is more of a puzzle. Divided government became rare after 1900 (four examples in twenty-six elections) as the Democrats and Republicans eliminated their third-party rivals, only to surge after 1952. Since then, it has become characteristic of American political life (even as third parties have almost vanished).[2] Fourteen of twenty-one governments between 1952 and 1994 have been divided. The immediate cause of these divided governments, ticket-splitting, is easy to identify. Reliable estimates of the incidence of ticket-splitting before 1952 are hard to come by, though districts which voted differently for president and Congress were so few (less than 15 percent prior to 1940) that it had to be smaller than it is today.[3] There is no difficulty in estimating ticket-splitting since 1952, however, and it has increased markedly. In the 1952, 1956, and 1960 elections, about 85 percent voted for the same party for president and the House; 82 percent were consistent in their votes for president, House, and Senate. By the 1980s, same-party president-House voting declined to 74 percent; same-party president-House-Senate voting, to 65 percent.[4]

The resulting divided government is accepted by most Americans. Whenever they have been asked during the past twenty years (see table 4.1), clear pluralities (of 10 percentage points or more) have chosen divided over unified government, whether the government has been unified (1977 and 1993) or divided (all the other years in the table). Differences in how the questions were worded are responsible for some of the variance in the choice of divided government. Cueing (e.g., a Democratic appeal to elect Democrats and thereby guard against Reagan policies or a Republican appeal to do the opposite) probably also shaped answers to the questions. The questions are so different, however, that it seems unlikely that the main effect—the choice of divided government—is an artifact of the question wording or a short-term reflection of the political environment in which the question was asked.

Theories of Ticket-Splitting and Support
for Divided Government

One prominent explanation of ticket-splitting and support for divided government views them as a conscious balancing strategy. This theory, which has been promoted by Alesina and Rosenthal, and supported by Erikson and Fiorina, treats voters as though they were sophisticated, risk-averse investors in a diverse policy portfolio.[5] "Investor voters" recognize the different programmatic interests of the Democrats and

TABLE 4.1
Support for Divided Government: 1972–1994

Source	Month/Year	% Choosing		Bias for divided government
		Divided	Unified	
Harris	Nov 1972	36	21	15
Roper	Feb 1977	48	36	12
Harris	Sep 1984	32	25	7
Harris	Oct 1985	33	20	13
Harris	Nov 1986	31	20	11
Roper	Dec 1986	61	25	36
WSJ/NBC	Nov 1988	54	32	22
WSJ/NBC	Apr 1992	60	30	30
NES	Jan 1993	38	31	7

Note: Bias for divided government is the arithmetic difference between the percentage who chose divided government and the percentage who chose unified. This measure is used throughout as the measure of support for divided government. These results are based on national samples of at least 1000 respondents.

Republicans. Some fraction of those voters—typically ideological centrists who are particularly uncomfortable with the more extreme positions in both parties—support Democratic *and* Republican candidates in order to balance the "extremist" tendencies of each party's wing.

In a political environment where candidates are quick to note the faults and failures of their opponents, it is easy to understand why the dangers posed by each party's extreme wing might loom large for some voters. "Yellow-dog" Democrats and Republican stalwarts may dismiss the charges of the opposition and comfortably vote for their party's candidates. But those who are not committed ideological partisans may find the dangers ascribed to each party memorable. Since people tend generally to be risk-averse for losses, it is easy to understand why they may follow a defensive strategy of voting for candidates from both parties (see Riker's discussion of risk-aversion and negative campaigning).[6] The resulting divided government (why divided government might be an almost deterministic outcome is argued by Ingberman and Villani) may be capable of fewer policy innovations and more easily thwarted.[7] But it is also less likely to pursue the "excesses" that are promoted by the extreme elements within each party. Just as the constitutional powers of each branch of the national government place limits on the misuse of power by the others, so divided government holds the diverging programs of the parties in check. Ladd has described this perspective on ticket-splitting as "a natural extension of the historic U.S. commitment to the separation of powers."[8]

A major alternative to the balancing view has been formulated by Gary Jacobson.[9] His theory joins images of the role differences between legislators and executives with images of the policy orientations of the parties. In this account, presidents provide public goods while members of Congress specialize in providing distributive benefits to their districts. Democrats, as a result, enjoy two significant advantages in legislative elections. First, the position of legislator is more attractive to Democrats because the role requirements match the Democratic Party's more positive disposition toward distributive goods. More Democrats are likely to seek legislative careers, and those who do are likely to be more skilled politicians. These greater numbers and skill levels give the Democrats important marginal advantages in any election. Second, it is easier for Democratic candidates to craft attractive campaign appeals. The typical Democratic candidate will, compared to the typical Republican, have a basketful of initiatives that he or she is prepared to undertake on behalf of programs that will distribute benefits to citizens. The Republican will frequently have fewer such plans and appear less imaginative and energetic to voters.

A third explanation of divided government emphasizes the issues raised in campaigns.[10] This theory of issue ownership agrees with Jacobson that each party has a reputation for handling some issues well and others less successfully. Most voters recognize and respond to these reputations when the issues become important elements in a campaign. When, for example, an issue owned by the Republicans is salient, the normal voting intention of Republican identifiers is reinforced, Democrats come under pressure to defect, and the less partisan have a strong incentive to support the Republican candidate. Elections, therefore, are decided by the relative salience of Democratic-owned versus Republican-owned issues. Democrats usually triumph when Democratic-owned issues dominate the public debate; Republicans, when the issue agenda favors the GOP.

In the theory of issue ownership, ticket-splitting occurs when the issues dominating the presidential election differ from those attracting attention in the congressional contest. Most susceptible to ticket-splitting are those voters who believe that the most important problem facing the *country* is a Republican-owned issue but the most important issue in the House election is Democratic-owned. Although this account resembles Jacobson's in its assumption that voters make positive choices among candidates based on the issues, it does not share Jacobson's assumption that these issues are inherent in the offices sought. Jacobson expects almost all House elections to focus on distributive issues that affect a district in some distinctive way and almost all presidential elections to focus on national collective goods that do not usually involve distributive benefits. In contrast, the theory of issue ownership expects the issue content of any House election to be variable. Circumstances and the strategic vision and tactical skill of the candidates will determine the issue content of the campaign. Although a severe recession, social disorder, and government corruption are often unavoidable issues that may harm or help the incumbent, many times the issue content is less determined by circumstances and emerges from the particular concerns candidates emphasize in their campaigns. At still other times, no issues capture the attention of the electorate. However it works out in any particular case, the campaign and the conditions of the moment, rather than some issue inherent in the office sought, pushes the vote toward the Democrat or the Republican. Assuming that factors such as incumbency and the partisan color of the district remain equal, a candidate from either party could do well in any particular contest—presidential or congressional. We would expect voters to split for the Republican congressional candidate and the Democratic presidential candidate in a district where the congressional election is dominated by GOP-owned issues and the national political environment by Democratic-owned issues. Mirror-image issue agendas would produce a mirror-image split-ballot outcome. We would expect straight-ticket voting when the issue agendas of the national and the congressional campaigns favor the same party.

The key to this theory is that ticket-splitting and support for divided government occur not because of the national policy debate, but because individual congressional candidates run campaigns that *separate* them from the national policy debate. Ticket-splitting could also occur when a congressional election turns on matters having little to do with issues. A presidential campaign that is concerned with social and cultural issues, taxes and government spending, and the adequacy of the national military defense might not even provide a dull echo in a congressional campaign. In fact, congressional campaigns have no significant issues so far as the voters can tell. Incumbent familiarity, widespread support for the incumbent by local business, labor, and social notables, and an unknown, underfunded challenger shape the outcomes in most congressional elections.

Our reading of the evidence leads us to conclude that voters do not pursue a balancing strategy with their ticket-splitting. Although the aggregate outcome is often consistent with a balancing interpretation, none of the supportive relationships required by the balancing theory are observed in the data. We think that ticket-splitting arises from largely isolated comparisons between candidates and that differences such as those between congressional and presidential elections, between two presidential elections, and between two adjacent Congressional races have more to do with issue ownership than with a desire to balance the ideology of the parties. The data examined below are not definitive in all respects. However, they overwhelmingly disconfirm the balancing theory and are consistent with cross-pressures induced by issue ownership.

Ticket-Splitting as a Balancing Strategy

The attribution of ticket-splitting to a balancing strategy is more compelling in theory than in the corroborating evidence. At the aggregate level alone, there is prima facie evidence against it. The balancing theory would expect risk-averse voters to be the most attentive to policy differences between the parties when the parties are most fully engaged, and that would be in presidential elections when each party's candidate is staking out the divisions between Democrats and Republicans. Off-year elections should present the opposite condition. The lower intensity of the off-year campaign effort, the more sparse media coverage, the hopelessness of most challenger efforts, and the positive regard local elites usually have for ever-helpful incumbents should make off-year elections less sensitive to the diverging policy tendencies of the parties. But actual election results are the reverse of the balancing theory. It is a commonplace fact that off-years are associated with congressional losses by the party holding the presidency, while on-years find the party that wins the presidency picking up a comparative surplus of seats in the House, more or less in proportion to the winning party's margin in the presidential election. Put differently, it is in the off-years—when the salience of each party's program is less—that the nonpresidential party acquires more seats to "balance" the president. Figure 1 shows the on-year pattern: the party that wins the presidency wins congressional seats in relation to the magnitude of the presidential victory. At the midterm elections, as figure 2 shows, the president's party suffers congressional seat losses roughly in proportion to the presidential victory margin of two years before (the apparent deviation in 1994 is addressed below). Erikson has attempted to formulate this pattern as evidence of balancing, but it is more easily interpreted as a surge-decline phenomenon. While the on-year surge for congressional candidates reflects the diffuse positivity enjoyed by the winning president's fellow candidates (perhaps aided by the strategic candidate effect described by Jacobson and Kernell), the off-year decline reflects the absence of the positivity associated with a presidential race, plus a midterm judgment against the president by all those who are dissatisfied with the policy initiatives (both successful and failed) of the president's first two years.[11]

Not only the aggregate pattern but individual survey data fail to support the balancing theory. That theory presumes a symmetry in perceptions and a level of information and political sophistication that we have yet to find among voters, even when we have believed they were attentive and inclined to see politics through ideological lenses. It assumes that policy issues are a principal determinant of presidential *and* congressional voting among centrists, a group known to be the least issue-motivated. It further assumes that this balancing preference is easily and accurately linked to candidates after exposure to national-level party programs, and that national-level programs are approximately equal in salience to voters making congressional choices and to those making presidential choices. These are large assumptions. More to the point, none of the proponents of the balancing theory of ticket-splitting have ever demonstrated that voters have the motivations and

John R. Petrocik and Joseph Doherty

FIGURE 1
Presidential Vote and Number of House Seats Won, 1960–1992

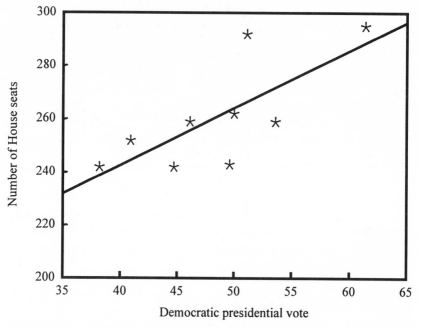

Democratic presidential vote

Note: Entries are Democratic percentages of the presidential vote and the number of Democratic House seats.

perceptions postulated by the theory, and systematic attempts to find them with individual-level data have left the theory without support.[12]

The balancing explanation persists, however, because it offers a fairly complete account of an otherwise intractable puzzle and because proponents remain attached to its theoretical utility (see the exchange between Fiorina and Born).[13] We believe that we can reinforce the evidence against the balancing strategy by also considering *attitudes* about divided government. The dependent variable in most analyses of divided government has been whether voters actually cast a split ballot. Although the failure to find the relationships postulated by the balancing thesis is a critical weakness, a proponent committed to the implications of the theory might hold out because actual votes may not test the *intentions* of voters—and that is what is critical. It is possible that the many advantages incumbents enjoy over their challengers, and the general weakness of challengers (especially GOP challengers), may

FIGURE 2
Off-Year Changes in House Seats as a Function of On-Year Deviations
from the Party Average, 1960–1992

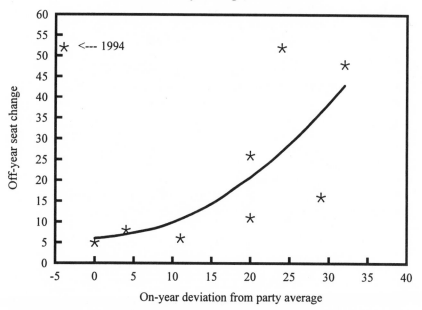

suppress the carrying out of an intention to balance the ideological tendencies of the parties. Some, perhaps many, voters may be inclined to balance the parties with ticket-splitting, but cannot because a flawed candidate, a weak campaign, and so forth make it difficult for voters to follow through on a balance-the-parties motivation. Thus a belief in the desirability of divided government might, nonetheless, be related to perceptions of the extremism of the parties and to dissatisfaction with this extremism, in which case, evidence of balancing might be observed by looking at intentions rather than behavior. The distinction is between *behavioral balancers*, whose ticket-splitting corresponds to a perception of ideological extremes in the parties, and *cognitive balancers*, who support the idea of divided government because of a belief that the parties represent ideological extremes.[14] A test of the balancing thesis that eliminates a whole class of confounding factors would require examining whether partisan ideological extremity leads people to support the *idea* of divided government. If support for the idea does not vary as the balancing theory suggests, it is even less likely that we will find evidence that ticket-splitting and divided government are the electorate's response to the policy extremism of the parties.

The 1992 National Election Survey (NES) enables us to examine the link between a balancing intention and perceived party extremism. In that study respondents were asked how they felt about divided party control—whether they preferred divided or unified control, or whether they believed it did not matter if one party controlled both branches of the national government or not. The NES marginals fit a pattern of consistent support for divided government over party government. However, as table 4.2 demonstrates, this sentiment does not have a large action component. Overall, a vast majority (78 percent) of voters in 1992 reported that they voted for the same party for president and the House (although a 7 percent plurality favored division), and almost as many (75 percent) among those who preferred divided control also voted a straight ticket. Straight-ticket voting was more common (at 84 percent) among those who preferred unified government, and the difference is statistically significant. However, the high rate of straight-

TABLE 4.2
Ticket-Splitting and Attitudes toward Divided Government

	Expressed preference about divided government		
	Prefer unified government (397)	Prefer divided government (421)	Other (308)
Straight ticket	84%	75%	74%
Republican for president/ Democratic for House	8%	15%	14%
Democratic for president/ Republican for House	9%	10%	12%

Note: The numbers from which the percentages were computed are in parentheses. Table entries are percentaged vertically.

ticket voting among divided government supporters is a troublesome result. If we assume that the 17 percent who mixed a split-ballot vote with an avowed preference for unified government is an error rate that also infects the 26 percent of divided government enthusiasts who voted a split ticket, as few as 6 percent of the voters might have cast a split ballot that was motivated by the idea that divided government was a good state of affairs. The prevalent attitude of support for divided government does not explain much of the actual behavior. Clearly, something is getting between the intent and the behavior. But does the intent proceed from a balance-the-parties concern?

Almost a third indicated that it did not matter to them whether the government was unified or divided. Having no interpretation of what that expression might indicate, we opted to treat those respondents as neutrals. Each supporter of divided government was coded as a positive one ($+1$), each supporter of unified government as a negative one (-1), and each who chose neither alternative as a zero (0). The arithmetic average of this coding produces a percentage difference in which support for divided government yields a positive value, while a preference for unified government generates a negative number. Scaled up by one hundred to eliminate the decimal value, the overall mean indicates that the population is more supportive of divided government by a margin of 8 percentage points.

The predisposition to balance is examined in two different ways, with both based on a perception of party policy positions. First, *party policy distance* is measured with four seven-point issue questions on which respondents characterized themselves and each party: liberal-conservative identification, attitudes toward levels of defense spending, preferences for more government services or lower spending, and attitudes as to the responsibility of the national government to assure jobs to all who want them. Party policy distance is the absolute value of the difference between the Democrats' score and the Republicans' score. For example, a respondent who believes the Democrats are extreme liberals will assign them a one on the liberal-conservative scale; if the same respondent believes the Republicans are extreme conservatives, they will receive a seven. The resulting difference of six is a measure of the parties' ideological distance as perceived by the respondent. The distance scores on all four measures are then averaged to produce a continuous scale (from zero through six) of party policy distance.

Second, in the balancing theory, a voter has a predisposition to offset the ideological tendencies of the parties to the extent that he or she holds moderate issue preferences *and* sees little to choose between in the extreme issue positions of the parties. The definition of a *moderate* is key, therefore, and after some experimentation, a self-placement in the middle of the rating scale (that is, at position four) on three of the four issue questions defined ideological moderates. Sorted thus, the minimal evidence for any tendency of voters to engage in balancing is a relationship between a divided government preference and the issue distance perceived between the parties. Those who see small average differences between the parties (e.g., a score of one) should have a weak predisposition to balance the parties. The disposition to balance should increase with the party difference score.

The basic findings are completely contrary to the balancing theory. Voters who differentiate between the parties prefer unified government, while voters who see little or no difference between them are the most likely to prefer divided government (figure 3). The pattern is virtually identical for moderates and nonmoderates. Figure 4 repeats the analysis, but categorizes the data to ease the visual inspection of the pattern. As the figure shows, moderates and nonmoderates who see no difference between the parties are almost equally likely to prefer divided government, by margins of 24 and 28 percentage points, respectively. Those who see the largest policy differences are the most likely to prefer unified government. Most troubling for the balancing theory is the finding that moderates who see the largest policy differences between the parties are absolutely the most likely to prefer unified government (by a margin of 27 percentage points). Put simply, nothing is as the balancing theory asserts; everything is the reverse. The voters who see the largest policy differences between the parties are the most supportive of unified government; the voters who should have the strongest predisposition for divided government (according to the balancing theory) are the most likely to oppose it.

These data cut straight to the heart of the intentional ticket-splitting model, for there can be no policy balancing when voters have nothing to balance. Voters must perceive differences between the parties before they can attempt to moderate those differences. The majority of divided government enthusiasts are largely unaware of policy differences between Democrats and Republicans and are unlikely to have been motivated to take their position by the Downsian-inspired calculus inherent in the balancing theory. In short, risk-averse attitudes based upon the policy orientations of the national parties do not appear to be a significant cause of voter preference for divided government.

FIGURE 3
Support for Divided Government and Perceived
Interparty Policy Distance

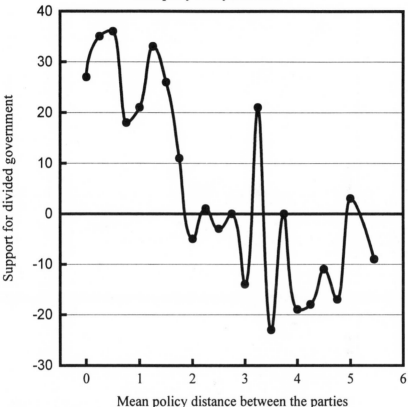

Note: Positive numbers indicate a percentage plurality of support for divided government.

Ticket-Splitting as Cross-Pressured Voting

The raw marginals in table 4.3 seem to make the cross-pressure perspective a promising alternative to the balancing theory. Most ticket-splitting pairs a Republican presidential vote with a Democratic House vote. As table 4.3 shows, Democratic-owned issues were about twice as common as Republican-owned issues in congressional elections in 1992—whether we look at all the issues mentioned or only the most important one. More important, there is a substantial relationship

FIGURE 4
Policy Differences and Divided Government:
Moderates and Nonmoderates

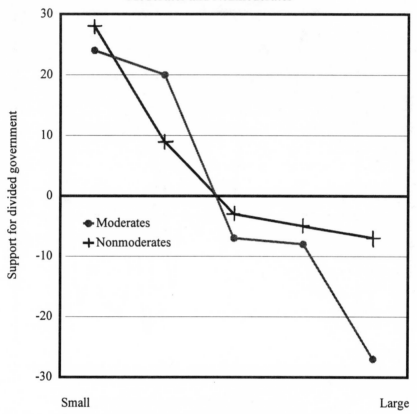

Perceived policy distances between the parties

between the issues that marked the House campaigns and the vote. Sixty-eight percent of those who recall a Democratic issue as the most important issue of the campaign voted for the Democrat; 60 percent of those who remember a Republican issue dominating the campaign voted for the Republican. Party identification affected, but did not eliminate, the pull of party-owned issues on the vote (table 4.4). When the voter was a Democrat, Democratic-owned issues reinforced partisanship and produced 86 percent support for the Democratic House candidate; the Democratic vote of Democratic identifiers declined to 78 percent when Republican issues held center stage in the

TABLE 4.3
Issues Recalled from the 1992 House Campaigns

	All Mentions	Most Important Issue
Mentions no issues	49%	49%
Mentions Democratic issues	33%	26%
Mentions Republican issues	15%	13%
Miscellaneous	12%	12%

Note: Total of first column exceeds 100% because of multiple mentions.

TABLE 4.4
Voting for Republican Congressmembers as a Function of Campaign Issues

Most important House campaign issue	Party identification			
	Democrat	Independent	Republican	Total
Democratic issue	14%	33%	66%	32%
Republican issue	22%	60%	83%	60%
No issues recalled	16%	39%	68%	41%

campaign. The effect for Republican identifiers was virtually identical. Eighty-three percent of Republicans voted Republican when the most important issue in the campaign was Republican; only 66 percent were loyal when the most important issue was Democratic. Independents were strongly affected by the issues.

That issue cross-pressures are more important than balancing is apparent when ticket-splitting is broken down by the voter's party identification and the major issue remembered in the congressional campaign (table 4.5). Democratic identifiers in congressional elections dominated by Democratic issues are overwhelmingly inclined (at 81 percent) to vote a straight ticket; only 9 percent voted for Clinton and the GOP House candidate. Ticket-splitting among Democrats increased to 15 percent when Republican issues dominated the House race, and 24 percent when no issues were prominent. The pattern is repeated for Republican identifiers, although they have slightly higher overall defection rates.

Data that bear more directly on the impact of issue cross-pressures on ticket-splitting appear in table 4.6. Consider the first part of the table, which singles out those who are concerned with national issues owned by the Democratic party. Sixty-five percent of this group voted straight Democratic when the congressional race was also focused on Democratic issues. Straight-ticket voting declined to 42 percent when the congressional race dealt with GOP issues; it was 46 percent when no issue was particularly memorable in the congressional campaign. The pattern was repeated for voters concerned with Republican-owned national issues. Sixty-six percent voted straight Republican when a Republican issue dominated the House race, 38 percent when a Democratic issue dominated it, and 54 percent when no issue domi-nated it.

Clearly, being cross-pressured by issues has an effect on ticket-splitting. But there is only partial evidence that ticket-splitting is the result of a strategy to obtain a divided government to deal with the GOP- and Democratic-owned issues of simultaneous concern to some voters. If it were a result of such a strategy, support for divided government ought to be greater when the issues of concern cross-pressure the voter. The data do not fully meet this reasonable expecta-tion. Table 4.7, which examines the preference for divided government by the issue contrast used in Table 4.6, shows only a partial relation-ship between support for the notion of divided government and the voters' national and congressional issue agendas. Voters whose Demo-cratic national agenda is reinforced by a Democratic agenda in the

TABLE 4.5
Ticket-Splitting as a Function of House Campaign Issues
and Voters' Party Identification

Most important House campaign issue	Voting pattern				
	President:	Dem	Dem	Rep	Rep
	House:	Dem	Rep	Dem	Rep
	Democratic identifiers				
Democratic issue		81%	9%	8%	2%
Republican issue		74%	15%	8%	4%
No issues recalled		73%	24%	0%	2%
	Republican identifiers				
Democratic issue		8%	7%	23%	63%
Republican issue		1%	2%	14%	84%
No issues recalled		5%	3%	24%	68%

Note: Table entries are percentaged horizontally.

House campaign prefer divided government slightly more than average; those whose Democratic national agenda is contradicted by a Republican House agenda also prefer divided government, but not as much. However, House issue agendas do seem to moderate GOP-owned national issue agendas in the predicted way. Voters who combined a GOP national agenda with a Democratic agenda for the House race preferred divided government, while those who reinforced their

TABLE 4.6
Ticket-Splitting as a Function of House Campaign Issues and Most Important National Issue

Most important House campaign issue	Voting pattern			
	President: Dem	Dem	Rep	Rep
	House: Dem	Rep	Dem	Rep
	Most important national issue was Democratic			
Democratic issue	65%	7%	12%	17%
Republican issue	42%	10%	15%	33%
No issues recalled	46%	12%	16%	27%
	Most important national issue was Republican			
Democratic issue	42%	8%	13%	38%
Republican issue	17%	3%	14%	66%
No issues recalled	27%	3%	17%	54%

Note: Table entries are percentaged horizontally.

GOP national agenda with a Republican agenda in the House race preferred unified government.

More consistent, but still not strong, evidence for strategic ticket-splitting emerges when cross-pressure is defined as a discrepancy between the party ownership of the major issue in the House campaign

TABLE 4.7
**Support for Divided Government and Issue Agendas in House
Campaigns and the Nation Generally**

Most important House campaign issue	Most important national issue	
	Democratic	Republican
Democratic issue	10	11
Republican issue	6	-4
No issues recalled	13	12

Note: Table entries are percentage differences between support for divided government and support for unified government. Positive numbers indicate that a plurality supports the concept of divided government.

and the voter's partisanship (see table 4.8). Democratic identifiers who confronted congressional races that emphasized Democratic issues preferred unified government; they were more inclined to support divided government when Republican-owned issues dominated the congressional campaigns (neither difference is statistically significant, however). The effect of the issue agenda on Republican identifiers was marginally stronger: an overall preference for divided government when campaign issues matched partisanship became substantial when Democratic-owned issues dominated the congressional campaign.

Some Conclusions and Observations

In his exchange with Richard Born, Fiorina drew a distinction between the more empirically and the more theoretically oriented observers of ticket-splitting.[15] Only slightly simplifying Born's argument and conclusions, Fiorina noted Born's inclination to reject a (policy-balancing) theory whose deductions were not supported by the data. Fiorina went on to note that his own "inclination [was] to retain any theory, some (even one) of whose interesting or nonobvious implications are

TABLE 4.8
Support for Divided Government as a Function of House Campaign Issues and Voters' Party Identification

	Most important House campaign issue	
	Democratic	Republican
	Democratic identifiers	
Prefer unified government	38%	41%
Prefer divided government	34%	42%
	Republican identifiers	
Prefer unified government	33%	38%
Prefer divided government	51%	40%

Note: Table entries sum vertically. The proportion who were unsure of their opinion on, or indifferent to, divided government is not reported.

consistent with the data . . . (since theories) . . . are precious things, not to be dismissed too casually, nor in the absence of viable competitors.''[16] While we agree with Fiorina's predisposition—anyone who has ever worked with data appreciates how inquiry without theory only produces sound and fury signifying nothing—we treat it only as a predisposition. And in the case of ticket-splitting, it is a predisposition that should be quietly set aside, for to continue championing the policy-balancing theory is to tell a tale in conflict with the evidence. Our analysis more than suggests that voters are not risk-averse cognitive balancers who consciously mix Democratic and Republican votes in direct proportion to their perception of issue differences between the parties, and that they are not behavioral Madisonians whose unplanned ticket-splitting is linked to perceived policy differences. Neither ticket-splitting nor support for the idea of divided government increases with perceived policy distances between the parties.

Our rejection of the policy-balancing theory of divided government is made neither "casually, nor in the absence of viable competitors." We think that divided government arises from several sources, but a plan on the part of voters is not one of them. Some part of it results from a biased recruitment of more energetic and talented Democratic candidates. Ehrenhalt and Jacobson have both outlined how the greater enthusiasm of Democrats for government careers and governmental action on public issues might bring this about.[17] Divided government is also a product of the marginal connection between the issues debated in the presidential and congressional elections. These different issue environments frequently allow voters to split for candidates of different parties, and feel no conflict about it, as the theory of issue ownership predicts. The minimal meaning of the overused (and, we believe, misleading) political folk wisdom that "all politics is local" is that congressional candidates can often (not always) separate themselves from a beleaguered presidential candidate. Its corollary is that their opponents usually have a hard time hitching on to the coattails of the presidential candidate with a political wind at his back. As hard as they might try, most congressional candidates, in most elections, cannot get voters to think about low-salience legislative elections in terms of the same issues voters use to judge presidential races. It is a perceptual disconnect that facilitates ticket-splitting and divided government. The 1994 election may be the exception that demonstrates the essential accuracy of this notion. Rarely do two congressional campaigns get decided by the same issues and concerns. The Republican Contract with America and a consistent emphasis in district after district on taxes, spending, and big government, coupled with a Democratic campaign against the contract, gave a national theme to elections that are rarely connected in the absence of recessions and such. The GOP tide may have been the consequence.

In all of this, it is difficult to find evidence for a plan by voters. There are very few correlates of expressed feelings about divided government. Party identification was one of the few things that did matter in 1992—and in a sensible way: Democrats tended to support united government; Republicans preferred division. Within both parties, the strong partisans tend to prefer unified government. Partisanship and situational rationalization, not a strategic vision, are the more plausible explanation for what Americans say when they are queried about divided government.

Notes

1. Morris Fiorina, *Divided Government* (New York: Macmillan, 1992), 7.

2. We recognize that far more than two parties field candidates in many elections in the United States. The counting rule that dismisses all of these third parties comes from Sartori. There is, he observes, no need to count any party that neither has a realistic prospect of forming or taking part in a government nor is capable of affecting the direction or specifics of competition among or between the parties. Giovanni Sartori, *Parties and Party Systems: A Framework for Analysis* (New York: Cambridge University Press, 1976).

3. Fiorina, *Divided Government*, 13.

4. Unless otherwise indicated, all of the survey data used in this chapter are from the National Election Studies. The data were made available through the Interuniversity Consortium for Political and Social Research. Neither the Consortium nor the principal investigators are responsible for our analysis or interpretations of the data. Most of the nonsurvey data were collected from the Statistical Abstract of the United States: 1992 (Washington, D.C.: U.S. Bureau of the Census, 1992).

5. Alberto Alesina and Howard Rosenthal, "Partisan Cycles in Congressional Elections and the Macroeconomy," *American Political Science Review* 83 (1989): 373–98; Robert S. Erikson, "The Puzzle of Midterm Loss," *Journal of Politics* 50 (1988): 1011–29; Fiorina, *Divided Government*.

6. William H. Riker, "Rhetorical Interaction in the Ratification Campaign," in *Agenda Formation* (Ann Arbor: University of Michigan Press, 1993).

7. Daniel Ingberman and John Villani, "An Institutional Theory of Divided Government and Party Polarization," *American Journal of Political Science* 37 (1993): 429–71.

8. Everett Carll Ladd, "Public Opinion and the 'Congress Problem,'" *Public Interest* 100 (summer 1990): 57–67; Gary C. Jacobson and Samuel Kernell, *Strategy and Choice in Congressional Elections*, 2d ed. (New Haven: Yale University Press, 1983).

9. Gary C. Jacobson, *The Electoral Origins of Divided Government: Competition in U.S. House Elections, 1946–1988* (Boulder, Colo.: Westview, 1990).

10. John R. Petrocik, "Divided Government: Is It All in the Campaigns?" in *The Politics of Divided Government*, ed. Gary W. Cox and Samuel Kernell (Boulder, Colo.: Westview, 1991); idem, "A Theory of Issue-Ownership and

the 1980 Presidential Election" (paper presented at the annual meeting of the American Political Science Association, New York, 1994).

11. Erikson, "Puzzle of Midterm Loss," 1011–29. On the strategic candidate effect see Gary C. Jacobson, "Strategic Politicians and the Dynamics of U.S. House Elections, 1946–1986," *American Political Science Review* 83 (1989): 773–93.

12. R. Michael Alvarez and Matthew M. Schousen, "Policy Moderation or Conflicting Expectations? Testing Intentional Models of Split-Ticket Voting," *American Politics Quarterly* 21 (1993): 410–38; Richard Born, "Split-Ticket Voters, Divided Government, and Fiorina's Policy-Balancing Model," *Legislative Studies Quarterly* 19 (1994): 95–115; Richard Born, "Rejoinder," *Legislative Studies Quarterly* 19 (1994): 126–29.

13. Born, "Split-Ticket Voters"; Morris P. Fiorina, "Response," *Legislative Studies Quarterly* 19 (1994): 117–25.

14. Ladd refers to this balancing of party issue extremity as *Madisonianism*, reflecting the constitutional ideal of interests and structures which balance each other and, thereby, protect liberty. It is an attractive term and may be a nice conceptual summary of the balancing theory. A preference for more modest language restricts us to the term *balancing*. Ladd, "Public Opinion and the 'Congress Problem.'"

15. Fiorina, "Response."

16. Ibid.

17. Alan Ehrenhalt, *The United States of Ambition: Politicians, Power, and the Pursuit of Office* (New York: Random House, 1991); Jacobson, *Electoral Origins of Divided Government*.

Chapter Five

It's the Constitution, Stupid! Congress, the President, Divided Government, and Policymaking

Leroy N. Rieselbach

Policy gridlock. Stalemate. Immobilism. Paralysis. Deadlock. Inefficiency. Numerous terms describe the symptoms, but the diagnosis remains the same: the American national government is incapable of enacting public policies that effectively resolve the nation's most pressing problems. Observers have identified several possible causes of the dread disease of deadlock, but the culprit of choice in recent years has been divided government. When one political party (until the 104th Congress, usually the Republicans) controls the presidency and the other (usually the Democrats) has a congressional majority, partisan animosity precludes innovative response to the issues of the day. Inaction is common; modest, incremental programs may become law but are insufficient to deal with difficult and demanding policy issues confronting the country. Thus, the budget deficit soars, millions of citizens lack health care, crime flourishes, and many other matters remain unresolved.

Yet the evidence linking divided government to policy paralysis is not entirely convincing.[1] In a highly influential work, David Mayhew identified 267 "major statutes" enacted between 1947 and 1990. He found, contrary to the received wisdom, that "on average, about as many major laws passed per Congress under divided control as under unified control."[2] Some have challenged Mayhew's conclusions, in whole or in part. Kelly, arguing that Mayhew defined "innovative policy" too broadly, uses "a more stringent definition" and finds that "there is less innovative policy enacted under divided government than united government."[3]

Other scholars have sought to move beyond a simple either-or view to assess particular circumstances when divided government seems important. For instance, Taylor, looking at domestic policy, finds that separate control matters less when the president and Congress are relatively close ideologically and when the branches agree "on each other's roles in the policy process."[4] Similarly, divided government may inhibit action on some specific substantive issues. It seems to lead to increased government spending and larger budget deficits.[5] It may thwart creative policymaking on items (e.g., social welfare, the environment, or defense) that fall along partisan and/or ideological lines; where issue cleavages reflect other dimensions (on agricultural or trade policy, for instance), split control may have minimal effects.[6] Finally, divided government may have indirect consequences: Epstein and O'Halloran suggest that Congress is less willing to delegate authority to the executive in periods of divided control, and in consequence, bureaucrats have less flexibility and are more prone to conflict with their political superiors.[7] In short, the impact of divided government on the policy process remains unclear. Moreover, split control is only one possible influence leading to policy stalemate. This chapter assesses the links of divided control, and those of other explanatory factors, to national policymaking, with particular attention to the 103rd Congress.[8]

The Constitutional Setting

The Constitution and convention shape and constrain the ways of policy formulation. The former, establishing, in Neustadt's classic formulation, "separate institutions sharing power," gives both the executive and the legislative branches the authority and opportunity to influence the substance of public policy.[9] The latter, reflecting the evolution of practice over two centuries, gives the president the policy-making initiative. The president, acting as "chief legislator," is to set the nation's policy agenda, and Congress is to react as it sees fit, with kindness or with hostility.

The constitutional allocation of authority and the expectation of presidential leadership set the stage for executive-legislative conflict and cooperation. To enact the administration's program, the president must both propose attractive bills and work to convince Congress to enact them. More specifically, his task is to assemble majorities, to construct winning coalitions (most commonly, but not always, 218 votes in the House of Representatives and 51 in the Senate) that will pass favored legislation or block undesirable bills.[10] This is no easy chore; the chief executive cannot command legislative obedience but rather must marshal an impressive, but not unlimited, array of resources in an effort to persuade Congress to comply with his policy requests.[11] Congress, of course, has ample resources of its own, particularly its authorization and appropriations powers, with which to resist presidential blandishments or to impose its own priorities on a reluctant executive. The president's authority, in short, rests on his "power to persuade," his capacity to elicit congressional support for the administration's program.

Executive-legislative relations, moreover, occur within a context defined by a number of relatively fixed features. For one thing, the basic organizational structure of Congress changes only very slowly. This means that the chief executive must maneuver his proposals through a decentralized institution—customarily characterized by bicameralism, individualistic members, independent committees and subcommittees, specific rules of procedure, widely observed informal norms of behavior, and weak political parties—in which action may occur only after considerable exertion. Similarly, the president is powerless to alter the nature of the constituencies that send the members of Congress to Washington. The kinds of people who live in the states and districts change slowly. To the extent that legislators feel the need, which elections induce, to react to local sentiments, they may respond to constituency pressures and resist presidential importunings. Finally, events, both foreign and domestic, lie beyond presidential control. The bombing of a federal installation in Oklahoma City, a Supreme Court decision overturning gun control legislation, strained trade relations with the nations of Europe and Asia, or unrest overseas (e.g., in Bosnia) will tax the president's leadership skills as he attempts to take account of such events. Thus, the president will have to contend with forces that congressional structure, constituency considerations, and the flow of events generate—forces that lie outside his power to shape to any great degree. Passing his program will not be easy.

Policy Gridlock: Four Explanations

Within the context that the constitutional setting defines, divided
government complicates policymaking. Without a congressional majority of his own party, the president lacks a solid foundation on which to
build winning coalitions. To secure passage of desired legislation, he
must court and win the votes of at least a few opposition members.
Even with unified government, when his party is the majority, the
chief executive may run afoul of the well-known incumbency effect;
individualistic members securely ensconced in safe constituencies are
largely free to vote as they wish without fear of reprisal from their
party.[12] In addition, divided government is only one of a number of
factors that may contribute to policy immobilism. Four separate, but
not mutually exclusive, explanations of policy inaction have been
proposed:

1. The partisan, or divided government, explanation: When one
   party controls the executive and the other the legislature, ideological differences between the two make policy agreement difficult,
   if not impossible. Polarized partisan positions make negotiating
   policy compromises problematic. Conversely, when there is unified government, the bases for interbranch cooperation are firmer
   and innovative lawmaking is more likely.
2. The electoral, or Tip O'Neill "all politics is local," explanation:
   Members' careers hinge on their ability to satisfy the "folks
   back home" in their states and districts, and their actions in
   Washington reflect the parochialism necessary to do so. Emphasis on "bringing home the bacon" and avoiding risky political
   stands that might offend constituency voters and interests undercuts policymaking creativity and effectiveness.
3. The structural, or "textbook congress," explanation: The organization of the legislature—featuring independent committees,
   complex rules of procedure, widely shared informal understandings (norms), and weak political parties—decentralizes the institution. Congress, with its individualistic members acting independently from a variety of power bases in a fragmented body, is
   better suited to resist than to adopt policy initiatives; innovative
   decision making suffers in consequence.
4. The presidential leadership, or Neustadt, explanation: Unless the
   president makes effective use of the available bases of persuasive
   power, Congress will protect and promote local concerns rather

than respond to national needs. The chief executive must bring his resources to bear on the lawmakers if he wishes to see his priorities enacted. If he fails to do so, legislative parochialism will subvert the administration's agenda.

Singly or in combination, these four factors—divided government, electorally-induced localism, congressional decentralization, and presidential leadership failure—may contribute to policy immobilism. The 103rd Congress offers one opportunity to explore the merits of these explanations.

Policymaking in the 103rd Congress

It may seem odd to assess divided government in a Congress of unified government. The 1992 election returned the Democrats to the White House, albeit with a modest plurality of the vote (43 percent) in a three-way race. The Clinton campaign offered a platform of change, to which the electorate seemed to respond positively. The Democrats retained a slightly reduced congressional majority, holding 256 House and 56 Senate seats. Moreover, the legislative party, energized by the restoration of one-party, unified government and a putative popular mandate, seemed committed to move ahead vigorously, not only on the high-profile items (health care, a middle-class tax cut, and welfare reform) of the Clinton agenda, but also on the second-tier matters (e.g., family leave legislation, anticrime measures, the North American Free Trade Agreement [NAFTA]). Conditions seemed propitious for successful presidential leadership. An inability of the chief executive to forge winning congressional coalitions under these favorable circumstances surely casts doubt on his capacity to achieve his purposes in the less conducive conditions, such as divided government, that have obtained more commonly in recent years (including the 104th Congress, elected in 1994). The 103rd Congress thus, in a sense, offers a conservative test for the influence of divided government. If the president cannot pass priority programs under unified government, he is surely no more likely (though not necessarily less so) to build majority coalitions when the opposition controls the legislature.

How effective was presidentially led policymaking under these promising circumstances? It is instructive to look first at the aggregate evidence. The initial lesson to emerge from the statistics of the 103rd Congress is that if he could get a vote on his favored proposals,

Clinton stood a strong chance of winning. One gauge of Congress's independent impact is the extent that it accepts or rejects the chief executive's initiatives. Lower levels of support for the president indicate that the lawmakers are prepared to block the administration's ideas or to modify them substantially. There has been wide variation, both between and within administrations and between periods of divided and unified government, in legislative compliance with presidential proposals.

The data in table 5.1 point to two fundamental conclusions. Most specifically, Bill Clinton achieved a higher success rate than any of his immediate predecessors; the 103rd Congress approved 86.4 percent of the measures the president supported.[13] More generally, the figures also reveal that divided government reduces presidential success. Democratic presidents, including Clinton, with Democratic congressional majorities, fared better than GOP chief executives who faced a Congress in which the opposition controlled at least one chamber. Even the allegedly weak leadership of Jimmy Carter secured a higher success rate (76.4 percent) than the most successful Republican president (Eisenhower, 72.2 percent).[14] Overall, then, Clinton won congressional approval of five out of every six of his requests in 1993 and 1994.

Turning to specific issues, Clinton compiled a mixed, but generally positive, record on his most significant initiatives. On many major matters, particularly in the House, he was able to get sufficient backing from Democrats alone to pass his preferred bills; on others, he was forced to rely on Republican votes (tables 5.2, 5.3, and 5.4). Of 20 high-priority bills, Clinton managed to get the House and Senate to vote on fourteen, and eleven became law; six others failed without getting a roll call in one or both chambers.[15]

Looking first to the House, it is obvious that the chamber leaders (Speaker Thomas Foley and his team), though much maligned inside the beltway, managed to provide the president with the votes needed to move the administration agenda forward. Seventeen of the twenty priority items cleared the House. The eleven that became law are listed in table 5.2. Of the six that passed the House but failed to become law, three were voted down in the Senate, and three others—telecommunications legislation, Safe Drinking Water Act amendments, and mining law reform—died without a direct vote in the Senate (table 5.4). Sixteen of the bills that the House enacted received roll call votes, and eleven of these would have passed without a single Republican vote. For example, Democrats alone provided 34 more votes (248) than the 214 needed (with 427 members voting) to enact the president's

TABLE 5.1
Presidential Success in Congress, under Unified and Divided
Government, 1953–1994

President	Years	% Success
Unified Government		
Eisenhower (R)	1953-1954	86.0
Kennedy (D)	1961-1963	84.6
Johnson (D)	1963-1968	82.6
Carter (D)	1977-1980	76.4
Clinton (D)	1993-1994	86.4
Divided Government		
Eisenhower (R)	1955-1960	66.5
Nixon (R)	1969-1974	67.2
Ford (R)	1974-1976	57.6
Reagan (R)	1981-1988	61.9
Bush (R)	1989-1992	51.6

Sources: Norman J. Ornstein, Thomas E. Mann, and Michael J. Malbin, *Vital Statistics on Congress, 1993–1994* (Washington, D.C.: CQ Press, 1994), Table 8–1; Steven Langdon, "Clinton's High Victory Rate Conceals Disappointments," *Congressional Quarterly Weekly Report,* 31 December 1994, 3619–23.
Note: These numbers represent, of all roll calls on which the president announced a clear stand, the percentage on which his position prevailed.

National Service Bill (table 5.2). Some votes were exceedingly close. In a widely reported case, Marjorie Margolies-Mezvinski of Pennsylvania cast the decisive 218th vote that ensured the adoption of the conference report on the administration's deficit reduction package (table 5.2);[16] in two votes on lobby disclosure legislation, Independent

TABLE 5.2
Clinton Victories in the House in the 103rd Congress

	Votes needed	Dem. Votes	Dem. "Surplus"	Rep. Votes
National service (conf. report)	214	248	+34	26
California desert protection (prev. q.)	213	241	+28	4
Balanced budget amendment	142	153	+11	1
Family leave	215	224	+9	40
Goals 2000 (recommittal)	214	223	+9	8
Deficit reduction (conf. report)	218	218	0	0
Abortion clinic access (conf. report)	208	200	-8	17
Anticrime Bill (rule: conf. report)	215	196	-19	42
Brady Bill (recommittal)	215	191	-24	37
GATT	218	167	-51	121
NAFTA	218	102	-116	132

Source: Congressional Quarterly materials.
Note: "Votes needed" is the number of votes needed for victory, given the number of members voting.

Bernard Sanders of Vermont cast the critical ballot (table 5.4). On the other five roll calls, Republican support put the Clinton proposals over the top. In the extreme case, on NAFTA, the Democrats came up 116 votes short, but were saved by the backing of 132 Republicans.

On the Senate side, the picture was about the same, although the president's success rate was lower. He secured passage of eleven of the bills that the House had passed (table 5.3). Of those, six victories required no Republican votes, though on one (the national service

TABLE 5.3

Clinton Victories in the Senate in the 103rd Congress

	Votes needed	Dem. Votes	Dem. "Surplus"	Rep. Votes
Family leave	51	55	+4	16
California desert protection	51	53	+2	16
Abortion clinic access (conf. report)	51	52	+1	17
Deficit reduction (conf. report)	51	51	0	0
National service (conf. report)	51	51	0	6
Balanced budget amendment	34	34	0	3
Brady Bill	51	47	-4	16
Anticrime Bill (cloture)	60	54	-6	7
Goals 2000 (cloture)	60	53	-7	9
GATT (budget waiver)	60	37	-23	31
NAFTA	51	27	-24	34

Source: Congressional Quarterly materials.

Note: "Votes needed" is the number of votes needed for victory, given the number of members voting. Vice-President Albert Gore cast the decisive tie-breaking vote on the deficit reduction conference report.

conference report), there were no votes to spare, and on another (the deficit reduction conference report), Vice-President Albert Gore cast the tie-breaking ballot. The remaining five wins depended on GOP support: Republicans provided 7 votes to invoke cloture and end debate on the Anticrime Bill and 34 votes to pass NAFTA. On the negative side, the president lost on nine occasions. On three measures—an economic stimulus package, reform of campaign finance, and regulation of lobbyists—the Democrats were unable to secure the 60 votes necessary to end late-in-the-session filibusters (table 5.4). Six other items expired in the Senate without a direct vote (table 5.4).

Overall, the president won on eleven of the twenty key issues.[17] Five

TABLE 5.4
Clinton Losses in the 103rd Congress

	Votes needed	Dem. Votes	Dem. "Surplus"	Rep. Votes
House votes				
Economic stimulus package	213	231	+18	3
Campaign finance (rule)	214	216	+2	3
Lobby disclosure (rule: passage)	212	211	-1	9
Lobby disclosure (rule: conf. report)	211	210	-1	5
Senate votes				
Economic stimulus (cloture)	60	56	-4	0
Campaign finance (cloture: passage)	60	55	-5	7
Campaign finance (cloture: conf. rep.)	60	51	-9	6
Lobby disclosure (cloture)	60	46	-12	9

No direct votes

Gays in the military, Health care reform, Superfund renewal,

Telecommunications reform, Safe drinking water, Mining law reform

Source: Congressional Quarterly materials.
Note: Independent Bernard Sanders of Vermont voted with the Democrats on the lobby disclosure bill (conference report and passage).

victories needed no Republican help in either chamber; two (Goals 2000 education and abortion clinic access legislation) required GOP votes in one house; and four passed only with bipartisan backing in both House and Senate. The implication of these aggregate figures is that the president can, at least in circumstances of unified government, use the available resources to win a significant number of his public policy struggles with Congress. Skillful leadership can overcome structural obstacles that a decentralized legislature raises, sometimes by rallying the party faithful, sometimes by constructing cross-party coalitions. On the other hand, unified government was not enough to secure passage of the most important elements (e.g., health care, campaign finance reform) on the Clinton agenda. A full assessment of the causes of policy failure, even under unified government, requires a closer look at the details of campaigns to pass specific pieces of legislation.

Clinton Victories

Even a casual examination of specific cases demonstrates conclusively that each piece of legislation necessitates a carefully tailored coalition-building effort. The president must lead skillfully, employing his resources in appropriate ways to win votes for his proposals. He needs to discover which members of Congress support him and which do not; he must shore up the backing of the former and, if he still lacks the requisite votes, he must induce those on the fence or convert those opposed. He may choose to "go public," seeking to arouse the public to bring pressure to bear on electorally sensitive lawmakers.[18] Some campaigns will be relatively easy, requiring only a minimal effort. Others will be fraught with peril and will demand an all-out struggle. Still others will be lost regardless of the time and energy committed to them. Unified government alone, it is clear, will not suffice.

The Clinton administration record in the 103rd Congress illustrates the fundamental distinctiveness of individual campaigns for particular bills. The Family and Medical Leave Act, for example, which allowed employees to take unpaid leave from their jobs to attend family members, was enacted without major controversy. Democratic majorities had passed the bill twice before, in 1990 and 1992, only to have George Bush's veto of it sustained on each occasion.[19] In 1993, the Democratic votes remained in place, and there was some Republican support as well (40 votes in the House, 16 in the Senate). With Clinton publicly committed to sign the bill, both the House and the Senate passed it easily, and the former accepted the latter's changes, obviating the need for a conference and clearing the bill for the president.

The administration also pursued a party-based coalition-building strategy on its deficit reduction (reconciliation) package, but this time there was far less margin for error.[20] The Republican minority was unanimously opposed; some conservative Democrats dissented on the grounds that the bill did not cut the deficit sufficiently; and the Congressional Black Caucus protested that social programs were scaled back excessively. In the House, the bill passed 219 to 213, without a single Republican vote and in the face of defections from 38 Democrats. To secure the narrow victory, Clinton "worked the phones incessantly," Vice-President Gore lobbied face to face out of his Senate office, and cabinet members made "repeated phone calls" to House members. Democrat Marcy Kaptur of Ohio received seven phone calls (two from Clinton, two from Gore, and three from Cabinet secretaries) and a personal visit from Dan Rostenkowski of Illinois, chair of the powerful Ways and Means Committee. She supported the administration after getting assurances that a controversial energy tax provision would be modified in the Senate. Clinton made other substantive concessions; he promised to add entitlement program cuts to the Senate version. The administration was prepared to use the "stick" as well as the "carrot." It "threatened some senior members with loss of their committee or subcommittee chairmanships" if they voted against the bill. Agriculture Secretary Mike Espy warned three California Democrats that he would cancel scheduled meetings with constituents in their districts (only one of the three voted for the bill). These efforts enabled the president to eke out a 6-vote victory.

The Democrats' partisan go-it-alone strategy was equally precarious in the Senate. Disdaining compromise with the Republican minority (and thus getting no GOP votes), the majority was hard put to pass the bill. It held its defections to 7 only after the president pledged to renegotiate several hotly contested items in conference, and even then the bill carried 50 to 49 on a tie-breaking vote by Vice-President Gore.

To win approval of the conference report was no simpler. In the House, Democratic leaders "cut a variety of deals to win votes." Their bill preserved social programs and thus mollified the Black Caucus. They agreed to allow two floor amendments to cut additional spending and supported Clinton's promise to propose further expenditure reductions later in the year. Representative Margolies-Mezvinski provided the critical vote after winning a commitment to hold a conference on cutting entitlement spending in her district. The administration survived 41 Democratic defections to win acceptance of the report, 218 to 216. In the Senate, the leadership, with no votes to spare, redoubled its efforts when Democrat David Boren of Oklahoma, who had voted for passage, announced his opposition to the conference report. They "redrafted or removed more than 100 provisions" to consolidate support. They prevailed, 51 to 50 (without a Republican vote), when Dennis DeConcini of Arizona reversed his earlier position to vote "aye," creating a tie that the vice-president broke in the administration's favor. "Both my arms feel twisted," DeConcini said, but he won a provision cutting back a tax increase that his upper-income retiree constituents would have to pay.

On some issues, relying on Democrats alone was infeasible. There were too many fissures within party ranks on an anti-crime package, and a bipartisan coalition-building strategy was the president's only recourse.[21] In general, controversy surrounded both the sums to be spent and the allocation of the funds between prevention (e.g., education) and punishment (e.g., more police). More specifically, the administration proposed to ban nineteen types of automatic assault weapons frequently used by criminals. The National Rifle Association (NRA) asserted that the ban infringed on Americans' Second Amendment "right to bear arms" and lobbied extensively against the provision. While the Black Caucus demanded inclusion of a "racial justice" title authorizing the courts to use statistics to demonstrate the unfairness of death penalty sentencing, Republicans pushed for an item reducing the use of habeas corpus provisions to appeal and delay endlessly the imposition of the death penalty. Polls revealed that the public demanded action against crime, giving both the executive and the legislative branches an incentive to pass some legislation.

The Senate acted first: a "two-week tougher-than-thou" bidding war produced a bill with an acceptable allocation of funds between prevention and punishment and a ban on assault weapons. The limitation of the use of habeas corpus appeals was abandoned. Republican votes provided the margins for the weapons ban and the deletion of the habeas corpus provision. The compromise passed easily, 95 to 4.

The going in the House was much rougher. The 285 to 141 passage belied considerable controversy. The Black Caucus was split, even after the racial justice provisions were narrowly retained, 217 to 212. The habeas corpus provisions were dropped, and the bill contained no assault weapons ban. The Republican motion to recommit failed, 192 to 235, with only 4 GOP votes against it; 65 Republicans eventually supported passage. In a surprising development, the House subsequently enacted the assault weapons ban as separate legislation. The administration played a major role in producing a 2-vote, 216 to 214, margin for the ban. Clinton "called dozens of members, as did Attorney General Janet Reno," relying on "moral persuasion" rather than conventional horse trading. Former presidents Jimmy Carter, Gerald Ford, and Ronald Reagan endorsed the ban. Only 4 Republicans supported the rule governing floor consideration of the measure, but when the roll was called for final passage, 38 Republicans, including Robert Michel, the party leader, supported it, perhaps unwilling to let the president claim full credit for a popular piece of legislation. Thirty members who had opposed a similar ban in 1991 reversed themselves and voted for it in 1994 (only five of them received NRA support). Freshman members, perhaps in tune with citizen sentiment, backed the ban 64 to 51.

Securing approval of the conference report was even more contentious. The administration suffered an embarrassing and almost fatal defeat when the House rejected the rule for consideration of the report. To protest, among other things, the dropping of the racial justice title, members of the Black Caucus voted 27 to 11 against the rule. Other Democrats objected to inclusion of the assault weapons ban. Overall, 58 Democrats opposed the rule. The administration lobbied the Republicans "intensely," but the GOP made crime a party issue—the bill spent too much on social programs aimed at prevention and too little on law enforcement—and only 11 of their number voted for the rule, which lost 210 to 225. Unable to convince enough Democrats to switch, the administration cut a deal with the Republicans. While insisting on retaining the ban on automatic weapons, the president agreed to reduce spending by $3.2 billion, most of it from the prevention side of the ledger. He accepted several other changes as well; for instance, the compromise called for the states to track sex offenders and notify local communities to which they moved. GOP moderates were reluctant to scuttle a popular measure; 42 of them voted for a revised rule (which passed, 239 to 189) and 46 joined 188 Democrats (64 Democrats deserted the president) to approve the conference report, 235 to 195. Republican moderates enabled the president to prevail in the Senate as well. After negotiations between Majority Leader George Mitchell and Minority Leader Robert Dole failed to produce an acceptable compromise, the GOP moderates cast their lot with the Democrats. Six voted (with 55 Democrats) to provide the three-fifths majority needed to waive a budgetary point of order against the bill, and 7 supported both cloture to end the debate and final passage of the conference report.

In extreme cases, such as that of NAFTA, the president secured a victory with greater support from the minority in Congress than from his own party.[22] On NAFTA, the administration needed only a single victory; the agreement was considered under "fast-track" procedures that allowed only one up-or-down vote on the text of the compact. On the other hand, there was massive opposition within Democratic ranks, particularly in the House. The labor movement, fearful of a huge loss of jobs to Mexico where wages were low, and environmentalists, worried that the pact would erode conservation efforts along the U.S.-Mexican border, strenuously opposed the agreement. The Republicans were divided as well. The bulk of the minority members, a "free trade" bloc, supported the agreement—originally negotiated during the Republican Bush administration—but a conservative faction was concerned that American commitment to specific dispute resolution procedures might cede the nation's sovereignty to an unfriendly international organization. Initially, the administration's prospects seemed bleak. Only one of the three House committees (Ways and Means, chaired by party loyalist Dan Rostenkowski) with jurisdiction over NAFTA reported it favorably. Worse still, the top House Democratic leaders (Majority Leader Richard Gephardt of Missouri and Whip David Bonoir of Michigan) declined to support Clinton. To gain acceptance of the agreement would be "a come from behind victory of impressive proportions." Yet many members seemed willing to listen to the president. "Right now my vote is no," said Republican Tom Lewis of Florida, "but the door's ajar."

Clinton orchestrated a major coalition-building campaign, featuring a "barrage of deal cutting" and considerable "arm twisting." He singled out some groups for special attention. "Many deals were struck to help farmers": the administration won over 9 members of the Florida delegation with arrangements to "help the state's citrus, sugar, and vegetable growers." Ten members from textile states responded to a promise to extend the phase-out of import quotas from ten to fifteen years by backing the agreement. The president also worked on individual members. Democrat Mike Kreidler of Washington announced his support, professing that the White House had convinced him that the agreement did not threaten jobs; Democrat Bart Gordon of Tennessee secured favorable publicity by announcing his conversion to the NAFTA cause at a press conference that Vice-President Gore attended; Democrat Floyd Flake of New York got a Small Business Administration pilot program for his district; Republican Peter King of New York won reversal of a decision to cancel a public works project in his constituency. When the dust from these and other arrangements settled, NAFTA triumphed 234 (132 Republicans, 102 Democrats) to 200 in the House and 61 (34 Republicans, 27 Democrats) to 27 in the Senate.[23]

Clinton Losses

If a president's skillful efforts, sometimes modest, often extensive, can regularly succeed, there remain instances when the legislative terrain is so hostile that the struggle for congressional backing seems fated to fail. In the 103rd Congress, the Clinton administration was unable to forge winning coalitions in a number of such circumstances, to which its own shortcomings contributed. Two issues stressed in the 1992 campaign, welfare reform and a tax cut targeted at the middle class, posed seemingly insuperable tactical problems and were quietly abandoned. In three instances, presidential programs, deftly steered through a House minefield, fell before the withering fire of a Senate filibuster. The president's economic stimulus package (fiscal 1993 supplemental appropriations bill) was one such defeat.[24] The Clinton proposals for "investment in America" did not generate an expected "groundswell of public support." The administration expected its 56-vote majority to prevail and was caught unprepared by a Republican filibuster. Clinton pursued a partisan strategy, typical of 1993, and refused to negotiate; he rejected a compromise offered by three middle-of-the-road Democrats. Senator Robert Byrd's use of obscure parliamentary procedures to preclude Republican amendments hardened the opposition. Three cloture votes fell short of the 60 votes needed to end debate (none got more than 55). The bill was then rewritten to cut spending one-fourth, but the minority would have none of it. A fourth cloture motion won only 56 votes, all from Democrats, and the bill was abandoned.

Campaign finance reform, a major 1992 Clinton campaign pledge, met a similar fate.[25] Both chambers enacted reform legislation in 1993, but no effort to convene a conference ensued until late in the 1994 session. Although a tentative House-Senate agreement on the ticklish issue of political action committee contributions was on the table, the Republican Senate minority chose to filibuster a motion to proceed to conference. The strategy was to deny Clinton a legislative victory to trumpet in the upcoming midterm elections. At the same time, "many Democrats," for obvious electoral reasons, opposed limits on contributions or campaign spending. In the end, 4 Senate GOP moderates and 6 Democrats refused to support a cloture motion, which garnered only 52 of the needed 60 votes, and the reform bill died. Though the administration had billed the measure as a "top priority," it did not seem to do much to round up support for the measure.[26]

If these measures got more lip service than serious persuasive effort from the president, health care was an entirely different story.[27] The issue dominated the 1992 Clinton-Bush campaign. The challenger promised a comprehensive reform bill within one hundred days of his inauguration. On taking office, he put Hillary Rodham Clinton in charge of a task force of more than five hundred experts charged with drafting the specifics of a reform plan. The issue proved nearly intractable. Eventually, well past the self-imposed deadline, the administration sent Congress a massive 1,342-page bill that truly boggled the mind. The proposal featured "employer mandates," "health care alliances," "managed care" options, a host of other arcane requirements, and a vast federal apparatus to run the program. The public found the bill incomprehensible; a widely broadcast series of television ads, featuring an ordinary couple, "Harry and Louise," pondering the possible pitfalls of health care change, played on public doubts and fear of unpredictable reform. Those affected—health care providers, insurance companies, employers—all found objectionable features in the proposals. An improving economy removed some of the sense of urgency that had animated early discussion of the issue. The question quickly became mired in controversy.

Five congressional committees (three in the House, two in the Senate) took up the confusing and contentious health care issue. Nothing remotely resembling consensus ever emerged, despite substantial prodding by the Clinton administration. After many hearings and much emotionally charged debate, four sharply contrasting bills, two in each house, were sent to the chamber floors. Eventually, in each house, the Democratic leadership produced a single plan; the House opted to let the Senate act first. Senate leader George Mitchell's bill was similar to the House (Gephardt) proposal, but Minority Leader Dole countered with a conservative bill that made only minimal reforms. A bipartisan "mainstream" group, led by Republican John Chafee of Rhode Island and Democrat John Breaux of Louisiana, weighed in with a middle-of-the-road measure. None commanded anything close to a majority. With no external pressure to act and with the Republicans seemingly prepared for a closing-days filibuster, Mitchell gave up. The House never returned to the issue. Two years of sustained effort failed to make any headway on the health care question.

Congress also rejected another high-priority Clinton campaign pledge, a promise to improve the lot of gays in the military.[28] Candidate Clinton had vowed to end discrimination against homosexuals serving in the armed forces, but his proposals to do so ran into heavy seas.

Public opinion was clearly hostile, the military resisted changing the existing policy, and social conservatives of both parties in Congress were unsympathetic to the president's initiative. In the end, not only did Clinton fail to get a vote on his proposals, but also the existing "longtime ban on homosexual conduct" was written into law "with only slight modifications" in the 1994 Defense Authorization Bill. Observers proclaimed the affair a major setback for the president.

Conclusion: Why Gridlock?

The foregoing analyses of the aggregate evidence and of specific cases strongly suggest that the causes of policymaking drift and deadlock are several and varied. Divided partisan control of government is one, but by no means the only, source of a slow-moving congressional decision process. It is not fatal; significant presidential initiatives do pass under divided control. But it is not helpful either. Presidents win on more roll calls when they have a legislative majority, but even then, as the 103rd Congress amply illustrates, they do not pass all their initiatives. Unified partisan control of government helps. It enabled Clinton to win some significant victories (on family leave and deficit reduction, for instance), especially in the House, but it could not facilitate passage of major proposals like health care reform or programs to protect the rights of gays in the military.

Policy innovation requires more than parliamentary majorities. The chief executive must exploit available resources adroitly to construct coalitions, often crossing party lines to do so (as on NAFTA). When leadership falters (as it did on health care) or is slack (as on campaign finance and lobby reform), members of Congress may feel free to respond to other pressures. If voters and interest groups are supportive (as they were on the Brady bill), electorally sensitive legislators may feel the need to act. If citizens are confused or divided (as they were on health care) or opposed (as they were on the economic stimulus package and gays in the military), lawmakers may prefer to avoid casting difficult votes and opt for inaction. Even when polls reveal support (as they did on campaign finance and lobbying reform), structural features of Congress, such as the Senate filibuster rule, may thwart lawmaking majorities. Opposition from influential legislative leaders (e.g., telecommunications) or independent committees (e.g., gays in the military) may defeat presidential proposals.

Thus, the Constitution creates conditions—executive and legislative branches sharing authority, a bicameral Congress featuring organizationally fragmented chambers, and locally based electoral arrangements—that hinder swift and easy policymaking. In other words, all four explanations (partisanship, electoral politics, legislative structure, and presidential leadership) contribute, on some issues at least, to the policy paralysis that critics decry. Unified partisan control facilitates creative policymaking; it provides the party in power with a foundation on which to construct legislative coalitions. If the public offers strong support for particular programs, electorally connected senators and representatives may respond positively to citizen sentiments. When loyal partisans or program proponents occupy critical positions in Congress, bills may move more smoothly through the procedural maze that a structurally decentralized legislature creates. Committed and forceful presidential leadership can exploit these possibilities and enhance the potential for significant policy change. Absent these facilitating conditions, and all four are seldom simultaneously present, the policy process is likely to be slow at best and to produce incremental, rather than radical, change.

This view of inefficient policymaking has provoked considerable commentary. On the one hand, some observers, citing the Madisonian pluralist argument that limited government is desirable, seem satisfied with the status quo. They see serious risk in precipitous policy change; they see no need to tamper with a process that avoids rushing into the unknown. Some, on the other hand, prefer action to caution; they propose reforms designed to energize decision making. A responsible party system offers one route to coherent policy; a disciplined partisan majority would pass its program subject to voter ratification or rejection in the subsequent election. Pragmatic reformers occupy intermediary positions. They put forth a series of proposals—term limits for legislators, campaign finance reform, and committee restructuring and rules changes within Congress—that might curb legislators' dependence on a volatile electorate and reduce organizational fragmentation that inhibits policy innovation.[29] These issues, inherent in the American constitutional system, seem certain to generate debate in the years ahead.

Epilogue: The 104th Congress

The remarkable Republican triumph in the 1994 midterm elections demonstrates dramatically and decisively that, within a constant con-

stitutional setting, the conditions for policymaking may change significantly. The 104th Congress differs in almost every respect from its
predecessor. The election restored divided control of government.
The Clinton White House confronted an opposition Congress.[30] The
Republicans, with their Contract with America, succeeded in overcom-
ing the "all politics is local" orientation of the majority Democrats,
making the election a referendum on the performance of the Clinton
administration. Their striking seizure of Congress was widely viewed
as a mandate for the bold policy changes the contract offered the
voters.

The House Republican leaders took firm control of the policy process. They curtailed committee independence, securing appointment
of party loyalists to the top posts and imposing term limits on service
as committee chairs. In sharp contrast to the usual "member individualism," rooted in the electoral safety of incumbents, the seventy-
three House Republican freshmen, many avid conservatives, displayed
unprecedented party loyalty. They voted cohesively for most elements
of the contract. The Senate was more inclined to "business as usual";
moderate Republican senators were less willing to abandon their policy
independence. The minority Democrats soon found ways to exploit
the rules, the filibuster in particular, to slow the progress of Republican
efforts to shrink the size and scope of the federal government. Nonetheless, to an unusual degree, congressional lawmaking in the 104th
Congress, at least on the broad philosophical matters of the contract
treated in the first hundred days of the new Congress, revolved around
legislative, rather than presidential, proposals. The new majority,
especially in the House, seemed singularly determined to reform
welfare, balance the budget, and deregulate the economy.

These changes forcefully challenged presidential leadership. Lacking a legislative majority and confronting a disciplined House opposition with a clear agenda, the Clinton administration was compelled to
adopt a defensive strategy. It was virtually powerless to block swift
House passage of the items in the Contract with America; a constitutional amendment imposing term limits was the only casualty. The
administration's focus instead was on the Senate. The president sought
to persuade loyal Democrats to employ the filibuster, negotiated with
moderate Republicans for agreements that softened House-passed
measures, and vetoed unacceptable bills that reached his desk. In the
first six months of the new Congress, despite unprecedented legislative
activity, only three relatively noncontroversial bills—applying regulatory statutes imposed on the private sector to Congress, limiting the

imposition of unfunded mandates on the states, and reducing federal paperwork—became law.

In the final analysis, these developments underscore a fundamental truth about public policymaking: the Constitution establishes a fluid decision process that cannot ensure a creative governmental response to issues that confront the country. The system of separation of powers, with its checks and balances, works to constrain the enactment of public programs. Partisanship (embodied in divided or unified government), the responsiveness of government to electoral considerations, the character of congressional organization, and the quality and commitment of presidential leadership conspire in distinctive ways to create a policy process prone to delay and deadlock. The adequacy of such a process is certain to remain a subject of considerable controversy.

Notes

1. James A. Thurber, "Representation, Accountability, and Efficiency in Divided Party Control of Government," *PS: Political Science & Politics* 24 (1991): 653–57.

2. David R. Mayhew, *Divided We Govern: Party Control, Lawmaking, and Investigations, 1946–1990* (New Haven: Yale University Press, 1991); David R. Mayhew, "Divided Party Control: Does It Make a Difference?" *PS: Political Science & Politics* 24 (1991): 637–40.

3. Sean Q Kelly, "Divided We Govern? A Reassessment," *Polity* 25 (1993): 475–88.

4. Andrew J. Taylor, "Understanding Madison's Curse: Divided Government and Domestic Policy, 1955–1992," (paper presented at the annual meeting of the American Political Science Association, New York, 1994).

5. Gary W. Cox and Mathew D. McCubbins, "Divided Control of Fiscal Policy," in *The Politics of Divided Government,* ed. Gary W. Cox and Samuel Kernell (Boulder, Colo.: Westview, 1991): 155–75.

6. Martha L. Gibson, "Politics and Divided Government," (paper presented at the annual meeting of the American Political Science Association, New York, 1994).

7. David Epstein and Sharyn O'Halloran, "Divided Government and the Design of Administrative Procedures," (paper presented at the annual meeting of the American Political Science Association, New York, 1994).

8. The extensive literature on the electoral roots of divided government—why the voters give the White House to one political party and Capitol Hill to the other—lies outside the scope of this essay. The focus here is on the impact, if any, of divided partisan control of government on policymaking. An

excellent overview of the electoral issue is provided by Gary C. Jacobson, *The Electoral Origins of Divided Government: Competition in U.S. House Elections, 1946–1988* (Boulder, Colo.: Westview, 1990); Morris Fiorina, *Divided Government*, 2d ed. (Boston: Allyn & Bacon, 1996), especially chapters 6 and 11; and other chapters in this volume.

9. Richard E. Neustadt, *Presidential Power and the Modern Presidents: Leadership from Roosevelt to Reagan* (New York: Wiley, 1990).

10. For stylistic convenience, and because to date all presidents have been men, I use the masculine pronoun throughout without pejorative intent.

11. Neustadt, *Presidential Power*.

12. The literature on the president and presidential leadership generally is extensive. Neustadt, *Presidential Power* (first published in 1960), remains the starting point. See also, inter alia, Bert A. Rockman, *The Leadership Question: The Presidency and the American System* (New York: Praeger, 1984); Theodore J. Lowi, *The Personal Presidency: Power Invested, Promise Unfulfilled* (Ithaca: Cornell University Press, 1985); Stephen Skowronek, *The Politics Presidents Make: Leadership from John Adams to George Bush* (Cambridge: Harvard University Press, 1983); Charles O. Jones, *The Presidency in a Separated System* (Washington, D.C.: Brookings Institution, 1994). On presidential leadership of Congress specifically, consult George C. Edwards, III, *At the Margins: Presidential Leadership of Congress* (New Haven: Yale University Press, 1989); Mark A. Peterson, *Legislating Together: The White House and Capitol Hill from Eisenhower to Reagan* (Cambridge: Harvard University Press, 1990); Jon R. Bond and Richard A. Fleisher, *The President in the Legislative Arena* (Chicago: University of Chicago Press, 1990). For recent scholarship on Congress, see Arthur Maass, *Congress and the Common Good* (New York: Basic Books, 1983); Barbara Sinclair, *The Transformation of the U.S. Senate* (Baltimore: Johns Hopkins University Press, 1989); R. Douglas Arnold, *The Logic of Congressional Action* (New Haven: Yale University Press, 1990); D. Roderick Kiewiet and Mathew D. McCubbins, *The Logic of Delegation: Congressional Parties and the Appropriations Process* (Chicago: University of Chicago Press, 1991); Keith Krehbiel, *Information and Legislative Organization* (Ann Arbor: University of Michigan Press, 1991); David W. Rohde, *Parties and Leaders in the Postreform House* (Chicago: University of Chicago Press, 1991); Gary W. Cox and Mathew D. McCubbins, *Legislative Leviathan: Party Government in the House* (Berkeley: University of California Press, 1993).

13. These percentages are the proportion of roll call votes on which the president's announced position prevailed. The figures must be taken as approximations. For one thing, the president may ask for something that he knows Congress will not pass. Second, the legislature may alter a proposal to barely recognizable form, but if the president initially suggested it, he will get credit for its passage. Finally, a president's success ratio will reflect the degree of controversy surrounding the administration's program; success may be inflated if requests include numerous less important items.

14. Interestingly, when Eisenhower had a Republican congressional majority in 1953 and 1954, he won on 89.2 and 82.8 percent, respectively, of his initiatives; once the Democrats reclaimed majority status, his success rate never exceeded 75.0 percent and fell to a low of 52.0 percent in 1959. Similarly, Ronald Reagan began well; in 1981 and 1982, with a Senate majority and working closely with conservative, mostly southern Democrats in the House, he secured passage of 82.3 and 72.4 percent, respectively, of his requests. By the end of his term, with the Democrats once again in control of the Senate, his success rate plummeted to 43.5 percent in 1987 and 47.4 percent in 1988.

15. "The 103rd Congress: What Was Accomplished, and What Wasn't," *New York Times*, 9 October 1994, 16; "The Record of the 103rd Congress," *Washington Post,* 9 October 1994, A21; "Assessing the 103rd Congress . . . What Passed and What Didn't," *Congressional Quarterly Weekly Report*, 5 November 1994, 3146–47. These three reviews of the 103rd Congress's performance identified the major elements of the Clinton program. The twenty bills analyzed in this essay include fourteen bills that appeared on all three lists, that the president favored, and that got roll call votes, one of which the *Congressional Quarterly Weekly Report* identified as a "key vote" on the floor of the House and/or the Senate. In addition, they include six additional measures that appeared on all three lists, that the president backed, and that failed to get record votes in one or both chambers.

16. Margolies-Mezvinski lost her seat in the 1994 midterm election, at least in part as a consequence of her challenger's attacking her as a "big spender" on the basis of this vote.

17. The 103rd Congress enacted several other significant bills—including "motor voter" registration, Hatch Act reform, student loan legislation, and reinstitution of investigatory independent counsels—on which there were no "key votes" and which, thus, were not included in the tabulations. If these are considered, the Clinton record appears substantially more impressive. On the other hand, the administration never pushed for a middle class tax cut or an "end to welfare as we know it," two of the most prominent themes in the president's 1992 campaign.

18. Samuel Kernell, *Going Public: New Strategies of Presidential Leadership*, 2d ed. (Washington, D.C.: Congressional Quarterly Press, 1992).

19. Jill Zuckman, "As Family Leave Is Enacted, Some See End to Logjam," *Congressional Quarterly Weekly Report*, 6 February 1993, 267–69.

20. References on the deficit reduction package are taken from David S. Cloud, "The Final Hours," *Congressional Quarterly Weekly Report*, 29 May 1993, 1343; George Hager and David S. Cloud, "Democrats Pull Off Squeaker in Approving Clinton Plan," *Congressional Quarterly Weekly Report*, 29 May 1993, 1340–45; George Hager and David S. Cloud, "Test for Divided Democrats: Forge a Budget Deal," *Congressional Quarterly Weekly Report*, 26 June 1993, 1631–35; and George Hager and David S. Cloud, "Democrats Tie Their Fate to Clinton's Budget Bill," *Congressional Quarterly Weekly Report*, 7 August 1993, 2123–29.

21. References on the anti-crime bill are taken from Holly Idelson, "More Cops, Jails: House Takes a $28 Billion Aim at Crime," *Congressional Quarterly Weekly Report*, 23 April 1994, 1001–5; Holly Idelson, "In Surprising Turnaround, House OKs Weapons Ban," *Congressional Quarterly Weekly Report*, 7 May 1994, 1119–23; Holly Idelson and Richard Sammon, "Marathon Talks Produce New Anti-Crime Bill," *Congressional Quarterly Weekly Report*, 20 August 1994, 2449–54; Phil Kuntz, "Tough-Minded Senate Adopts Crime Crackdown Package," *Congressional Quarterly Weekly Report*, 20 November 1993; Phil Kuntz, "Hard-Fought Crime Bill Battle Spoils Field for Health Care," *Congressional Quarterly Weekly Report*, 27 August 1994, 2485; David Masci, "$30 Billion Anti-Crime Bill Heads to Clinton's Desk," *Congressional Quarterly Weekly Report*, 27 August 1994, 2488–93.

22. References on NAFTA are taken from David S. Cloud, "As NAFTA Countdown Begins, Wheeling, Dealing Intensifies," *Congressional Quarterly Weekly Report*, 13 November 1993, 3104–7; David S. Cloud, "Decisive Vote Brings Down Trade Walls with Mexico," *Congressional Quarterly Weekly Report*, 20 November 1993, 3174–78; David S. Cloud, "Routine Approval in Senate Wraps Up NAFTA Fight," *Congressional Quarterly Weekly Report*, 27 November 1993, 3257.

23. On the other major piece of trade legislation, the General Agreement on Tariffs and Trade (GATT), the administration overcame the opposition somewhat more easily. See Bob Benenson, "GATT Pact Lurches Off Course As Hollings Hits the Brake," *Congressional Quarterly Weekly Report*, 1 October 1994, 2761–64; Bob Benenson, "Free Trade Carries the Day as GATT Easily Passes," *Congressional Quarterly Weekly Report*, 3 December 1994, 3446–50; Alissa Rubin, "Dole, Clinton Compromise Greases Wheels for GATT," *Congressional Quarterly Weekly Report*, 26 November 1994, 3405. It "spent months fine-tuning the legislation in a consultive process with key congressional committees." The president negotiated a deal with Minority Leader Dole that gave Congress the opportunity to instruct the chief executive to withdraw from the World Trade Organization, the arbiter of GATT, if it acted arbitrarily. In return, Dole promised to urge "every Republican Senator" to support the pact and to send them copies of letters from administration officials outlining acceptable adjustments to the agreement. The public seemed largely indifferent to the arcane trade matters. Acting under "fast track" provisions, a bipartisan House coalition (167 Democrats and 121 Republicans) easily passed the bill, 288 to 146. In the Senate, Chairman Ernest Hollings of the Commerce Committee, a stout defender of the textile interests in his state of South Carolina, manipulated the rules to force a delay that required a lame-duck, postelection session. But in the end, the Clinton-Dole deal held. A bipartisan coalition of senators (37 Democrats and 31 Republicans) supported a budget waiver required to override technical requirements of the rules and a larger coalition (41 Democrats and 35 Republicans) approved the agreement.

24. References on the economic stimulus package are taken from Jon

Healey and Chuck Alston, "Stimulus Bill Prevails in House, but Senate Battle Awaits," *Congressional Quarterly Weekly Report*, 20 March 1993, 649–52; Jon Healey, "Democrats Look to Salvage Part of Stimulus Package," *Congressional Quarterly Weekly Report*, 24 April 1993, 1001–4; Jon Healey, "Saga of a Supplemental," *Congressional Quarterly Weekly Report*, 24 April 1993, 1002.

25. Beth Donovan, "Republicans Plan Filibusters, Imperiling Senate Schedule," *Congressional Quarterly Weekly Report*, 24 September 1994, 2655; Beth Donovan, "Democrats' Overhaul Bill Dies on Senate Procedural Votes," *Congressional Quarterly Weekly Report*, October 1, 1994, 2757–58.

26. The story of the administration's lobbying disclosure legislation was nearly identical. See David S. Cloud, "Leaders Turn to Arm-Twisting to Pass Gift Ban in House," *Congressional Quarterly Weekly Report*, 1 October 1994, 2756; David S. Cloud, "GOP and Interest Groups Dig In to Dump Ban in Senate," *Congressional Quarterly Weekly Report*, 8 October 1994, 2854–55. Despite "private misgivings," both chambers enacted restrictions on lobbyists, but waited until adjournment was at hand before producing a conference agreement. In support of Republican obstructionist tactics, intended to deny victory to the administration, eight Democrats declined to support cloture, and the filibuster killed the bill. Similarly, a "prolonged effort" to sort out telecommunications policy—to redefine relationships among the long distance and local telephone companies, the cable television industry, the press, and the Hollywood filmmakers—petered out in the crush of business as adjournment neared. The House easily passed two telecommunications bills, but agreement in the Senate proved elusive. Although Senate Commerce Chair Hollings sought a compromise, three senators threatened a filibuster. Minority Leader Dole proposed a "non-negotiable" amendment that the bill sponsors refused to consider. In the end, Hollings "pulled the plug on a committee-approved bill" without pushing for a floor vote.

27. Adam Clymer, Robert Pear, and Robin Toner, "For Health Care, Time Was a Killer," *New York Times*, 29 August 1994, A1, A8.

28. Pat Towell, "Months of Hope, Anger, Anguish Produce Policy Few Admire," *Congressional Quarterly Weekly Report*, 24 July 1993, 1966–70; Pat Towell, "Battle over Gay Ban Policy Moves into the Courts," *Congressional Quarterly Weekly Report*, 31 July 1993, 2075; Pat Towell, "The Legislative Word on Gays," *Congressional Quarterly Weekly Report*, 31 July 1993, 2076.

29. For fuller treatment of the consequences of divided government and proposals to remedy its alleged defects, see James P. Pfiffner, "Divided Government and the Problem of Governance," in *Divided Government: Cooperation and Conflict between the President and Congress*, ed. James A. Thurber (Washington D.C.: Congressional Quarterly Press, 1991): 39–60; M. Stephen Weatherford, "Responsiveness and Deliberation in Divided Government: Presidential Leadership in Tax Policy Making," *British Journal of Political Science* 24 (1994): 1–31; James L. Sundquist, "Needed: A Political Theory for the New Era of Coalition Government in the United States,"

Political Science Quarterly 103 (winter 1988–89): 613–35; Lloyd N. Cutler, "Some Reflections about Divided Government," *Presidential Studies Quarterly* 18 (1988): 387–402.

30. After Democratic Senators Richard Shelby of Alabama and Ben Nighthorse Campbell of Colorado and Representatives Nathan Deal of Georgia and Greg Laughlin of Texas bolted to the GOP, the Republicans held 232 House and 54 Senate seats.

Chapter Six

The New Deal, the Modern Presidency, and Divided Government

Sidney M. Milkis

Studies of divided government have become prominent in the last dozen years. This growth industry among political scientists is understandable, as divided party control of the executive and legislature has become a more regular feature of American political life since the Second World War. Indeed, in every national election between 1968 and 1992 (Jimmy Carter's one term in the White House being the only exception), the voters delivered a split verdict, handing control of the presidency and of the Congress to the Republicans, as well as of most state and local offices, to the Democrats. Divided government did not occur in 1992, when the voters installed Democrat Bill Clinton in the White House while keeping Democratic majorities in the House and the Senate. With the 1994 elections, however, which saw the Republicans assume command of both houses of Congress for the first time in forty years, divided government was restored, this time in a form that had not occurred since Harry Truman confronted the Republican-controlled Eightieth Congress.

No clear consensus has emerged on what effect divided government has on public authority and policy, but many commentators view partisan cohabitation of the councils of government with alarm. Benjamin Ginsberg and Martin Shefter argue that the routine existence of separate partisan realms between 1968 and 1992 encouraged "institutional combat" that made it impossible for presidents to govern. Even Reagan, the only president during this period to complete two full terms in office, saw his second term disrupted by the Iran-Contra affair and by battles to control social regulation that were marked, not just by differences between the president and Congress about policy, but by each branch's efforts to weaken the other. Despite Bush's promise to pursue a "kinder, gentler version" of conservatism that would encourage a spirit of bipartisanship in executive-legislative relations, these institutional battles continued during his presidency.[1]

In the aftermath of this pitched warfare between the two branches, the authors of a leading textbook of American constitutional history called "divided government under the separation of powers the central constitutional problem of the 1980s."[2] By the 1992 elections, this view was widely accepted, apparently contributing to the Democratic Party's first successful presidential campaign since 1976. Since 1968, the public's striking ambiguity about the parties usually had left the government in a cross fire between a Republican president and a Democratic Congress. In 1992, however, an exit poll revealed that 62 percent of the voters now preferred to have the presidency and Congress controlled by the same party, in the hope that the ideological polarization and institutional combat encouraged by separate partisan realms would be brought to an end.[3]

Yet as the presidency of Jimmy Carter had revealed, one-party control of the White House and Congress does not ensure harmony between the branches of government. To be sure, Clinton cultivated his party leaders in Congress more than did his Democratic predecessor, and his efforts were rewarded with rather strong partisan unity during the first two years of his presidency.[4] But congressional support for his programs was sometimes undercut by recalcitrant moderate Democrats, many of whom shunned the president's ambitious health care initiative. More damaging to Clinton was the steadfast opposition of the Republican minority in both the House and the Senate. Clinton's determination during the early days of his administration to fight "an exclusively Democratic holy war" to reshape national economic policy aroused a militant Republican reaction. Indeed, Senate Republican leader Robert Dole resorted to the filibuster as a tool of party opposition on key Clinton proposals such as the economic stimulus package and health care reform. The willingness of Senate Republicans to resort to the filibuster to block many of Clinton's initiatives was a mark of the fundamental conflicts that divided the parties in Congress and prevented harmonious relations between the executive and the legislature. Such a course was virtually unprecedented; historically, the filibuster had been employed by mavericks or regional minorities to obstruct party leaders. That its use was orchestrated by the Republican

Party to ensnare President Clinton testified to the bitter partisanship that lingered from the Reagan-Bush era, as well as to Clinton's failure to move the country beyond the institutional conflicts spawned by partisan estrangement.[5]

The 1994 congressional elections did not enhance Clinton's ability to govern effectively.[6] Indeed, the new Republican majority's program completely eclipsed the president's. No longer in control of Congress's agenda, the Clinton administration switched from offense to defense on Capitol Hill. Resorting to the very same tactics that Reagan and Bush had used to withstand Democratic majorities in Congress, the Clinton administration faced the Republicans in a bitter partisan showdown that set the stage for the 1996 presidential election.

Curiously, these partisan battles within the beltway occurred amid the declining influence of the Democrats and Republicans on the perceptions and habits of the American people. The decline of partisan loyalties became especially pronounced in the late 1960s as the McGovern-Fraser reforms, which expanded the number of presidential primaries, and the rise of mass media politics led to an emphasis on candidate-centered, rather than party, campaigns.[7] Indeed, the 1992 presidential campaign of H. Ross Perot, whose 19 percent of the vote was the most significant challenge to the two-party system since Theodore Roosevelt's Progressive Party campaign of 1912, was dominated by thirty-minute and hour-long commercials and appearances on talk shows that set a new standard for direct, plebiscitary appeal. Disdaining pleas to form a third party from those interested in party renewal, Perot required no nominating convention to launch his candidacy.[8] Instead, he called his supporters to arms on the popular Cable News Network talk show *Larry King Live*.

Thus, as one astute observer of executive-legislative relations has written, "there is a basic disconnection between the [parties'] lack of a role in the government's relationships with the public and [their] increasingly important role in the government's relationship with itself."[9] If we are to make sense of the causes and consequences of divided government, we have to explain the seemingly contradictory patterns of party decline and renewal.

The New Deal Realignment and the Decline of Partisanship

I have argued elsewhere that a reexamination of Franklin Roosevelt's presidency and the New Deal can help solve the puzzle of contemporary party politics.[10] Paradoxically, the New Deal both strengthened parties and attenuated partisanship. On the one hand, it marked one of the periodic "critical partisan realignments" in American history. Occurring at critical junctures of American history—1800, 1828, 1860, 1896, and 1932—realignments have been animated by fundamental and polarizing conflict, thus severely testing the broad liberal consensus that so many scholars and pundits have portrayed as the essential genius of American politics. During these episodes, which Walter Dean Burnham has characterized as "America's surrogate for revolution," political parties in the United States, usually engaged in limited battles over personalities and policies, get caught up in something big that invigorates partisanship. The 1860 episode led directly to the outbreak of the Civil War, and every one of the others has been marked by acute political tension.[11] In the case of the New Deal realignment of the 1930s, a governing philosophy emerged that made legitimate, for the first time in American history, the expansion of social welfare policies. On the basis of this "programmatic liberalism," the Democratic Party became the majority party, and the Republicans were relegated to minority status after commanding the political system for most of the previous seventy years. There followed a program dedicated to guaranteeing the basic security of the American people—to building the welfare state.

On the other hand, the New Deal represented the culmination of efforts, which began in the Progressive era, to loosen the grip of partisan politics on the councils of power, with a view to shoring up the administrative capacities and extending the programmatic commitments of the federal government. In effect, Roosevelt and his key advisors viewed the American party system as an archaic institution that reinforced what liberal reformers considered outmoded constitutional understandings and mechanisms. The American party system was forged on the anvil of Jeffersonian principles, dedicated to establishing a "wall of separation" between the national government and society. As a result, it was, from its inception in the early 1800s, wedded to constitutional arrangements, such as legislative supremacy and states' rights, that were designed to constrain the expansion of national administrative power. Beginning with Woodrow Wilson, therefore, twentieth-century reformers criticized American political parties as an obstacle to the development of a significant progressive program.[12]

As such, the New Deal represents a secular change in party politics—one that was deliberately pursued to counteract the traditional pattern of realignment and the habits that sustained that pattern. Simply put, political parties were dispossessed of their status as the leading agents of democracy in the United States. Thereafter, the American people looked to a refurbished, "modern" presidency and newly formed administrative agencies to play that role.

There is a real sense, therefore, in which the New Deal was a realignment to make future partisan realignments unnecessary. Previous realignments had strengthened the national resolve and significantly altered the terms of American politics, but had not transformed the principles and institutional arrangements that historically had impeded the development of the "modern" state, that is, of a national political power with expansive programmatic obligations. The New Deal realignment, however, was the first to focus national attention on the capacity of the president and administrative agencies to extend the political capability of the American people. Especially during Roosevelt's second term, the New Deal emphasized a political program to make party politics less important and, concomitantly, to create a "perfected" system of public administration more significant in organizing the work of American constitutional government. As FDR put it in his 1932 campaign address at the Commonwealth Club in San Francisco, "the day of enlightened administration has come."[13]

In this pursuit of "enlightened administration," New Dealers created a more prominent and powerful presidency, which has strengthened the capability of the national government to tackle the pressing domestic and international challenges of the twentieth century. Yet the emergence of the "modern" presidency came at the cost of weakening the decentralized political parties that, for all their shortcomings, had long served as primary schools of democracy, in which Americans learned the art of association, or citizenship, and formed attachments to governing institutions.[14] In the end, the New Deal strengthened the national purpose while weakening certain fundamental principles and institutions of republican government. It is this deterioration of political associations and affiliations, and not divided government, that is the root cause of Americans' present discontent. Unified party government is not the solution to this crisis; in fact, divided government represents an understandable, if not fully effective, response to the disjunction between zealous partisanship within government and the deterioration of partisan affiliation outside of it.

"Programmatic Liberalism" and Party Politics
in the United States

The public philosophy of the New Deal provides the key to under-standing the New Deal's legacy for party politics and the separation of powers. Above all, the New Deal represented a redefinition of the social contract, a doctrinal change that presupposed an increase in administrative authority and efficiency and, concomitantly, the decline of the traditional two-party system. Roosevelt first spoke about the need to modernize elements of the old faith in his Commonwealth Club address. His theme was that the time had come—indeed, had come three decades earlier—to recognize the "new terms of the old social contract." It was necessary to rewrite the social contract to take account of a national economy remade by industrial capitalism and the concentration of economic power and to establish a countervailing power—a stronger national state—lest the United States steer "a steady course toward economic oligarchy."[15]

The creation of a national state with expansive supervisory powers would be a "long, slow task." The Commonwealth Club address was sensitive to the uneasy fit between energetic central government and the Constitution. It was imperative, therefore, for the New Deal to be informed by a public philosophy in which the new concept of state power would be carefully interwoven with earlier conceptions of American government. The task of modern government, FDR announced, was to "assist the development of an economic declaration of rights, an economic constitutional order."[16] The traditional emphasis in American politics on individual self-reliance ("natural" rights) should therefore give way to a new understanding of individualism, in which the government acted as a regulating and unifying agency, guarantee-ing individual men and women protection from the uncertainties of the marketplace. Thus, the most significant aspect of the move from natural rights to programmatic liberalism was the association of consti-tutional rights with the extension, rather than the restriction, of the programmatic commitments of the national government.

The need to construct an economic constitutional order, first articu-lated in the Commonwealth Club address, was a consistent theme of Roosevelt's long presidency. Significantly, it was the principal message of Roosevelt's first reelection bid in 1936, a decisive triumph that established the Democrats as the dominant party in American politics. The Democratic Party's platform for that campaign, drafted by Roose-velt, was written as a pastiche of the Declaration of Independence, thus emphasizing the need for a fundamental reconsideration of rights. The platform set forth as a new "self-evident truth" of the American constitutional order "that the test of representative government is its ability to promote the safety and happiness of the people" and announced the Democrats' determination to erect on the foundation of the 1935 Social Security Act "a structure of economic security" for all of America's citizens.[17]

As FDR would later detail in his 1944 State of the Union address, constructing a foundation of economic security meant that the inalienable rights secured by the Constitution (speech, press, worship, due process, and so on) had to be supplemented by a "second bill of rights," so to speak, "under which a new basis of security and prosperity can be established for all—regardless of station, race, or creed." Among these new rights were the right to a useful and remunerative job, the right to a decent home, the right to a good education, the right to adequate protection from the economic fears of old age, sickness, accident, and unemployment, the right to earn enough to provide adequate food, clothing, and recreation, and the right to adequate medical care.[18]

Although the Progressive tradition anticipated many elements of this understanding of government, Roosevelt was the first advocate of an active federal government to "appropriate" the term liberalism and make it part of the common political vocabulary.[19] Before the New Deal, American liberalism was associated with its Jeffersonian origins, which identified positive government with conservative efforts, beginning with Hamilton's economic policy, to advantage unjustly business enterprise. Even Woodrow Wilson's progressivism, the so-called New Freedom, remained in its essentials committed to decentralization of power. Herbert Croly and Theodore Roosevelt expressed an alternative progressive understanding, one that envisioned a "New Nationalism" as the "steward of the public welfare." From Croly's perspective, the victory of Wilson over Theodore Roosevelt in the 1912 election, in which the latter as the standard-bearer of the Progressive Party advocated "the substitution of frank social policy for the individualism of the past," ensured the triumph of "a higher conservatism over progressive democracy."[20]

The political genius of Franklin Roosevelt was to transform American politics without seeming to. The distinction between progressives and conservatives, as most boldly pronounced by Croly, all too visibly placed reformers in opposition to limited constitutional government and the self-interested basis of American politics. The use of the term liberalism by Roosevelt gave legitimacy to progressive principles by embedding them in the parlance of constitutionalism and interpreting them as the expansion, rather than the transcendence, of the natural rights tradition.[21]

Of course, these new programmatic rights were never formally ratified as amendments to the Constitution, nor were they fully codified in statutes and policies. But they became the foundation of political dialogue, redefining the role of the national government. The new social contract heralded by FDR marks the beginning of what has been called the "rights revolution"—a transformation in the governing philosophy of the United States that has brought about major changes in American political institutions.[22]

Roosevelt's reappraisal of values is important in understanding the New Deal, but it is also important in understanding FDR's impact on political parties and the separation of powers. The new understanding of the Declaration of Independence required an assault on the established party system, which had long been allied with constitutional forms that favored a decentralization of power. This effort to weaken traditional partisan organizations began during the Progressive era, but it fell to FDR and the architects of the New Deal to make progressivism an enduring part of American politics.

Party politics in the United States originated in an endeavor by Thomas Jefferson and his political allies, the most important being James Madison, to protect local freedom from the challenge to it they perceived in Alexander Hamilton's project to strengthen the national government. As secretary of the Treasury in the Washington administration, Hamilton had proposed a program of economic nationalism, based on a bank and a system of tariffs. Jefferson and Madison opposed his plan, claiming that it would unfairly benefit commercial interests. Yet the attack on Hamiltonian nationalism, which led to the founding of the Democratic-Republican Party, was not undertaken merely to get the government off the people's backs. Rather, it was based on a political doctrine dedicated to strengthening the democratic character of the Constitution. The "consolidation" of responsibilities in the national government that would follow from Hamilton's commercial and international objectives presupposed dominant executive leadership in formulating and carrying out public policy. The power of the more decentralizing institutions—Congress and state governments—would necessarily be undermined in this process. In order to keep power close enough to the people for republican government to prevail, Jefferson and Madison formulated a public philosophy to support a strict interpretation of the national government's powers. This also became a party doctrine, and the principal task of the Democratic-Republicans after the critical election of 1800 (or, as Jefferson called it, the "revolution of 1800") was to dismantle Hamilton's program for a strong executive. The purpose of presidential leadership in the Jeffersonian mold was to capture the executive office in order to contain and minimize its constitutional potential. This system, in its appeals and organization, as James Pierson has written, created a "tension between party politics, on the one hand, and governmental centralization and bureaucracy on the other."[23]

With Jefferson, American political parties were organized as popular institutions, but they were formed when popular rule meant limiting the role of the national government. Whereas modern party politics in Great Britain and Europe began at the end of the nineteenth century with the effort to reform a state that presumed the existence of strong national controls, political parties in the United States matured as the cornerstone of a political order that celebrated democratic individualism and presumed the absence of centralized administrative authority. Both the Democratic and the Republican Parties traced their origins to the Democratic-Republican Party, and were thus wedded to principles and constitutional arrangements dedicated to resisting centralized administration, to consolidating public opinion against the "state." Consequently, before the New Deal, presidents who sought to exercise executive power to expand national administrative power were thwarted, as Stephen Skowronek has written, "by the tenacity of this highly mobilized, highly competitive, and locally oriented democracy."[24]

The origins and organizing principles of the American party system established it as a force against the creation of the modern state. The New Deal commitment to building such a state—a national political power with expansive programmatic responsibilities—meant that the party system had to be either weakened or reconstituted. As Croly wrote in *The Promise of American Life*, the task was to give "democratic meaning and purpose to the Hamiltonian tradition and method" and thereby "emancipate American democracy from its Jeffersonian bondage."[25]

When Franklin Roosevelt displaced Jefferson as the patron saint of the Democratic Party, that party became the instrument of greater national purpose. This led many scholars and commentators to believe that a single-party, presidency-centered government was evolving in the new century as the common solution to the problems they identified with the existing constitutional system.[26] But those who held this evolutionary perspective misjudged the long-term objective of New Deal party politics. Ultimately, the Democratic Party was dedicated to the creation of a presidency-centered administrative state that would displace partisan politics with "enlightened administration."

This attempt to transcend, rather than reform, the American party system sheds light on the limited prospects of establishing party government in the United States, as well as the current paradoxical state of party politics. For New Dealers, the idea of the welfare state was not a partisan issue. It was a "constitutional" matter that required eliminating partisanship about the national government's obligation to provide economic security for the American people. Nevertheless, the displacement of partisan politics required a major partisan effort in the short run in order to generate popular support for the economic constitutional order. To a point, this made partisanship an integral part of New Deal politics, for it was necessary to remake the Democratic Party as an instrument to free the councils of government, particularly the president and administrative agencies, from the restraints of traditional party politics and the constitutional understanding they reflected.

Party Responsibility and the Creation of the "Modern" Presidency

In part, Roosevelt undertook an assault on the party system to make it more national and principled in character. He wanted to overcome the state and local orientation of the party system, which was suited to congressional primacy and poorly organized for progressive action by the national government, and to establish a national, executive-oriented party, which would be more suitably organized for the expression of national purposes. With such a task in mind, the Roosevelt administration modified traditional partisan practices in an effort to make the Democratic Party, as FDR put it, one of "militant liberalism." This, in turn, would bring about a structural transformation of the party system, pitting a reformed Democratic Party against a conservative Republican Party. As Roosevelt wrote in the introduction to the seventh volume of his presidential papers, "Generally speaking, in a representative form of government there are generally two schools of political belief—liberal and conservative. The system of party responsibility in American politics requires one of its parties to become the liberal party and the other be the conservative party."[27]

The most dramatic moment in Roosevelt's challenge to traditional party practices was the so-called purge campaign of 1938. This involved FDR directly in one gubernatorial and several congressional primary campaigns (twelve contests in all) in a bold effort to replace conservative Democrats with candidates who were "100 percent New Dealers."[28] The special concern of this campaign was the South (the Southern Democracy), a Democratic stronghold since the Civil War but, given the commitment to states' rights in that region, one that also represented, as a prominent journalist of the time, Thomas Stokes, put it, "the ball and chain which hobbled the party's forward march."[29]

As the press noted frequently after the 1938 purge campaign, no president had ever gone as far as Roosevelt in striving to stamp his policies upon his party. In the context of American politics, where presidential dominance over the decentralized party system was a cardinal vice, this was an extraordinary partisan effort. With the purge and other initiatives, such as the elimination of the "two-thirds" rule, the Roosevelt administration initiated a process whereby, increasingly, the party system evolved from predominantly local to national and programmatic party organizations.[30]

Yet at the same time, the New Deal made partisanship less important. Roosevelt's partisan leadership, though it effected important changes in the Democratic Party, envisioned a personal link with the public that would enable the president to govern from his position as leader of the nation rather than just the leader of the party.[31] For example, in all but one of the 1938 primary campaigns in which he personally participated, Roosevelt chose to make a direct appeal to public opinion rather than attempt to work through or reform the regular party apparatus. His ability to appeal broadly to the nation was enhanced by Progressive reforms, especially the direct primary, that had begun to weaken the grip of party organization on the voters. FDR supported and hoped to advance further the loosening of candidates and voters from party organizations. As he made clear in the fireside chat initiating the purge, he favored a selection process that abolished the convention system and gave "party voters themselves the chance to pick their candidates."[32]

The spread of the direct primary gave the president the opportunity to make a direct appeal to the people over the heads of congressional candidates and local party leaders. Thus, it provided an attractive vehicle for Roosevelt to put his own stamp upon the party. Radio broadcasting had made the opportunity to appeal directly to large audiences even more enticing. Of course, this was bound to be especially tempting to an extremely popular president with as fine a radio presence as Roosevelt.

In the final analysis, the "benign dictatorship" Roosevelt sought to impose on the Democratic Party was corrosive to the American party system. Indeed, the emphasis Roosevelt placed upon forging a direct link between himself and the public reflected a lack of faith in party politics and a conscious attempt to supplant collective responsibility (based upon the give-and-take between the president and Congress) with executive responsibility. In part, such a view stemmed from practicality. Roosevelt viewed the traditional party apparatus as incorrigible, so wedded was it to Congress and local politics. Even if the intransigent localism of the party system could be eliminated and a more national party system formed, moreover, there would still be federalism and separation of powers to overcome. These institutional arrangements, even with nationalized parties, would still encourage the free play of rival interests and factions, thus making ongoing cooperation between the president and Congress unlikely.

The failure of the purge to imprint the New Deal indelibly on his party majority only reinforced FDR's disinclination to seek a fundamental restructuring of the party system. The purge campaign was successful in only two of the twelve states targeted, Oregon and New York, and it galvanized opposition throughout the nation, apparently contributing to the heavy losses the Democrats sustained in the 1938 general elections. Former Wisconsin Governor Philip LaFollette, one of several Progressives who went down to crushing defeat in 1938, concluded: "The results of the so-called purge by President Roosevelt showed that the fight to make the Democratic party liberal is a hopeless one."[33]

E. E. Schattschneider, chairman of the American Political Science Association Committee on Political Parties, drew a different conclusion. Viewing the purge campaign as "one of the greatest experimental tests of the nature of the American party system ever made," he believed that a more comprehensive effort supported by the whole body of national party leaders "could bring overwhelming pressure to bear on local party leaders who control congressional nominations."[34] But neither FDR nor any president since has risked a similar effort, let alone a more expansive one, to hold his fellow partisans to a national party program. The purge campaign and its aftermath suggest how resistance to party government is not merely built into the Constitution and laws. It is deeply rooted in a regime that gives preference to a different way of governing.[35]

Indeed, the Roosevelt administration's rejection of party government developed from principles as well as practical reasons. Party government would require subordinating rights to a national party majority, yet FDR's party politics rested on a new, expansive concept of rights that was not congenial to such partisanship. The "economic constitutional order" conceived of New Deal programs such as Social Security as rights. In principle, these programs were to be permanent entitlements, like speech and assembly, beyond the vagaries of public opinion, elections, and party politics. "No damn politician," FDR once remarked, "can scrap my social security program."[36] Such programmatic rights, he believed, would be practically and morally beyond the reach of conservative party leaders. As one New Dealer prophetically observed:

> We may assume the nature of problems of American life are such as not to permit any political party for any length of time to abandon most of the collectivist functions which are now being exercised. This is true even though the details of policy programs may differ and even though the old slogans of opposition to governmental activity will survive long after their meaning has been sucked out.[37]

For practical and principled reasons, the Roosevelt administration did not seek to remake American party politics; rather, it championed the executive as the guarantor of a "second bill of rights," as the steward of an administrative constitution. This explains why the most significant institutional reforms of the New Deal did not promote party government but fostered instead a program that would enable the president to govern in the absence of party government.

This program, as embodied in the 1937 executive reorganization bill, was based on the Brownlow Committee Report.[38] It proposed measures to expand significantly the staff support of the executive office and to greatly extend presidential authority over the executive branch, including the independent regulatory commissions. The strengthened executive that emerged in this report would also be delegated responsibility to govern, so that as Luther Gulick, a member of the Brownlow committee, anticipated, laws would be little more than "a declaration of war, so that the essence of the program [would be] in the gradual unfolding of the plan in actual administration."[39]

In effect, the enactment of the executive reorganization bill would mean that party politics would be displaced by executive administration, by an executive-centered administrative state generated by the

Sidney M. Milkis

activities of a dominant and dominating president. A reconstituted party system would strengthen ties between the executive and the legislature, but in the administrative design of the New Deal, the president and executive agencies would be delegated authority to govern, making unnecessary the constant cooperation of party members in Congress and the states. To be sure, party politics were not irrelevant to the task of strengthening national administration. In fact, the administrative reform program became, at FDR's urging, a party program. Thus, ironically, a policy aimed at making party politics less important became a major focus of party responsibility. So strongly did Roosevelt favor this legislation that House Majority Leader Sam Rayburn appealed for party unity before the critical vote on the executive reorganization bill, arguing that the defeat of this legislation would amount to a "vote of no confidence" in the president.[40]

FDR lost this vote of confidence on administrative reform. In April 1938, the House of Representatives, with massive Democratic defections, voted down the legislation. It was a devastating defeat for Roosevelt. Together with the defeat of the "court-packing" plan, also closely linked to strengthening administrative power, it led FDR to undertake the purge campaign.[41] The purge failed at the polls, but it scared recalcitrant Democrats, who became more conciliatory toward their president on a few matters after the 1938 election. Administrative reform was one of these, and in 1939, an executive reorganization bill passed Congress. This legislation (the Executive Reorganization Act of 1939) was, in effect, the organic statute of the "modern" presidency. Roosevelt's extraordinary leadership was, so to speak, institutionalized by the administrative reform bill, for this statute ratified a process whereby public expectations and institutional arrangements established the president as the center of governmental activity. The statute not only provided authority to create the Executive Office of the President, which included the newly formed White House Office and a strengthened and refurbished Bureau of the Budget, but also enhanced the president's control over the expanding activities of the executive branch. As such, this legislation represents the genesis of the "administrative presidency," which was better equipped to govern independently of the constraints imposed by the separation of powers.[42]

The battle for the destiny of the Democratic Party during Roosevelt's second term, therefore, was directly tied to strengthening the presidency and the executive branch as the vital center of governmental action. FDR's success transformed the Democrats into a party of administration, dedicated to enacting an institutional program that would make parties less important. Traditional localized parties had provided presidents with a stable basis of popular support and, episodically during critical partisan realignments, with the opportunity to achieve national reform. What was once episodic must now become routine. As the Brownlow report put it: "Our national will must be expressed not merely in a brief, exultant moment of electoral decision, but in a persistent, determined, competent day-by-day administration of what the nation has decided to do."[43]

For a time, the modern presidency was at the center of this new political universe. With the strengthening of executive administration, the presidency became distanced from party politics, undermining the latter's importance. In effect, personnel in the Executive Office of the President transformed the presidency into an alternative political organization that gradually preempted many of the limited but significant tasks of party leaders: linking the president to interest groups, staffing the executive department, developing policy, and most important, providing campaign support. Presidents no longer won election and governed as heads of a party; instead they won and governed as heads of a personal organization they created in their own image.

But the purpose of New Deal reforms was not to strengthen presidential government per se. Rather, it was to strengthen the presidency under the assumption that as the national office, it would be an ally of progressive reform. Consequently, executive power was refurbished in a way compatible with the objectives of programmatic liberalism, and administrative reform was intended to insulate reformers and reforms from the presidential election cycle. By executive orders issued with authority granted by the 1939 Executive Reorganization Act, many of the emergency programs of the New Deal were established as permanent institutions. Moreover, the Roosevelt administration obtained legislative authority in the 1940 Ramspeck Act to extend civil service protection to the New Deal loyalists who were brought to Washington to staff the newly created welfare state. Whereas the original objective of administrative reformers, who first became prominent after the Civil War, was to separate politics and administration—to further "neutral competence"—the New Deal transformed the character of administrative politics. Previously, the choice was posed as one between party politics and spoils, on the one hand, and nonpolitical administration, on the other. The New Deal celebrated an administrative politics that denied nourishment to the regular party apparatus but fed instead an executive department oriented toward expanding liberal programs. As the administrative historian Paul Van Riper has noted, the new practice created another kind of patronage, "a sort of intellectual and ideological patronage rather than the more partisan type."[44]

The future of the American political system, then, was predicated on the emergence of a policymaking state; party politics and debate were subordinated to a "second bill of rights" and to the delivery of services associated with those rights. Indeed, the New Deal was placed beyond partisan politics to such a degree that Republican presidents, even an ardently conservative one such as Ronald Reagan, oftentimes felt as though they were relegated to managing the liberal state.

The "Modern" Presidency and Divided Government

Of course, these Republican presidents faced, not only a recalcitrant bureaucracy and a public philosophy that celebrated an expansive understanding of rights, but a Congress, as well as a majority of state and local governments, that was controlled by the Democratic Party. The institutional and policy disputes between Republicans in the White House and Democrats in Congress and the states testify to the partial resurgence of partisanship in the 1970s and 1980s.

As a party of administration, the Democrats established the conditions for the end of parties unless, or until, a party sprang up that was antiadministration. No such party has arisen in American politics, although the Republicans have slouched toward that role. As programmatic liberalism began to lose support, the Republicans under Richard Nixon and especially Ronald Reagan embraced programs, such as the new federalism and regulatory relief, that challenged the institutional legacy of the New Deal. This bolder conservative posture coincided with the construction of a formidable national Republican organization with strength at the federal level that is unprecedented in American politics. After 1976, the Republican National Committee and the two other Republican campaign bodies, the National Republican Senatorial Committee and the National Republican Congressional (House) Committee, greatly expanded their efforts to raise funds and provide services at the national level for state and local candidates. Moreover, these efforts carried the national party into activities, such as the publication of public policy journals and the distribution of comprehensive briefing books for candidates, that demonstrated its interest in generating programmatic proposals that might be politically useful. The Democrats lagged behind in party-building efforts, but the losses they suffered in the 1980 election encouraged them to modernize the national political machinery, openly imitating some of the devices employed by the Republicans. Arguably, a party system had finally evolved that was compatible with the national polity forged on the anvil of the New Deal.[45]

Nevertheless, the importance of presidential politics and unilateral executive action suggests that Nixon and Reagan essentially continued the institutional legacy of the New Deal. Thus, Republican presidents, intent upon transforming the liberal political order, have conceived of the presidency as a two-edged sword that could cut in a conservative, as well as a liberal, direction. Indeed, given that the New Deal was based on a party strategy to replace traditional party politics with administration, it is not surprising that the Republican challenge to liberal policies produced a conservative administrative presidency, which also retarded the revival of partisan politics.

The administrative ambition of Republican presidents was encouraged by, and in turn helped perpetuate, the condition of divided government that prevailed virtually without interruption between 1968 and 1992. Prior to 1994, the challenge to programmatic liberalism never extended beyond the presidency, leaving Congress, as well as most states and localities, under Democratic control. Republican presidents, facing hostility, not only in the bureaucracy, but also in Congress and the states, were, even more than Democrats, encouraged to pursue policy goals by seeking to concentrate executive power in the White House.

But reinforcing this bow to practicality is conviction, revealing modern conservatives to be products of the New Deal revolution. Republican administrative aggrandizement is supported by a modern conservative movement, with which the Reagan administration frequently expressed common cause, whose advocates prefer, not to limit the national state forged on the New Deal realignment, but to put it to new uses. Consequently, the Reagan administration, while promising to bring about "new federalism" and "regulatory relief," was stalled in these tasks by the conviction that a strong national state was necessary to foster economic growth, oppose communism, and "nurture" family values. The Iran-Contra scandal, for example, was not simply a matter of the president's being asleep on his watch. Rather, it revealed the Reagan administration's determination to assume a more forceful anticommunist posture in Central America in the face of a recalcitrant Congress and bureaucracy.

The Reagan administration's assertion of the "administrative presidency" was hardly an aberration. As a matter of course, when the president and his advisors confronted legislative resistance on an issue, they charted administrative avenues to advance their goals. Indeed, often they did not even try to modify the statutory basis of a liberal program, relying instead on administrative discretion as a first resort. Even in the area of regulatory relief, a project ostensibly designed to "get government off the backs of the people," the Reagan administration's efforts came, not through legislative change, but through administrative action, delay, and repeal. President Reagan's Executive Orders 12291 and 12498 mandated a comprehensive review of proposed agency regulations by the Office of Management and Budget.[46] Reagan also appointed a Task Force on Regulatory Relief, headed by Vice-President Bush, to apply cost-benefit analysis to existing rules. This pursuit of conservative policy options through the administrative presidency continued with the accession of George Bush to the White House. The burden of curbing environmental, consumer, and civil rights regulations fell on the Competitiveness Council, chaired by Vice-President Quayle, which, like its predecessor, the Task Force on Regulatory Relief, required administrative agencies to justify the costs of existing and proposed regulations.[47]

The conservative administrative presidency did not go unchallenged. As designed by the Democrats, the modern presidency was conceived as an ally of programmatic rights. When this supposition was seemingly violated by Vietnam and its aftermath, reformers set out to protect liberal programs from unfriendly executives. By the time Lyndon Johnson left the White House, support for unilateral executive action had begun to erode, occasioned by the controversial use of presidential power in Vietnam, and it virtually disappeared under the strain of divided government. The result was a "reformation" of New Deal administrative politics, which brought Congress and the courts into the details of administration. The institutional reforms in Congress during the 1970s that devolved policy responsibility to subcommittees and increased the number of congressional support staff members were compatible with the attention being paid by legislators to policy specialization, which increased congressional oversight of the administrative state while making Congress more administrative in its structure and activities. Similarly, the judiciary's decreasing reliance on constitutional decisions in its rulings affecting the political economy and its emphasis on interpreting statutes to determine the responsibilities of executive agencies were symptomatic of its post–New Deal role as "managing partner of the administrative state." Consequently, the efforts of Republicans to compensate for their inability to control Congress by seeking to circumvent legislative restrictions on presidential conduct were matched by Democratic initiatives to burden the executive with smothering legislative and judicial oversight.[48]

The opposition to programmatic liberalism, then, resulted, not in a challenge to national administrative power, but in a virulent, enervating battle for the administrative state's services. The political toll of this battle is seen all too readily in the 1992 election and its aftermath: a badly frayed connection between American government and its citizenry, a frightening deterioration of American civil society. Political parties, which once provided a connection between the governing institutions and the public, are certainly not absent from the administrative politics spawned by the New Deal and the opposition it aroused. But in the wake of the New Deal, parties have been weakened as electoral institutions; both parties have shifted much of their attention from the building of constituencies (from the building of a vital link with the public) to an "inside the beltway" administrative politics. Moreover, this administrative politics has been associated with expansion of new rights, which has further shifted partisan disputes away from parties as associations that organize public sentiments as an electoral majority. Even conservatives in the abortion debate talk of the rights of the unborn in a way that requires centralized administration—consider the so-called gag rule of the Reagan and Bush administrations.[49] When rights dominate policy discourse, majority sentiments are commonly viewed as a problem and not the solution.

Thus far, therefore, divided government has been obsessed with a politics of entitlements. This politics has belittled efforts by Democrats and Republicans alike to define a collective purpose with a past and a future. Instead, it yields a partisanship joined to a form of administrative politics that relegates electoral conflict to the intractable demands of policy advocates. Indeed, a partisanship that emphasizes national administration in support of programmatic rights has little chance to reach beyond the Washington beltway and influence the perceptions and habits of the American people. This development does not mean, certainly, that the Democrats and Republicans consider elections unimportant and have despaired of extending their influence through them. It does suggest that as parties of administration, the Democrats and Republicans are hobbled in their efforts to form vital links with the public. The emergence of parties of administration has strengthened the national party organization and created more discipline among party members in Congress but at the cost of weakening party loyalties among the electorate. The tendency for growing numbers of voters to split their tickets or stay at home on election day represents their estrangement from these parties of administration—a plague on both your houses.[50]

The indecision at the polls, and the concomitant perpetuation of divided government, also reflects the fact that more is at stake in American politics than at any other time in U.S. history, with the notable exception of the Civil War. The commitment to limited government that prevailed until the New Deal tended to reduce the stakes of political conflict in the United States, to confine political battles to "safe issues." Yet the emergence of activist government after the 1930s attenuated the constitutional boundaries that once contained political conflict in the United States, and the Reagan "revolution" further eroded the wall that separated politics and society. The checks that divided government has imposed on the parties has not led to "policy gridlock"; during the Nixon, Reagan, and Bush presidencies, a number of important laws were passed in spite of, and in some cases because of, the persistence of separate partisan realms.[51] Indeed, to a point, divided government has restrained the extreme tendencies of the Democrats and Republicans, thus providing some protection against the abuses of centralized administration. But this security did not come without its costs. As the extraordinary budgetary evasions and the jarring nomination fights of the past two decades reveal, the dark side of divided government is that it tends to obscure political responsibility and to mire government in petty, virulent clashes that undermine respect for American political institutions.

Clinton and the 1994 Elections: Can There Be Still Another Realignment in American Politics?

Bill Clinton dedicated his 1992 campaign to principles and policies that "transcended," he claimed, the exhausted left-right debate that had afflicted the nation for two decades. During the mid-1980s, Clinton was a leader of the Democratic Leadership Council, a moderate group in the Democratic Party that developed many of the ideas that became the central themes of his run for the presidency. As Clinton declared frequently during the campaign, these ideas represented a new philosophy of government that would "honor middle class values, restore public trust, create a new sense of community and make America work again." He heralded "a new social contract," a "new covenant," one that would seek to constrain, in the name of responsibility and community, the demands for rights summoned by the Roosevelt revolution. Invoking Roosevelt's Commonwealth Club address, in which FDR first outlined the "economic constitutional order," Clinton declared that the liberal commitment to guaranteeing economic security through entitlement programs such as Social Security, Medicare, Medicaid, and Aid to Families with Dependent Children had gone too far. The objective of the New Covenant was to correct the tendency of Americans to celebrate individual rights and government entitlement programs without any sense of the mutual obligations they had to each other and their country.[52]

Clinton's commitment to educational opportunity best exemplified the objective of restoring a balance between rights and responsibilities; its central feature, a National Service Corps, was emblematic of the core New Covenant principle: national community. According to Clinton, a trust fund would be created, out of which any and all Americans could borrow money for a college education, so long as they paid it back either as a small percentage of their life's income or with two years of service as teachers, police officers, or child care workers, or by participating in other activities that "our country desperately needs."[53] Clinton's campaign, thereby, promised to correct and renew the progressive tradition as shaped by the New Deal. Vital parties require some compromise between a deep and abiding commitment to rights and a due attention to common deliberation and choice; some decisions must be left to a party majority. Roosevelt's party politics, however, rested on a new understanding of rights, one associated with the expansion of national administrative power, that is not congenial with such partisan responsibility. In challenging the explosion of rights and the hidebound bureaucracy that arose from the New Deal and the opposition it spawned, Clinton pledged to dedicate his party to a new public philosophy that might redress many of the troubling aspects of the New Deal legacy: the decline of parties as civic associations, the rise of virulent administrative politics, and the deterioration of public trust in American political institutions.

Although Clinton pledged to dedicate his party to the new concept of justice he espoused, his words and actions during the early days of his presidency seemed to betray this commitment. No sooner had he been inaugurated than Clinton announced his intention to lift the long-standing ban on homosexuals in the military. The president soon learned, however, that there was no prospect that such a divisive issue could be resolved through the stroke of a pen. To be sure, the development of the administrative presidency gave presidents more power to exercise domestic policy autonomously. Yet with the expansion of national administration to issues that shaped the direction and character of American public life, this power proved to be illusory. Intense opposition from the respected head of the Joint Chiefs of Staff, Colin Powell, and the influential chair of the Senate Armed Services Committee, Sam Nunn of Georgia, forced Clinton to defer the executive order for six months while he sought a compromise. But the delay and the compromise aroused the ire of gay and lesbian activists who had given strong financial and organizational support to Clinton during the election. Most damaging for the new president was that the issue became a glaring benchmark of his inability to revitalize progressive politics as an instrument to redress the economic insecurity and political alienation of the middle class.

The bitter partisan fight in the spring and summer of 1993 over the administration's budgetary program served only to reinforce doubts about Clinton's ability to lead the nation in a new, more harmonious direction. Even though Clinton's budget plan promised to reduce the deficit, it involved new taxes and an array of social programs that Republicans and moderate Democrats perceived as tax-and-spend liberalism. The Republicans marched in lockstep opposition to Clinton's economic program, especially to his $16 billion stimulus package, which he offered as a partial antidote to the economic contraction that he feared deficit reduction would cause. In April 1993, Senate Republicans unanimously supported a filibuster that killed the stimulus package. Congress did enact a modified version of the president's budgetary plan a few months later, albeit by razor-thin margins and without any support from Republicans, who voted unanimously against it in the House and Senate. Clinton won this narrow, bruising victory only after promising moderate Democrats that he would put together another package of spending cuts in the fall. But this uneasy compromise failed to dispel the charge of his political opponents that Clinton was a wolf in sheep's clothing—a conventional liberal whose commitment to reform had expired at the end of the presidential campaign.[54]

In fact, Clinton said and did little about a New Covenant during the first two years of his presidency. He appointed Donna Shalala to head the Department of Health and Human Services, even though she had not expressed support for reshaping social welfare policy. And in a February 1993 address to Congress, in which he laid out his administration's goals, Clinton, instead of trumpeting reciprocal obligations between citizens and their government, proposed instead a new set of entitlements in the form of job training, a college education, and health care. Clinton's proposal to make college loans available to all Americans did include the much touted plan to form a National Service Corps. But the enactment of a scaled-down version of this educational reform program in August was lost amid Clinton's promises to expand the welfare state. In fact, the reciprocal obligation Clinton expected of the beneficiaries of college loans seemed almost apologetic. They will be able to pay the country back with a small percentage of their income, thereby avoiding service as teachers, police officers, or community workers. This option to avoid public service greatly dilutes the concept of national community.[55]

The apologetic stance that Clinton displayed in the face of traditional liberal causes was, to a point, understandable; it was a logical response to the modern institutional separation between the presidency and the party. The moderate wing of the Democratic Party that he represented—including the members of the Democratic Leadership Council—was a minority wing. The majority of liberal interest-group activists and Democratic members of Congress still preferred entitlements to obligations and regulations to responsibilities. Only the unpopularity of liberal groups and the emphasis on candidate-centered campaigns in presidential politics had made Clinton's nomination and election possible. The media-driven caucuses and primaries that dominate the presidential nomination process had given him an opportunity to seize the Democratic label as an outsider candidate but offered no means to effect a transformation of his party once he took office. Clinton's Democratic predecessor, Jimmy Carter, who tended to be fiercely independent and a scourge to traditional liberal approaches, had faced a situation of nearly complete political isolation during his unhappy term in office.

To bring about the new mission of progressivism that he advocated during the election, Clinton would have had to risk a brutal confrontation with the major Democratic Party, a battle that might have left him even more vulnerable politically than Carter had been.[56] In truth, no president had risked such a confrontation with his party since Roosevelt's failed purge campaign. It is not surprising, therefore, that Clinton's allies in the Democratic Leadership Council urged him to renew his "credentials as an outsider" by going over the heads of the party leadership in Congress and taking his message directly to the people. Most important, the president needed to take his New Covenant message directly to the large number of independents in the electorate who had voted for Perot, they argued, so as to forge "new and sometimes bipartisan coalitions around an agenda that moves beyond the polarized left-right debate."[57]

In the fall of 1993, Clinton took a page from his former political associates in his successful campaign to secure congressional approval of the North American Free Trade Agreement (NAFTA). The fight for NAFTA caused Clinton to defend free enterprise ardently and to oppose the protectionism of labor unions that still represented one of the most important constituencies in the national Democratic Party. Clinton's victory owed partly to the active support of the Republican congressional leadership; in fact, a majority of Republicans in the House and Senate supported the free trade agreement, while a majority of Democrats, including the House majority leader and majority whip, opposed it.

No less important, however, was the Clinton administration's mobilization of popular support that transcended party lines. Indeed, the turning point in the struggle came when the administration challenged Perot, the leading opponent of NAFTA, to debate Vice-President Gore on *Larry King Live*. Gore's optimistic defense of open markets was well received by the large television audience, rousing enough support for the treaty to persuade a bare majority of legislators in both houses of Congress to approve the trade agreement.[58]

With the successful fight over NAFTA, moderate Democrats began to hope that Clinton had finally begun the task of dedicating his party to principles and policies he had espoused during the campaign. But the next major legislative battle was over the administration's health care program, which promised to "guarantee all Americans a comprehensive package of benefits over the course of an entire lifetime." The formulation of this program marked the apotheosis of New Deal administrative politics; it was designed behind closed doors by a Health Care Task Force headed by First Lady Hillary Rodham Clinton and the president's longtime friend Ira Magaziner. Moreover, it would have created a new government entitlement program and an administrative apparatus that would have signaled the revitalization, rather than the reform, of traditional welfare-state policy.[59] Although the administration made conciliatory overtures to the plan's opponents, hoping to forge bipartisan cooperation on the Hill and a broad consensus among the general public, the possibilities for comprehensive reform hinged on settling differences over the appropriate role of government that had divided the parties and the country for the past two decades. In the end, this proved impractical. The health care bill died in the 103rd Congress when a compromise measure, negotiated between Senate Democratic leader George Mitchell of Maine and Republican Senator John Chafee of Rhode Island, could not win over enough Republicans to break a threatened filibuster.[60]

By proposing such an ambitious health care reform bill, Clinton enraged conservatives. By failing to deliver on his promise to provide a major overhaul of the health care system, he dismayed the ardent liberals of his party. Most significant, the defeat of the president's health care program created the overwhelming impression that he had not lived up to his campaign promise to transcend the bitter philosophical and partisan battles of the Reagan and Bush years.

The president and his party paid dearly for this failure in the 1994 election. In taking control of Congress, the Republicans gained fifty-two seats in the House and eight in the Senate. Moreover, they won dramatic victories at the state and local level: Republicans increased their share of governorships to thirty, their first majority since 1970; they also reached near parity in state legislatures, a status they had not enjoyed since 1968. Significantly, Republicans achieved this in-depth victory after running a national, ideological campaign, which promised to fulfill the failed promise of the Reagan revolution—to get government off the backs of the American people. The national character of the campaign owed largely to the House minority leader, Newt Gingrich of Georgia. Gingrich, his party's choice to be the new Speaker of the 104th Congress, persuaded more than three hundred House candidates to sign a Republican Contract with America, a "covenant" with the nation that promised to restore limited government by eliminating programs, ameliorating regulatory burdens, and cutting taxes. Clinton's attack on the Republican program during the campaign seemed to backfire, serving only to abet Republicans in their effort to highlight the president's failure to "reinvent government." Examining exit polls that suggested that a "massive anti-Clinton coalition came together" to produce the "revolution" of 1994, political analyst William Schneider wrote of the voters' desire for change, "If the Democrats can't make government work, maybe the Republicans can solve problems with less government."[61]

The dramatic Republican triumph in the 1994 midterm election led scholars and pundits to suggest that the nation might be on the threshold of a critical partisan realignment.[62] Speculating that the Republican landslide in 1994 was analogous to midterm Democratic gains in 1930, which marked an end to a long period of one-party dominance in the House, conservative intellectual William Kristol waxed hopeful that his party's midterm triumph signaled an end to the New Deal and the emergence of a new conservative governing coalition. Just as 1930 was a prelude to the critical victories of Roosevelt in 1932 and 1936, so 1994 would culminate in a full-scale Republican realignment in 1996.[63] Surprisingly, few ardent liberals disagreed. "The 1994 midterm election is not yet the epochal realignment that prefigures a governing coalition," wrote the editor of the liberal journal, *The American Prospect*, Robert Kuttner. "But if Democrats sleep through the wake-up call and the Republicans win the White House in 1996, realignment will be complete."[64]

It remains to be seen, of course, whether the New Deal realignment and its aftermath have left room for still another critical partisan realignment in American political life. The emphasis on rights and administrative politics that characterizes contemporary political struggles would seem to belie the sort of collective partisan affiliations that have made partisan transformations of American political life possible in the past. To be sure, the obstacles to partisan realignment have not displaced party conflict. We have noted how the New Deal, and the erosion of traditional decentralized parties that followed from it, has made possible a new blending of partisanship and administration, one in which administration has become a vehicle for partisan objectives. Yet the American people had become alienated from these parties of administration by the 1990s, so much so that the renewal of partisan loyalties in the electorate, let alone a full-scale partisan transformation, remains a most difficult prospect.

The new Republican majority in Congress and the states promised to pursue a program dedicated to rebuilding the wall of separation between government and society and to cultivate a vital debate about the role of the state in promoting the general welfare. Significantly, the Republican Contract with America was silent on the abortion issue. The failure to mention the rights of the unborn in this covenant with the electorate suggested a new determination on the part of some conservative leaders to avoid the language and programmatic ambition that presupposed new uses of, rather than a fundamental challenge to, the centralized administrative power created in the aftermath of the New Deal realignment.

The determination of the new conservative majority to challenge the administrative state was also apparent in the sweeping changes that the new Speaker and his allies made in the House rules. House Republicans reduced standing committees and their staffs, limited the tenure of committee chairs, and prohibited closed door hearings and unrecorded votes. These reforms promised to restrain the institutions that had encouraged the House to focus excessively on management of the executive, at the expense of serious public debate over major issues of national policy. Indeed, Speaker Gingrich pledged to Democrats and moderate Republicans a renewed emphasis on a legislative debate that would "promote competition between differing political philosophies."[65]

Although the new Republican majority promised to rededicate the government to the principles of limited government and states' rights, they were hardly unreconstructed Jeffersonians. The Republican contract proposed to strengthen national defense in a form that would require the expansion rather than the rolling back of the central government's responsibilities; and the GOP's proposals to reduce entitlements targeted at the poor and to get government off the back of business demanded the creation of alternative national welfare and regulatory standards.[66] Finally, the Republican party was reluctant to challenge middle class entitlements such as Social Security and Medicare, which dwarfed the spending programs that guaranteed a minimum standard of living to the destitute, thus making unlikely a serious reexamination of the core assumptions of the New Deal.[67]

In the absence of a meaningful debate between conservative and liberal principles, the new chapter of divided government threatened to degenerate into the same sort of visceral administrative politics that had corroded the legitimacy of American political institutions for the past twenty-five years. The battle between Clinton and the Republican Congress became especially fierce in a contest over legislation to balance the budget. More than any other idea celebrated in the GOP's Contract with America, Republicans believed that a balanced budget bill would give them their best opportunity to control Congress for years to come. But their proposal for a constitutional amendment to require a balanced budget died in the Senate, where, facing stiff resistance from the president and his Democratic allies, it failed, by one vote, to get the necessary two-thirds support.

Eventually, the GOP's commitment to a balanced budget, even as it pursued substantial tax reductions and increased military spending, forced it to reexamine its cautious approach to entitlements. In the fall of 1995, Republicans in the House and Senate put their faith in a plan to balance the budget by 2002. The most controversial part of this program was a proposal to scale back the growth of Medicare, a federal health insurance program for the elderly and disabled, by encouraging beneficiaries to enroll in health maintenance organizations and other private, managed health care systems. Rallied by their militant partisan brethren in the House, Republicans sought to pressure Clinton to accept their priorities on the budget by twice shutting down government offices and even threatening to force the U.S. Treasury into default. These confrontational tactics backfired. Clinton's veto of a sweeping budget bill in December, which would not only overhaul Medicare, but also remake decades of federal social policy, roused popular support for the administration. Most important, Clinton's budgetary stand, signaling his growing willingness to draw sharp differences between his priorities and those of the Republican Congress, appeared to preserve the essential characteristics of the Medicare program; indeed, to end the efforts of the 104th Congress to curtail the major programs of the New Deal and the Great Society. In attacking Medicare and social policy, such as environmental programs, the Republicans' militant assault on programmatic liberalism went beyond what was promised by the Contract with America, thus giving Clinton the opportunity to take a political stand that was supported by most of the country.

When Congress returned for the second session of the 104th Congress in January 1996, it was not to Speaker Gingrich's soaring agenda of reducing the role of Washington in the society and economy, but to the measured, yet dramatic tones of Clinton's third State of the Union message. On the one hand, the President embraced many of the themes of his Republican opponents, boldly declaring, "the era of big government is over." On the other hand, warning that "we cannot go back to the time when our citizens were left to fend for themselves," Clinton called for a halt to Republican assaults on basic liberal programs dedicated to providing economic security, educational opportunity, and environmental protection. Thus, as the Democratic Leadership Council's Al From observed, the president "spoke to the main concerns of the millions of disaffected voters in the political center" who were estranged from the ideological and institutional combat between liberals and conservatives and "were likely to be the margin of difference in the [1996] election."[68] Winning the support of these alienated citizens, however, would require Clinton to transform his rhetoric into government action, to bring about a smaller federal government, albeit one that would "enable all our people to make the most of their lives with stronger families, more educational opportunity, economic security, safer streets, a cleaner environment, and a safer world."[69]

Clinton's annual message appeared to depart from weeks of venomous dialogue between the White House and Republican leaders over a balanced budget plan. But this surface calm, as Senate majority leader Robert Dole acknowledged in the Republican response to the president's speech, barely hid "starkly different philosophies of government and profoundly different visions of America." Setting the tone for the 1996 national campaign, Dole, the all but certain nominee of his party for president, characterized Clinton as "the rear guard of the welfare state," and the "chief obstacle to a balanced budget and the balanced-budget amendment." Far more pragmatic than his partisan brethren in the House, Dole had opposed the use of government shutdowns and holding the debt ceiling hostage to Republican demands during the first session of the 104th Congress. But he now proclaimed that there were times "when even practical statesmen must refuse to bend or yield." That time, apparently, had come for Senator Dole, who now sought to position himself not only as the leader of his party, but also of the conservative movement.[70] Indeed, frustrated by the responsibilities of leading the Senate in petty and mean-spirited skirmishes with the White House, Dole resigned his seat in May, hoping that he could better lead a charge against the liberal establishment as a private citizen than he could as a Washington insider.

If the recent past is prologue, this assault on the liberal state would end in a raw and disruptive struggle to control national administration. Confronted with the challenge of maintaining his command of the nation in the face of a fierce Republican opposition, Clinton might be pushed into a more aggressive defense of his party's policies. He might resort to an aggressive use of the administrative presidency to circumvent Republican majorities in congress. In response, the Republicans in the House and Senate would be tempted to use, rather than curtail, the levers of administrative power accumulated on Capitol Hill since the 1960s—to torment a Democratic president with the same sort of investigations and "micromanagement" of domestic and foreign policy with which Democratic congresses assaulted Reagan and Bush. This battle for control of national administrative power might very well continue beyond the 1996 election, should this contest, as now seems likely, maintain the existing state of divided government.

A renewal of institutional confrontation would only intensify the people's alienation from partisan politics. A strong third-party movement might arise from such popular disaffection. It is more likely, however, that the people's disappointment would advance the plebiscitary politics championed by Perot during the 1992 campaign. Perot's call for better planning and "electronic town halls" as solutions to government "gridlock" testified to the powerful appeal of simplified notions of "enlightened administration" in contemporary democratic politics. He hinted broadly at an even bolder new order in which, a historian has warned, "the president, checked only by direct expressions of popular desire, [would] role up his sleeves and solve the nation's problems."[71] In the face of this threat to constitutional government, the challenge for Clinton and Dole is to lead their parties in a great contest of opinion, to engage the people in public deliberation and choice over the appropriate understanding of their rights. This challenge is unlikely to be met, however, unless Democrats and Republicans alike recognize the limits of national administrative power to solve the nation's problems.

Notes

1. Benjamin Ginsberg and Martin Shefter, *Politics by Other Means: The Declining Importance of Elections in America* (New York: Basic Books, 1990); Benjamin Ginsberg, Walter R. Mebane, Jr., and Martin Shefter, "The Presidency and Interest Groups: Why Presidents Cannot Govern," in *The Presidency and the Political System*, ed. Michael Nelson, 4th edition (Washington, D.C.: Congressional Quarterly Press, 1995). Defenders of divided government reject the critique of Ginsberg and Shefter. In a careful empirical study, David R. Mayhew was able to show that laws were passed with equal frequency under divided and unified forms of party control. His conclusion is that divided control makes no important difference in government performance. *Divided We Govern: Party Control, Lawmaking, and Investigations, 1946–1990* (New Haven: Yale University Press, 1991). I agree with Mayhew that divided party control has not caused "gridlock," but I would not go so far as to say it does not make a difference. As suggested in this essay, divided government is a symptom of, if not a solution to, Americans' "love-hate" relationship with the "state" forged on the anvil of the New Deal.

2. Alfred H. Kelly, Winfred A. Harbison, and Herman Belz, *The American Constitution: Its Origins and Development*, 7th ed. (New York: W. W. Norton, 1991), 705.

3. William Schneider, "A Loud Vote for Change," *National Journal*, 7 November 1992, 2544.

4. For example, see Phil Duncan and Steve Langdon, "When Congress Had to Choose, It Voted to Back Clinton," *Congressional Quarterly Weekly Report*, 18 December 1993, 3427–34.

5. Alan Brinkley, "The 43 Percent President," *New York Times Magazine*, 4 July 1993, 22.

6. Todd S. Purdum, "A Crippled President Seeks Not to Become a Lame Duck," *New York Times*, 8 December 1994, A1, B21.

7. Martin P. Wattenberg, *The Rise of Candidate-Centered Politics* (Cambridge: Harvard University Press, 1991).

8. See, for example, Theodore Lowi, "The Party Crasher," *New York Times Magazine*, 23 August 1992, 28, 33.

9. Michael J. Malbin, "Was Divided Government Really Such a Big Problem?" in *Separation of Powers and Good Government*, ed. Bradford P. Wilson and Peter W. Schramm (Lanham, Md.: Rowman & Littlefield, 1994), 233.

10. Sidney M. Milkis, *The President and the Parties: The Transformation of the American Party System since the New Deal* (New York: Oxford University Press, 1993).

11. The two seminal presentations of critical realignment theory are found in V. O. Key, Jr., "A Theory of Critical Elections," *Journal of Politics* 17 (February 1955): 3–18; and Walter Dean Burnham, *Critical Elections and the Mainsprings of American Politics* (New York: W. W. Norton, 1970).

12. For example, see Woodrow Wilson, *Constitutional Government in the United States* (New York: Columbia University Press, 1908), especially Chapters 3 and 8; Herbert Croly, *Progressive Democracy* (New York: Macmillan, 1914).

13. Franklin D. Roosevelt, "Address at the Commonwealth Club in San Francisco," 23 September 1932, *Public Papers and Addresses*, ed. Samuel J. Rosenman, 14 vols. (New York: Random House, 1938–1950) 1: 751–52.

14. Even when political parties were relatively indifferent to broad moral questions and were dedicated to the personal ambitions of their members, Tocqueville found them to be valuable political associations in which individuals learned the art of cooperation and became citizens. See Alexis de Tocqueville, *Democracy in America* (New York: Doubleday, 1969), 189–95, 509–13, 520–24; see also Wilson Carey McWilliams, "Parties as Civic Associations," in *Party Renewal in America*, ed. Gerald Pomper (New York: Praeger, 1980).

15. Roosevelt, "Address at Commonwealth Club," 751.

16. Ibid., 752.

17. "Democratic Platform of 1936," in *National Party Platforms*, ed. Donald Bruce Johnson (Urbana: University of Illinois Press, 1978), 360.

18. Franklin D. Roosevelt, "State of the Union Address," 11 January 1944, *Public Papers*, ed. Rosenman, 13: 40.

19. Ronald D. Rotunda, "The Liberal Label: Roosevelt's Capture of a Symbol," in *Public Policy*, ed. John D. Montgomery and Albert O. Hirschman (Cambridge: Harvard University Press, 1968), 17: 399; Samuel Beer, "In Search of a New Public Philosophy," in *The New American Political System*, ed. Anthony King (Washington, D.C.: American Enterprise Institute, 1979); James Ceaser, "The Theory of Governance of the Reagan Administration," in *The Reagan Presidency and the Governing of America*, ed. Lester M. Salamon and Michael S. Lund (Washington, D.C.: Urban Institute, 1981).

20. Croly, *Progressive Democracy*, 15.

21. In the *Discourses*, Machiavelli counsels, "He who desires or attempts to reform the government of the state, and wishes to have it accepted and capable of maintaining itself to the satisfaction of everybody, must at least retain the semblance of the old forms; so that it may seem to the people that there has been no change in the institutions, even though in fact they are entirely different from the old ones." *Discourses*, (New York: Modern Library, 1950), Book I, Chapter 25, p.182.

22. As R. Shep Melnick has observed, "The 'rights revolution' refers to the tendency to define nearly every public issue in terms of legally protected rights of individuals. Rights of the handicapped, rights of workers, rights of students, rights of racial, linguistic, and religious minorities, rights of women, rights of consumers, the right to a hearing, the right to know—these have become the stock and trade of political discourse." See his "The Courts, Congress, and Programmatic Rights," in *Remaking American Politics*, ed. Richard A. Harris and Sidney M. Milkis (Boulder, Colo.: Westview, 1989), 188.

23. James Piereson, "Party Government," *Political Science Reviewer*, 12 (fall 1982): 51–52.

24. Stephen Skowronek, *Building a New American State: The Expansion of National Administrative Capacities, 1877–1920* (Cambridge: Cambridge University Press, 1982), 40. Madison and Jefferson did not abandon their view, expressed during the founding of the Constitution, that a strong majority party—and raw and disruptive partisan conflict—posed a threat to individual liberty. They hoped that once Hamilton and his allies in the Federalist Party were defeated at the polls, the party system would wither away. During the Jacksonian era, however, Martin Van Buren, supported by a forceful and popular president, defended the party as a legitimate constitutional institution, one that would take its shape from Jeffersonian principles.

25. Herbert Croly, *The Promise of American Life* (1909; Reprint, New York: Dutton, 1963), 169.

26. Charles O. Jones, *The Presidency in a Separated System* (Washington, D.C.: Brookings Institution, 1994), 282.

27. Franklin D. Roosevelt, introduction to *Public Papers*, ed. Rosenman, 7: xxix.

28. Arthur Krock, "New Deal Victory Laid to Federal Money Lure," *New York Times*, 28 May 1938, section 4, p. 2.

29. Thomas Stokes, *Chip Off My Shoulder* (Princeton: Princeton University Press, 1940), 503.

30. The two-thirds rule of the Democratic Party required support from two-thirds of the delegates for the nomination of president and vice-president. This rule had been defended in the past because it guarded the most loyal Democratic region—the South—against the imposition of an unwanted ticket by the less habitually Democratic North, East, and West. The Roosevelt administration's successful push to abolish the two-thirds rule, therefore, weakened the

influence of southern Democrats and facilitated the adoption of a national reform program.

31. Morton J. Frisch, *Franklin D. Roosevelt: The Contribution of the New Deal to American Political Thought and Practice* (Boston: St. Wayne, 1975), 79.

32. Franklin D. Roosevelt, radio address, 24 June 1938, *Public Papers and Addresses*, ed. Rosenman, 9: 28.

33. Philip LaFollette, Elmer Bensen, and Frank Murphy, "Why We Lost," *The Nation*, 3 December 1938, 587. In the general election, the Democrats lost eighty-one seats in the House and eight in the Senate, as well as thirteen governorships. See Milton Plesur, "The Republican Congressional Comeback of 1938," *Review of Politics* 24 (1962): 525–62. On the results of the purge campaign, see John Edward Hopper, "The Purge: Franklin D. Roosevelt and the 1938 Nominations," (Ph.D. diss., University of Chicago, 1966).

34. E. E. Schattschneider, "The Struggle For Party Government," in *The Party Battle*, ed. Leon Stein (New York: Arno, 1974), 40.

35. On the limits of party government in the United States, see James Sterling Young and Russell L. Riley, "Party Government and Political Culture" (paper presented at the annual meeting of the American Political Science Association, San Francisco, 1990).

36. Franklin D. Roosevelt as quoted in Martha Derthick, *Policymaking for Social Security* (Washington, D.C.: Brookings Institution, 1983), 230.

37. Joseph P. Harris, "Outline for a New York Conference," 8 April 1936 (*Papers of the President's Committee on Administrative Management*, Franklin D. Roosevelt Library, Hyde Park, New York).

38. *Report of the President's Committee on Administrative Management* (Washington, D.C.: U.S. Government Printing Office, 1937). The President's Committee on Administrative Management, headed by Louis Brownlow, played a central role in the planning and politics of institutional reform between 1936 and 1940.

39. Luther Gulick, "Politics, Administration, and the New Deal," *Annals* 169 (September 1933): 64.

40. *Congressional Record*, 75th Cong., 3d Sess., 8 April 1938, 83: 5121.

41. Significantly, the two Supreme Court cases that triggered the dispute between Roosevelt and the judiciary were *Humphrey's Executor v. United States*, 295 U.S. 602 (1935), and *Schecter Poultry Corp. v. United States*, 295 U.S. 553 (1935), both of which imposed constraints on the executive authority of the president.

42. The term *administrative presidency* was coined by Richard Nathan to describe the strategic use of administrative power in the Nixon and Reagan presidencies. See his *The Administrative Presidency* (New York: John Wiley, 1983).

43. *Report of the President's Committee on Administrative Management*, 53.

44. Paul Van Riper, *History of the United States Civil Service* (Evanston, Ill.: Row, Peterson, 1958), 327.

45. See A. James Reichley, "The Rise of National Parties," in *The New Direction in American Politics*, ed. John E. Chubb and Paul E. Peterson (Washington, D.C.: Brookings Institution, 1985). By the end of the 1980s, however, Reichley was much less hopeful that the emergent national parties were well suited to perform the parties' historic function of mobilizing public support for political values and substantive government approaches and policies. See his *The Life of the Parties: A History of American Political Parties* (New York: Free Press, 1992), especially chapters 18–21.

46. Nixon transformed the Bureau of the Budget into the Office of Management and Budget (OMB) by executive order in 1970, adding a cadre of presidentially appointed assistant directors for policy to stand between the OMB director and the bureau's civil servants. Consequently, the budget office both attained additional policy responsibility and became more responsive to the president. In the Reagan administration, the OMB was given a central role in remaking regulatory policy.

47. Richard A. Harris and Sidney M. Milkis, *The Politics of Regulatory Change: A Tale of Two Agencies*, 2d ed. (New York: Oxford University Press, 1996).

48. Richard B. Stewart, "The Reformation of American Administrative Law," *Harvard Law Review*, 88, no. 8 (June 1975): 1712; Allen Schick, "Congress and the 'Details of Administration,'" *Public Administration Review*, 36 (September–October 1976): 516–28; Jeremy Rabkin, "The Judiciary in the Administrative State," *Public Interest*, 71 (spring 1983): 662–84; Melnick, "The Courts, Congress, and Programmatic Rights."

49. The gag rule, first issued by the Reagan administration's Department of Health and Human Services in 1988, declared that a program that received federal funds "may not provide counseling concerning the use of abortion as a method of family planning or provide referral for abortion as a method of family planning." The Reagan administration was thwarted in this policy by the lower courts, which delayed the regulation for three years. But in late May 1991 the Supreme Court upheld the gag rule in *Rust v. Sullivan*, 500 U.S. 173 (1991) and the Bush administration prepared to carry it out. Congress quickly passed legislation to stop the administration from enforcing it; however, the House failed by a dozen votes to override Bush's veto of the legislation. Soon after his inauguration, President Clinton issued an executive order reversing Reagan and Bush's policy of forbidding abortion counseling at federally funded clinics.

50. David Shribman, "Tsongas Suggests Third Party, Sees Powell as a Candidate," *Boston Globe*, 13 December 1994, 1, 28.

51. See, for example, Malbin, "Was Divided Government Really Such A Big Problem?"; Mayhew, *Divided We Govern*; Richard M. Vallely, "Divided They Govern," in *The American Prospect: Reader in American Politics*, ed. Walter Dean Burnham (Chatham, N.J.: Chatham House, 1995).

52. William Clinton, "The New Covenant: Responsibility and Rebuilding the American Community," Washington, D.C., 23 October 1991. This speech marked the first pronouncement of these "sacred principles." From then on, Clinton repeated them at every defining moment of his journey to the White House: the announcement of Senator Albert Gore, who shared his ideas, as his running mate; his promotion of the party platform; his acceptance speech at the Democratic Convention in New York; and his victory remarks in Little Rock on election night.

53. Similar ideas and attendant policy proposals are spelled out in detail in Will Marshall and Martin Schramm, eds., *Mandate for Change* (New York: Berkeley Books, 1993).

54. Sidney Blumenthal, "Bob Dole's First Strike," *New Yorker*, 3 May 1993, 40–46; Douglas Jehl, "Rejoicing Is Muted for the President in Budget Victory," *New York Times*, 8 August 1993, 1, 23; David Shribman, "Budget Battle a Hollow One for President," *Boston Globe*, 8 August 1993, 1, 24.

55. William Clinton, "Address before a Joint Session of Congress on Administration Goals," 17 February 1993, *Weekly Compilation of Presidential Documents*, 17 February 1993, 215–24; Jill Zuckman, "Pared Funding Speeds Passage of National Service," *Congressional Quarterly Weekly Report*, 7 August 1993, 2160–61.

56. Indeed, during the early days of his presidency, Clinton sought to identify with his party's leadership in Congress and the national committee—partly, one suspects, to avoid the political isolation from which Carter suffered. Whereas Carter kept party leaders in Congress and the national committee at arm's length, Clinton sought both to embrace and to empower the national organization. The White House lobbying efforts on Capitol Hill focused almost exclusively on the Democratic caucus, and the administration relied heavily on the Democratic National Committee to marshal public support for its domestic programs. Interviews by author with White House staffer, 3 November 1994 (not for attribution); with David Wilhelm, chairman, Democratic National Committee, 18 October 1993; and with Craig Smith, political director, Democratic National Committee, 19 October 1993. Also see Rhodes Cook, "DNC under Wilhelm Seeking a New Role," *Congressional Quarterly Weekly Report*, 13 March 1993, 634.

57. Al From and Will Marshall, *The Road to Realignment: Democrats and the Perot Voters*, (Washington, D.C.: Democratic Leadership Council), 1 July 1993, section 1, p. 3–5.

58. David Shribman, "A New Brand of D.C. Politics," *Boston Globe*, 18 November 1993, 15; Gwen Ifill, "Fifty-Six Long Days of Coordinated Persuasion," *New York Times*, 19 November 1993, A27.

59. William Clinton, "Address before a Joint Session of Congress on Health Care Reform," 22 September 1993, *Congressional Quarterly Weekly Report*, 25 September 1993, 2582–86; Robin Toner, "Alliance to Buy Health Care: Bureaucrat or Public Servant?" *New York Times*, 5 December 1993, 1, 38.

60. Adam Clymer, "National Health Program, President's Greatest Goal, Declared Dead in Congress," *New York Times*, 27 September 1994, A1, B10. For a sound and interesting case study of the Clinton health care program, see Cathie Jo Martin, "Mandating Social Change within Corporate America" (Paper presented at the annual meeting of the American Political Science Association, New York, 1994). Martin's study shows that health care reform became the victim of a battle between "radically different world views about the state and corporation in modern society," p. 1.

61. William Schneider, "Clinton: The Reason Why," *National Journal*, 12 November 1994, 2630–32. Schneider cites a nationwide poll by Voter News Service revealing that voters who approved of the job Clinton was doing as president (44 percent of all those who voted) cast their ballots for Democrats in House elections by 82 to 18 percent. Those who disapproved of his performance (51 percent of all who voted) chose Republicans by 83 to 17 percent.

62. Stephen Gettinger, " '94 Elections: Real Revolution or Blip on Political Radar?" *Congressional Quarterly Weekly Report*, 5 November 1994, 3127–32; Richard L. Berke, "Epic Political Realignments Often Aren't," *New York Times*, 1 January 1995, section 4, p. 3.

63. Remarks of William Kristol, lecture at Harvard University, 2 December 1994. In 1930, the Democrats gained fifty-three seats in the House, giving them a majority in that legislative chamber for the first time since 1918. In the Senate, the Democrats gained eight seats but were still one vote short of a majority. See A. James Reichley, *The Life of the Parties: A History of American Political Parties* (New York: Free Press, 1992) 243–44.

64. Robert Kuttner, "Up from 1994," *American Prospect*, 20 (winter 1995): 7.

65. Michael Wines, "Republicans Seek Sweeping Changes in the House's Rules," *New York Times*, 8 December 1994, A1, B21; idem, "Moderate Republicans Seek an Identity for Gingrich Era," 26 December 1994, 1, 22; Richard E. Cohen, "The Transformers," *National Journal*, 4 March 1995, 528–29, 531.

66. Republicans are ambivalent about whether the appropriate path to reform is federalism or a national conservative policy. With respect to reforming Aid to Families with Dependent Children (AFDC), for example, the Republican Contract with America proposes to expand the flexibility of the states, allowing them to design their own work programs and to determine who participates in these programs. In fact, states have the option to opt out of the AFDC program and convert their share of AFDC payments into fixed annual block grants, thus removing federal control over the program. For those states that stay in the program, however, the contract calls for national standards to determine eligibility, to attack illegitimacy and teen pregnancy, and to establish work requirements. As John J. Dilulio and Donald Kettl argue in their analysis of the contract, "every relevant study indicates that nationally

initiated contract-style welfare reforms can be achieved only where significant resource increases are made in the government bureaucracies that administer the programs." *The Contract with America, Devolution, and the Administrative Realities of American Federalism* (Washington, D.C.: Brookings Institution, 1995), 49. Similarly, with respect to regulatory policy, the contract envisions strengthening federalism by ending the imposition of unfunded federal mandates on state and local governments. At the same time, the contract calls for the protection of property rights against "takings," a protection that would greatly reduce the discretion of states and localities to control land use. See Harris and Milkis, *Politics of Regulatory Change*, chapter 7. Warning conservatives against committing the same sins for which they had condemned their political opponents, William Kristol urged "federalism," rather than "conservative micromanagement from Washington," as a solution to liberal "statism." Lecture at Harvard University.

67. Although many pundits were quick to view the 1994 election results as the end of the New Deal, neither Democrats nor Republicans proposed changes in the largest entitlement program, Social Security, or an end to the entitlement status of Medicare. See Robert Pear, "Welfare Debate Will Re-Examine Core Assumptions," *New York Times*, 2 January 1995, 1, 9.

68. Al From, "More than a Good Speech: The State of the Union Address Could Have Marked a Turning Point in History," *The New Democrat*, March–April 1996, 35–36.

69. William Clinton, "Address Before a Joint Session of Congress on the State of the Union," 23 January 1996, *Congressional Quarterly Weekly Report*, 27 January 1996, 258–62.

70. Robert Dole, "Republican Response to President Clinton's State of the Union Message," ibid., 262–63.

71. Alan Brinkley, "Roots," *New Republic*, 27 July 1992, 45.

Chapter Seven

Unity versus Division: The Effect of Divided Government on Policy Development

Roberta Q. Herzberg

"How does divided government affect policy success?" and "how well do our theories of divided government predict the policy formation process?" are questions at the heart of the debate about the role of divided government in executive-legislative decision making. Those who have focused on divided government suggest that it is a meaningful electoral concept for voters and, as such, forms the basis of policy agreement and conflict once governing coalitions are established. Unified government is argued to be more effective in policy formation than divided government, but voters wary of activist government may actually choose divided parties as a means to increase bargaining around a more moderate position.[1]

For divided government to be a major factor in shaping the policy arena, a secondary set of assumptions must follow: First, the party affiliation of voters and candidates must be directly correlated with individual policy preferences. Individuals therefore, must be able to define what is meant by Republican policy positions and distinguish them from Democratic preferences, which then allows them to place each of these party positions relative to their own positions in the policy space. Second, party cohesion is assumed to be correlated with policy cohesion. The more meaningful the party labels in identifying specific policy positions, the more likely that a party will be successful in achieving that policy preference. Finally, we assume that unified

173

government presents a more favorable policymaking environment in terms of passing positive policy positions. In other words, presidents do better when they face a congressional majority of their own party than when they face an opposing majority.

While these assumptions each present part of the truth, they over-look meaningful factors in the U.S. policymaking process that affect the outcome of any policy deliberation. A theory based on divided government assumes that party divisions are most relevant for under-standing policy outcomes and that Congress and the executive each operate as monolithic actors. A focus on differences in party control between the executive and the legislative branch may obscure the many internal divisions within the legislature and even within the executive branch that obstruct positive policy action.[2] Anyone observ-ing the intricate methods used by policymakers to slow and stop policy has to ask how meaningful a simple overlay such as divided government is for understanding the task of coalition building and policy formation.

While a desire for divided government may be the cause of the electoral division between executive and legislative parties, it is hardly necessary for the creation of policy division. There is little chance of a positive policy agenda sweeping through our divided system regardless of whether policy control is divided by party or not. As Robert Bendiner argued over thirty years ago, the institutional structure favors inaction:

> A United States Congressman has two principal functions: to make laws and to keep laws from being made. The first of these he and his colleagues perform only with sweat, patience and a remarkable skill in the handling of the creaking machinery; but the second, they perform daily with ease and infinite variety. Indeed, if government is best that governs least, then Congress is one of the most perfect instruments of government.[3]

While divided government may add to the problem of policy frustra-tion, the elimination of party division, in the absence of institutional and constitutional change, will not result in active policy change. Thus, we should not expect performance under divided control to be markedly different than under unified control, and Democrats should not have been disappointed with the somewhat low level of policy success under Clinton and a Democratic Congress. Divided govern-ment is but one factor in determining policy success or failure.

Comparing Policy Performance across the Great Divide

For students interested in the policy effects of divided government, one could hardly ask for a better empirical test than that created by the national electoral shake-ups during the 1990s. Since 1990, we have experienced policymaking under a Republican president/Democratic Congress, Democratic president/Democratic Congress, and a Democratic president/Republican Congress. The question remains, how have these dramatic shifts in divided government translated into the policy arena? Is policy markedly different under the unified government of 1993 and 1994 than under divided control? Does the makeup of division (Republican president/Democratic Congress versus Democratic president/Republican Congress) matter for the degree of policy success and the type of policy produced? To address these questions, I examine two major policy issues during this period to consider how divided or unified government affected policy outcomes. The first area selected is health care reform, with special attention paid to the proposed health security act. The second policy area is budgetary policy, in which I focus on the continuing policy divisions in the 104th Congress. While these are by no means the full extent of legislation considered during this period, they represent two visible policy areas that were central to the electoral debate that led to the unified and divided governing episodes.[4] If electoral decisions regarding divided government and unified party control are integral to explaining policy outcomes, then these two areas should certainly provide evidence of it.

Two factors make this a particularly good time for a test of this approach. First, having unified government sandwiched between two different forms of divided government presents an important opportunity to evaluate the effects of divided and unified government under similar political and policy conditions. At times, analyses have relied on comparisons virtually decades apart, and the time difference introduces a variety of alternative explanations for policy success or failure. Second, the concept of divided government requires an underlying party cohesion that has been lacking for most of the modern period but is now renewed, at least with respect to congressional politics. Newt Gingrich implemented partisan division as a minority strategy response to Democratic domination of Congress. Rather than seek compromise to influence Democratic policy, Gingrich initiated a strategy of opposition and obstruction intended to accentuate the ideological differences between the groups. He used this stark division both for electoral politics (the campaign in 1994) and for governing. The

Contract with America, for example, provided a policy platform rarely used in congressional elections or in organizing the congressional agenda. Relying on this strategy, Congress as policymaker was elevated in the attention of the public and the press, and the issue of divided or unified control of the branches became increasingly relevant to the debate. Rarely in the modern era had a congressional platform assumed an importance in the public eye comparable with the president's agenda.

Clinton's election in 1992 was believed by political observers to be a response to the inability of government to respond to the economic and social concerns on the agenda. The time seemed right for a more positive response to the nation's problems, with a plan for health care at the top. At the time Clinton took office, public opinion polls showed overwhelming support for action on health care (almost 80 percent characterized health care as a serious problem in need of major overhaul).[5] What Clinton and the nation were to find out is that unified government, while important, is not sufficient to control the flow of policy outcomes. Moreover, the 1994 electoral results suggested that voters, faced with the prospects of a positive Democratic agenda, were not sure that they wanted the action promised by unity.

Whether voters in 1994 were explicitly choosing divided government to check the Democratic agenda or whether they were taking the first step towards a broader shift to unified Republican control cannot be answered definitively. What is clear is that the response to the 1996 budget stalemate suggests that voters were not pleased with the lack of policy outcomes possible when two strong party opponents line up against each other.[6] While Congress has fielded most of the public's fury, the voters seem torn between a desire to check extreme actions by Congress or the president, which may mean stalemate, and a hope that "the politicians quit acting like children and reach a decision."[7] To sort out these many confusing signals, I turn to a closer examination of health care reform and budgetary policy.

The Long and Winding Road to Health Reform

Health care reform has been an important policy issue for a number of years but was finally brought to the front of the policy agenda during the presidential election of 1992. In 1991 in Pennsylvania, the surprise election of Democratic Senator Harris Woford in response to a theme of health care security and universal coverage suggested that the time for considering a major reform of our health care system had arrived. Candidate Bill Clinton made this issue a centerpiece of his campaign, and George Bush's efforts to bring a Republican plan forward during 1992 seemed to be too little, too late.[8] Democrats had traditionally enjoyed an advantage on this issue, and its rise in 1991 helped set the stage for the Democratic candidate to be favored. Certainly, health care was not the only factor in Clinton's victory over President Bush, but Clinton's focus on the issue during the definition of his electoral mandate and of his promises to deliver complete reform within "100 days" suggests the importance he believed health care had played in his electoral victory.[9] In many ways, the behavior of the Clinton administration on health care suggests that Clinton himself believed in the power of unified government. Democratic control of Congress and the executive would provide an opportunity for reversing the frustrations of delayed policymaking during the 1970s and 1980s. Several analysts believed this as well. Mark Peterson, for example, argued that the time was indeed right for putting forward and passing significant health care reform.[10] Several changes in congressional membership and electoral politics, combined with an activist president, converged to make proponents of reform optimistic, even giddy.

Confidence among reformers resulted in a complex proposal (1,342 pages of detail) designed behind closed doors with virtually no input from Republicans. Such an approach depends heavily on an assumption that majority rule is the relevant decision-making institution and ignores both serious divisions in the Democratic Party and the institutional complexity of the congressional policymaking process. There were a number of problems with the way in which the plan was introduced, with the degree of detail included in the proposal, and with the reading of the level of public sentiment. The defeat of the proposal, however, did not depend on these mistakes. The failure of Clinton's health security bill occurred on the day it was introduced into the Congress under the normal rules of decision making. The policy was doomed because of the many opponents placed in veto positions throughout the system. Virtually everyone had some problem with at least a part of the proposal. A significant number had concerns about relying on private insurers and about the concept of managed competition. Others feared the huge quasi-public bureaucracy the plan would require. Still others opposed employer mandates, or standard benefit packages, or problems of cost containment, or the need for new revenues to cover the large cost requirement. Many opposed all of it. It is little wonder that the coalition to pass major reform was quickly divided on what had to be retained. Trying to amend such a complex proposal while it was being considered in so many different congressional arenas became problematic. Changes made to address the concerns of labor supporters led to greater concerns in the business community. Providers who favored universal coverage opposed the managed-care assumptions underlying much of the implementation. When the problems began to outweigh the positive aspects, the unified governing coalition was unified no more.

The mechanisms that were used to bring down health care reform were well entrenched in Congress long before the Democrats gained unified control. They were not specific to the health care decision process but were available for delaying and defeating policy in virtually any arena. The difficulty with the theory of divided or unified government as a way of predicting policy outcomes is that it reduces complex policy struggles to a dichotomous choice between two opposing positions. At the level at which the electorate is involved, such dichotomies may be appropriate. Health reform is turned into a thirty-second sound bite in which the problem becomes increasingly simplistic. In any given election, the ability of individual candidates to define the issues of interest and to focus on those in which the electorate and those candidates are in agreement helps shape victories. It is oversimple, however, to believe that all candidates who were elected because they favored (or opposed) governmental action on a given issue took similar positions on that issue. If the issue were unidimensional, then even dissimilar positions could be defined in terms of a single proposal. Duncan Black and Anthony Downs each showed that policy preferences over a single policy dimension can be evaluated in terms of distance between two policymakers' ideal policy.[11] If most voters' preferences were closer to the Clinton plan than to its Republican alternative, then even single-payer advocates would support it in a dichotomous choice. However, as the policy arena expands beyond a single dimension, the likelihood that a stable policy majority can be constructed drops precipitously.[12]

To say that the 1,342-page health security act proposal was multidimensional is undoubtedly a great understatement. Congressmembers who supported health reform in theory rejected the specifics of the Clinton managed-competition plan. Among Republicans, three primary camps emerged. The first group opposed the Clinton plan only as a matter of degree. They wanted a slightly less regulatory, but largely bipartisan, approach in which employers or individuals covered their health care costs.[13] The second group believed the direction of change should be towards freer markets and towards using medical savings accounts and tax reforms. They argued that the problem with health care was a function not of market failure, but of the failure to use a market for making health care decisions.[14] The final group of Republican opponents wanted individual insurance mandates and vouchers, rather than employer mandates, to bring consumers closer to the decision regarding health care value.[15] Mandates were required to bring everyone (including the young and healthy) into the common insurance pool. Consumers would not be allowed to shift the costs of their care to others except in the case in which care was subsidized for low-income or unhealthy individuals.

If opposition had been contained within the Republican Party, Clinton's health reform might have survived. But Democrats were equally sensitive to the various ways in which health care reform could be structured. While many were willing to support their president in his attempt at reform, a larger coalition favored a more regulatory single-payer approach. They agreed on the issue of universal coverage but differed on the delivery system for that insurance product. Over one hundred Democratic congressmembers signed on as cosponsors of Congressman Jim McDermott's single-payer approach to health reform before the president had even introduced his proposal. While not opposed to the president's intentions, they argued that his approach was "bad policy" and far too complicated. In order to overcome the many factions opposing the move to a nationalized insurance system, the Democratic Party would have to stand united. Yet many within the ranks argued that the managed-competition plan favored by Clinton was simply inadequate to solve the problems of access and cost. Remembering the failures of the 1970s, some feared that this might be their only chance at creating a national health care system, and they wanted that system to include all the features for which they had fought so long.[16]

As the debate expanded beyond the simple yes or no of health reform, the potential policy divisions grew. But policy failure requires more than simply the desire to defeat a policy. The policy's opponents must also have a means to defeat it. Congress possessed almost unlimited means to change and stall the president's health package. While we frequently discuss our political system using the language of majority rule, the reality is that policy requires positive action at numerous decision stages before it reaches the point of potential congressional-executive agreement or disagreement. Policy requires positive support at the subcommittee and committee stages. Usually any bill requires at least two to three committees in each body: at a minimum, the authorizations and appropriations committees in both houses and the Rules Committee in the House. Changes in the tax code require, in addition, the relevant revenue committees. Budgetary impacts bring in the budget committees. The scope of health care reform involved all of these and more. Each decision point provided an opportunity for opponents of the Clinton plan to delay action to provide time for interests to mobilize. Negative decision powers such as these make it far easier to stop legislation than to move it forward.[17] When the issue is complex and the opponents many, as in this case, negative decision powers associated with the normal decision process make change virtually impossible. Without changing the process or imposing strong leadership to centralize the decision, complex policy will fail.

Furthermore, policy debate does not stop inside the beltway. As supporters started to debate the Clinton proposal in Congress, affected industries and interests outside of Washington got into the mix. From providers, to insurers, to small employers and labor unions, almost everyone had some concern about the specific proposal put forward. Most had not been involved in the actual drafting and thus had little stake in this proposal. By targeting those aspects they disliked, this amalgam of diverse interests started pulling at the threads of the complex tapestry of the proposed health security act, and it started to unravel. Change designed to shore up support with one group inevitably created greater opposition from another arena. By the end of 1994, the coalition opposed to the Clinton plan had turned around public support as well. While voters still favored health care reform, they had lost faith in Clinton's ability to design and deliver such a plan. It is little wonder that unified government is so frequently insufficient to create significant policy change at this level.

Health Care Reduced: The Republicans Get Their Turn

If health care reform contributed to Bill Clinton's election in 1992, it almost certainly was equally important to the loss of the Democratic majority in the 1994 midterm elections. Again, this speaks to the negative decision bias that permeates our complex policy system. After President Clinton had raised expectations for policy action, his highly visible policy defeat on health care, along with a public perception of his actions as too liberal, set the stage for an electoral defeat during the midterm elections. The Republican minority under the direction of Newt Gingrich was able to shape a national campaign against Clinton.[18] The opposition strategy they had developed during 1992 and 1993 became the rallying cry for their campaign to place a check on the decisions of President Clinton. One of the important distinctions between the 1994 election and previous midterm elections is the degree to which the Republican leadership was able to national-ize the contest. If anything, the 1994 electoral result would seem to suggest that voters do seek a counterbalance in federal policymaking consistent with party division. But the form the division took pre-sented a very different set of policy expectations. Many scholars of divided government have argued that the Democratic majority in Congress was sustained because congressional elections are usually more localized than presidential contests and, thus, less open to the more volatile national trends of the presidential contests.[19] The ques-tion remains whether the theory of divided government is sufficiently robust to deal with the new balance brought about by a Republican Congress.

Republicans felt confident following the defeat of the Clinton health care proposal. But political observers should not be surprised that no conservative health reform proposal has succeeded after the Republi-can's 1994 electoral success. That the Republicans were unified against the Clinton plan does not imply that they are either willing or able to devise policy that bridges their own policy differences. The divisions in their own reasons for opposing the Clinton health care plan were secondary when their purpose was to defeat Clinton. They shared almost universal agreement that the Clinton plan was a serious mis-take. However, when the Clinton plan was removed from the table, the divisions over what should replace it came immediately to the foreground. Without any meaningful policy consensus, and with the memory of the Clinton failure fresh in everyone's mind, health care slipped to the back burner. Again, the loose coalitions and small policy fiefdoms sufficient to bring a policy down are woefully inadequate when directed at positive action.[20]

Currently, health reform advocates have rallied behind a relatively small bipartisan effort incorporated in the Kennedy-Kassebaum reform bill. This bill is an obvious response to the 1994 policy defeat. It focuses on the heart of the public's concern with respect to their own health care: insurance reform. The fear of losing coverage, of the lack of portability, or of an insurer's refusal to cover a sick or disabled family member is at the heart of the average citizen's frustration with the health care system. Most people like their own coverage and providers and thus were unwilling to support changes to those parts of the system. They do not like insurance companies, and the arbitrariness of illness makes everyone feel vulnerable. Thus, reforms that would address these narrower concerns are consistent with continuing public sentiment for health reform. Change beyond this minimum is increasingly difficult.

Yet even this more limited change is more than the ideological center of the new Republican Party seems willing to support. Some conservative groups worry about the cost implications of insurance reforms and the unfairness of shifting costs from older to younger Americans at a time when so many economic burdens have already been shifted in that direction. Others worry that the Kennedy-Kassebaum legislation represents the nose under the tent that will drive the system to a more regulatory state approach.[21]

In addition to their lack of a consistent party policy on health care, the Republican leadership was not eager to stray far from the economic theme that had brought them to majority status. Republicans sought an agenda that focused on the central questions of fiscal conservatism that tied them together. That focus implied a reform policy that cut costs in health care and reduced the federal commitment to health funding, not increased it. Reforms directed at reducing the costs of Medicare and Medicaid became the centerpiece of the Republican health care strategy. Expanding beyond current policy would be inconsistent with the Republican theme of less government. Only compromise and bridge building across the party divisions will make any health care reform emerge, and these are the commodities that are most scarce in this new era of divided government. Insurance regulation and other issues of the previous health care debate will have to wait until the central economic issues are resolved.

The Republican Revolution of 1994: Delivering on the Economic Contract

The Republican revolution of 1994 is suggestive of how divided government arises as an electoral strategy in which voters desire a balance in the policy directions of the Washington establishment. Perhaps more than any recent example, the midterm election of 1994 posed the issue of checking the power of a president by balancing him with a decisive majority of the opposing party. The literature on divided government, based on the long periods in which Republican presidents faced Democratic congresses, poses many alternative explanations for this particular pattern. The first set of explanations deal with structural advantages of the parties that favor Republicans for the presidency and Democrats for Congress. Wattenberg argues that the Republicans' presidential advantage can be tied to that party's greater ideological consistency and their winner-take-all primary structure.[22] Similarly, Gary Jacobson argues that political advantages of Democratic congressmembers, along with incumbency, have made it hard to break the Democratic majority in Congress.[23] An alternative explanation put forward by John Petrocik suggests a division of issues between presidential and congressional races that lead to the selection of different parties.[24] Presidents run on national economic and international issues, while contests for Congress are decided on more local fare or constituency-based issues. Republicans have traditionally been advantaged by "presidential" issues, while Democrats are more successful on the "congressional" issues. The question remains, what happened in 1992 and 1994 to reverse this pattern, and what does this imply about the policy effects of divided government? In other words, should we expect a different policy pattern emerging as a result of "the new divided government"?

Arriving in a flurry of new majority status, the Republican Party of the 104th Congress, under the direction of Speaker Newt Gingrich, made it clear that politics as usual would not be the order of the day. Organizing the 1994 election as a referendum on Bill Clinton and nationalizing the message through the use of the Contract with America, the Republicans demonstrated that national party politics could play an important role even in a midterm election. While the 1994 election caught almost everyone by surprise, the revolution of change had begun years before in the selection of more conservative party leaders and the increasing ideological consistency of the party activists. There is little question that the change from a Democratic majority to a Republican majority had significant policy effects. The Republicans who won office were not as likely as past challengers to be drawn from the ranks of politicians familiar with the art of compromise. Rather, they were business people and outsiders recruited to the cause by GOPAC and other conservative organizations.[25] As such, the new Republicans were more likely to owe their allegiance and their victories to the party leadership and to Newt Gingrich, in particular. Moreover, the districts where change occurred were usually those in which each political party was competitive and, thus, those districts more likely to have a moderate Democrat replaced by a moderate-to-conservative Republican. Those Democrats who survived tended to be from very safe Democratic districts and, therefore, were more likely to be ideologically liberal than those who were defeated. The election losses of 1994 returned a Democratic class more liberal and more cohesive than the previous congresses. The result is that the 104th Congress is increasingly divided between distinct policy positions of the two parties. Republican leadership attacked their new policy agenda with an attitude that if playing opposition politics was good for electoral success in 1994, then it would be right for governing in 1995 and 1996.[26] This is not a recipe for compromise and bipartisanship. The stage was set for the holiday budget battle of 1995.

Confident in their electoral strategy, Republican lawmakers took the lead in developing and following a legislative agenda based on the tenets of the Contract with America. Having been in the minority for decades, Republicans were familiar with the strategies and techniques of obstruction. Unwilling to be brought down by the same institutional tools they had used against the Democrats, they rushed to adopt a series of institutional and party reforms that would strengthen and consolidate power in the party leadership. They reduced committee and subcommittee power relative to the leadership, and they reduced staff that could provide a competing source of policy ideas and research. The result was a streamlined partisan force, more cohesive than the one the Democrats had had available in 1993.

Quickly, they set to work passing the Contract with America, with Newt Gingrich acting as much like a president as one can outside the Oval Office.[27] Success came quickly in the House. However, as Clinton had overestimated the ability of unified government in 1993, Gingrich overestimated the revolution of a unified Congress in 1995. Gingrich had made many needed changes and had strengthened House control, but that left virtually unlimited possibilities for delay and change in the Senate, and there remained the issue of separation of powers and the presidential veto.

The ingredients of Gingrich's revolution are very visible in the Republicans' proposed budget for the 1996 fiscal year. The plan called for balancing the budget in seven years, cutting entitlements such as Medicaid and Medicare by hundreds of millions of dollars, reforming welfare and cutting its growth, eliminating departments to reduce the size of the federal government, reducing regulation, streamlining agencies, and providing significant tax relief. While many elements of the Republican proposal were popular (e.g., balancing the budget, welfare reform), others proved impossible to sell (e.g., Medicare cuts). Again, using the mechanisms of negative decision power, Clinton was able to turn the tables on the Republican leadership: he focused on the fight against the unpopular changes proposed in the Republican budget and, at the same time, agreed "in spirit" to the popular cuts. The lesson Clinton learned about the power of opposition from the defeat of his health care proposal became an important force in his stand against Gingrich and the Republican revolution. Although the budget compromise reached in December 1995 dramatically changed Clinton administration policy (Clinton accepted the seven-year deadline for balancing the budget and the use of Congressional Budget Office [CBO] estimates in future budget agreements), Clinton emerged victorious as a check on the rush to extreme policy. If the public opinion polls are to be believed, Clinton improved his image among American voters by playing a strategy of negative policy and putting himself up as the last best hope against extremism.[28] The result is that no agreement has been reached on the 1996 budget, that Clinton's budget for 1997 returns to much of his previous agenda, and that government continues to operate on a series of continuing resolutions and threats of economic troubles from rising inflation and stagnant growth.

In the end, Gingrich's revolution, while changing the direction of the debate, was insufficient to change policy outcomes. Major legislation such as welfare reform has fallen to the veto of an opposition party president. Thus, Gingrich's ability to reduce the points at which actions could be internally vetoed in the House was insufficient to overcome the continued veto point represented by divided partisan control of government. As the Republican agenda ran into the brick wall of divided government, the solidarity of the party coalition began to falter as well. The unity so marked in 1995 began to wane as the natural divisions in the Republican Party became relevant for setting the boundaries of the budget compromise. As Clinton found in facing unified government, party cohesion is hard to maintain in the absence of positive gain. As party agendas fail, those who had been subordinating their own positions to the party stand in the name of unity become less willing to make concessions. If no action is going to occur, then why not be true to one's own principles?

While comments from voters continue to suggest disgust with the inability of Washington policymakers to respond to the needs of the American people, voters' choices in the 1994 elections and their response to polls in 1995 and 1996 indicate a desire for restraint. They support divided government or any other mechanism that slows change in the status quo. Revolution may make a desirable campaign strategy, but it ignores the realities of an institutional system designed around many necessary decision stages. Perhaps Clinton's best hope for 1996 is that he presents the best vehicle for slowing the Republican revolution. In late 1995, over twice as many people worried that Congress would go too far as worried that Congress would be prevented from making changes.[29] Following on the stalemate of the 1996 budget debates and the president's positioning as a check on Republican policies, Clinton's success or failure in the 1996 elections may be the best empirical measure to date of whether or not voters truly desire divided government for its policy implications.

Notes

1. David R. Mayhew, in his *Divided We Govern: Party Control, Lawmaking, and Investigations, 1946–1990* (New Haven: Yale University Press, 1991), argues that divided government has not resulted in significantly different policy outcomes than are achieved under unified government. By contrast, Sean Q Kelly, in his "Divided We Govern? A Reassessment," *Polity* 25 (1993): 475–88, and Morris Fiorina, in his *Divided Government* (New York: Macmillan, 1992), argue that policy differences do emerge if we focus on key issues or ideologically sensitive areas. In this volume, Leroy Rieselbach examines several of these competing views and finds general support for improved success under unified party control.

2. Roberta Herzberg, "Blocking Coalitions and Policy Change," in *Congress and Policy Change*, ed. Gerald C. Wright, Jr., Leroy Rieselbach, and Lawrence Dodd (New York: Agathon, 1986), 201–21.

3. Robert Bendiner, *Obstacle Course on Capitol Hill* (New York: McGraw Hill, 1964), 15.

4. The central place of health care in the election campaign of 1992 and in Clinton's inaugural address and his State of the Union address suggests the importance of health care reform as a national issue during his tenure. Similarly, the dominance of economic issues in the Republicans' Contract with America argues for an examination of budgetary issues as a mechanism for evaluating Republican success or failure.

5. Karlyn Bowman, "Public Attitudes on Health Care Reform: Are the Polls Misleading the Policy Makers?" (Washington, D.C.: American Enterprise Institute, 1994).

6. Public opinion polls suggest that large majorities favored compromise by Congress and the president (68 to 78 percent in the period from November 1995 to January 1996). *National Journal*, 2 December 1995, 3000, and 20 January 1996, 142. However, when queried, a majority of those polled (58

percent) favored Clinton's decision to veto the budget to protect Medicare and education. *National Journal,* 2 December 1995, 3000. More respondents blamed the Republicans for the stalemate (50 percent blamed Republicans, 27 percent Clinton). *National Journal,* 20 January 1996, 142.

7. *CBS Evening News,* 19 December 1995.

8. Bush proposed a rather extensive health care reform plan that would individualize health insurance coverage and provide vouchers for low-income recipients based on a blueprint developed by the Heritage Foundation. However, the plan's introduction in 1992, without extensive consultation with congressional leaders and at a time when the Democratic Congress was in a partisan election mode, meant that it had little chance of even serious consideration, much less passage. Moreover, voters responded to it as an opportunistic attempt to capture a relevant part of the electoral agenda without any serious policy commitment.

9. William Clinton, "Address before a Joint Session of Congress on the State of the Union," 25 January 1994, *Congressional Quarterly Weekly Report,* 29 January 1994, 194–98; "Address before a Joint Session of Congress on Health Care Reform," 22 September 1993, *Congressional Quarterly Weekly Report,* 25 September 1993, 2582–86.

10. Mark Peterson, "Institutional Change and the Health Politics of the Nineties" in *Health Care Reform in the Nineties,* ed. Pauline Rosenau, (Thousand Oaks, Calif.: Sage Publications, 1994), 149–75.

11. Duncan Black, *The Theory of Committees and Elections* (Cambridge: Cambridge University Press, 1958); Anthony Downs, *An Economic Theory of Democracy* (New Haven: Yale University Press, 1957).

12. Charles Plott, "A Notion of Equilibrium and Its Possibility under Majority Rule," *American Economic Review* (1967): 787–806.

13. This group was composed of moderate Republicans, led by Senator John Chaffee of Rhode Island. They worked with southern Democrats, led by Jim Cooper of Tennessee, throughout the 103rd Congress to develop a moderate alternative to the Clinton plan. Eventually, these efforts collapsed under opposition from both sides of the political spectrum.

14. This group's plan is supported by some of the more conservative members of the party (including Speaker Gingrich) and is based on analysis and theory developed by John Goodman and Gerald L. Musgrave, *Patient Power* (Washington, D.C.: Cato Institute, 1992); and the National Center for Policy Analysis, *An Agenda for Solving America's Health Care Crisis* (Dallas: National Center for Policy Analysis, May 1990).

15. The Heritage Foundation argued for adoption of a system based on the structure of the Federal Employees Health Plan. It believed that if the market for health insurance was to be truly competitive, health insurance had to be removed from the employer and mandated for individuals in terms of both selection of the plan and financing. This plan was the basis for the Bush health reform proposal in the 1992 campaign.

16. Health care reform had been an important issue for a number of senior legislators, but for no one more than Senator Edward Kennedy. Having fought for twenty-five years for universal health care coverage based on a national health insurance system comparable to the Canadian system, he was hesitant to see legislation that would not accomplish the goals of state-guaranteed coverage.

17. Roberta Herzberg, "Blocking Coalitions and Institutional Equilibrium," (Ph.D. diss., Washington University in St Louis, 1985).

18. A frequently used technique of the 1994 campaign was to "morph" the image of the Democratic congressional candidate into the image of Bill Clinton, suggesting that every Democratic candidate was the equivalent of Bill Clinton. The underlying message was that if you opposed Clinton's proposals, then you should oppose this Democratic congressional candidate as well. Certainly, party affiliation is meaningful under such a strategy.

19. Gary C. Jacobson, "The Persistence of Democratic House Majorities," in *The Politics of Divided Government*, ed. Gary Cox and Samuel Kernell (Boulder, Colo.: Westview, 1991), 57–84.

20. While many moderate plans continued to circulate during this time, there seemed to be little enthusiasm for taking on the health care system directly as Clinton had done. The problem the Republicans faced, however, was that the budgetary dilemma imposed by existing health care programs and spiraling costs had not disappeared. Republicans would have preferred to ignore health care altogether, but the budgetary promises made in the Contract with America required that they take on the cost problems of Medicaid and Medicare at the very minimum.

21. While public support for insurance reforms remains high, conservative Republicans see many serious problems with the Kennedy-Kassebaum legislation.

22. Martin P. Wattenberg, "The Republican Presidential Advantage in the Age of Party Disunity" in *Politics of Divided Government*, ed. Cox and Kernell, 39–55.

23. Jacobson, "Persistence of Democratic House Majorities," 57–84.

24. John Petrocik, "Divided Government: Is It All in the Campaigns?" in *Politics of Divided Government,* ed. Cox and Kernell, 13–38.

25. Jeff Shear, "United They Stand," *National Journal*, 28 October 1995, 2646–50.

26. Richard Cohen and William Schneider, "Voting in Unison," *National Journal*, 27 January 1996, 179–85.

27. Rarely in the modern Congress has a Speaker of the House attracted as much attention and controversy as Speaker Gingrich. His selection as *Time's* "Man of The Year" for 1995 was based on the national presence he attained as the recognized leader of the Republican Party. *Time*, 25 December 1995, 48–99. He is credited with House legislative successes, including the Contract with America, and with obtaining concessions from Clinton on the seven-year

time frame for balancing the budget. William Newkirk, "Americans Crave Leadership, but What Is It? Candidates Cultivate Hard-to-Define Trait," *Chicago Tribune*, 24 December 1995, 1.

28. Clinton has been very effective in characterizing himself as a guard against extremism while adopting many of the general goals at the heart of the Republican platform. This strategy, attributed to Dick Morris, Clinton's close advisor and Republican electoral consultant, appears to be working well in reframing the president's electoral position for the 1996 election. Again, it suggests the efficacy of policies designed to prevent positive action, both as a legislative and as an electoral strategy.

29. In October 1995, 26 percent feared that Congress would be prevented from making changes, while 64 percent worried that it would go too far. In November 1995, the figures were 29 percent and 62 percent, respectively. *National Journal*, 16 December 1995, 3118.

Chapter Eight

Doing One's Job: A Constitutional Principle and a Political Strategy for an Uncertain Future

Peter McNamara

One factor that has contributed mightily to the saliency of the divided government issue is that the persistence of divided government in recent decades has seemed to add weight to a long-standing critique of the Constitution's separation of powers. That critique originated with Walter Bagehot, but it was adapted and elaborated in the United States by Woodrow Wilson and then embraced by generations of scholars and reformers, not to mention political leaders such as Franklin Roosevelt.[1] It is still very much alive today both in academia and in the political arena. Books and articles proposing major constitutional reform in the area of separation of powers just keep on coming.[2] Consider as well the virulence of H. Ross Perot's attack on the Constitution in the 1992 presidential election campaign. Like Wilson, Perot emphasized the tendency of the American system towards gridlock and attributed it to the eighteenth-century origins of the Constitution.

But this volume, along with other recent research, presents considerable evidence that the divided government issue is complex.[3] For example, gridlock might be an illusion. Despite divided government, significant new laws continue to be passed. Divided government might even increase the number of laws passed by intensifying the natural institutional rivalry between Congress and the president. This effect is particularly clear in the case of proposals for new tax cuts! Two other

191

considerations are relevant. First, it is very plausible that divided government has prevented certain bad laws from being passed. Second, it must always be remembered that there is little evidence that the chief alternative to the American system, parliamentary government, is any better at dealing with the fundamental problems that confront modern democracies.[4]

Two reasons, however, suggest that we should continue to take seriously the issue of divided government. First, perhaps the most cogent argument that divided government is a real problem is that it makes it difficult to assign praise and blame for the conduct and performance of government. Voters become confused about who is responsible. And it might be in the interest of politicians to keep them in that state. A second and related reason for taking the issue of divided government seriously is that confidence in the American system of government seems to be at a low ebb. Public opinion polls continually show that there is a widespread feeling that government is remote, unresponsive, inefficient, and corrupt. Divided government intensifies this reaction against "gridlock," "politics," "rhetoric," and "insiders" because divided government puts partisan differences front and center in political debate. If anything, the momentum of the reaction against "politics as usual" seems to be growing. Witness the strong public sentiments in favor of a third party, the growth of populist campaigning, and the surprising level of public openness to candidates with little or no political experience, simply on the grounds that they are true "outsiders."

A common response among the public, the media, and politicians is to decry partisanship and call for an end to gridlock. There are two serious difficulties with this response. First, it assumes that partisan differences are not real differences of principle. This difficulty grows in significance when we recognize that the so-called political center is elusive. The problem is, not so much that there is no center, but rather that the center is often incoherent and therefore cannot provide a basis for good policy. The public, for example, seems to want tax cuts, spending increases, *and* a balanced budget. Second, calling for bipartisanship can be a very effective partisan weapon in the hands of a politician who can smile, stake out allegedly centrist or bipartisan ground, and at the same time skewer the opposition. When such calls for bipartisanship are transparently self-serving or when announcements about the breaking of gridlock seem always to be premature, the result can only be ever greater public dissatisfaction with government.

It probably goes too far to say that the present juncture represents a crisis for constitutional democracy. But these are nevertheless troubling developments, especially because the present electoral situation suggests that the continuation of divided government is as likely as any realignment. The two major parties have strong foundations in particular sections of American society, but neither can command a steady majority of voters. This has come about at a time when the lines between the two parties have become increasingly clear, especially at the congressional level. On the one hand, this clear ideological division means that sharp partisan conflicts will continue to be a conspicuous feature of American politics. But on the other hand, and more important, it means that at each election a large and free-floating bloc of voters will be up for grabs. Given the disenchantment of these voters with the major parties, it seems unlikely that they will be easily or quickly incorporated into either major party.

With these prospects in mind and as an alternative to the strategy of moving to the center, I would like to make a suggestion as to how to deal with the present discontents. Public officials should do their constitutionally assigned jobs. This suggestion is offered on the basis of a hunch that doing their jobs—an obvious constitutional principle—is also a good political strategy. This hunch, in turn, grows out of the realization that whatever the changes in American government and society since the nation's founding, it is still the Constitution that structures the incentives and shapes the possibilities available to public officials. One of the basic premises of the constitutional scheme was that the "best security for the fidelity of mankind is to make their interest coincide with their duty."[5] Given the current level of dissatisfaction with politics, a reconsideration of this basic principle is in order. To develop these thoughts, I first consider the framers' understanding of both the separation of powers and partisanship. I then turn to the efforts of President Clinton and Speaker Gingrich to reshape the American political landscape. I conclude that each man has operated on a faulty and ultimately self-defeating understanding of his constitutional role.

The Constitution, the Separation of Powers, and Partisanship

The gist of the Wilsonian critique was that the separation of powers reflected an eighteenth-century outlook on politics which embraced the theory of checks and balances. Because the checks-and-balances approach created a cumbersome governmental process, it could not deal adequately with a fundamental fact of political life, namely, change. Change meant, first of all, the necessity of quick and systematic responses to political and social problems. But it also meant that the political system, including the Constitution, must change with the times. After an early embrace of cabinet government, Wilson settled on presidential leadership as the way to make the Constitution adequate to the task of change. He argued that the president must become a popular and national leader for the purpose of imposing order and system on the government's policy agenda. He believed Congress to be simply incapable of order and system. Only the president could provide these qualities. Wilson lamented that since 1789, the president's leadership functions had waxed and waned according to "men and circumstances," that is, according to the talents and abilities of the incumbent and the circumstances that he confronted.[6] Wilson wanted to make presidential leadership the normal state of affairs. His project did not require a new constitution, but it did require that the presidency acquire new sources of power outside of the formal sources of power granted by the Constitution. Perhaps the key task of a Wilsonian president would be the mobilization of public support for a legislative agenda.

While Wilson's progressive agenda was superseded by the New Deal, his reinterpretation of the Constitution has shaped the behavior of most of this century's presidents, both Democrats and Republicans.[7] Because the separation of powers is the most visible obstacle to presidential leadership, it must be acknowledged that Wilson's view of the presidency has contributed greatly to the widespread frustration with the Constitution and with the separation of powers. Furthermore, by making divided government possible, the separation of powers seems, not only to frustrate presidential leadership, but also to incite an unseemly and unproductive level of partisanship. The question is whether Wilson's view of the separation of powers as based simply on the theory of checks and balances is correct. What did the framers have to say about the separation of powers and partisanship?

Separation of Powers

The government of the United States consists of a number of more or less independent parts. Just how these parts constitute a whole is the critical question for evaluating the separation of powers. Focusing solely on the legislative and executive branches and using the *Federalist* as our guide, let us turn to the reasons given by the framers in favor of such a separation. There were two: safety and effectiveness. Separation contributes to the preservation of liberty because it makes less likely dangerous concentrations of power. The framers did not separate powers completely or, in places, all that sharply. They feared the power of the legislative branch above all and, as a result, took steps to strengthen the hands of the other branches through a certain mixing and balancing of powers.[8] In addition, separation, because it assigns to different branches different kinds of tasks, was thought to contribute to safety by making it easier for the public to assign "responsibility"—to praise or blame, and to reward or punish, public officials—for the good or ill that government does.[9] If, for example, the laws are not being well executed, then prima facie the executive is responsible.

The idea that powers are divided by function brings us to the second rationale for a separation of powers: effectiveness. Power was not simply divided; "powers" were divided into their different kinds and assigned to different institutions designed specifically for exercising those particular kinds of powers.[10] As Publius described the distinction between the legislative power and the executive power:

> Those politicians and statesmen who have been most celebrated for the soundness of their principles and the justness of their views have declared in favor of a single executive and a numerous legislature. They have with great propriety, considered energy as the most necessary qualification of the former, and have regarded this as most applicable to power in a single hand; while they have, with equal propriety, considered the latter as best adapted to deliberation and wisdom, and best calculated to conciliate the confidence of the people and to secure their privileges and interests.[11]

The power to legislate was lodged in an institution designed for lawmaking; the executive, in one designed for execution.

Not only does each institution have a distinct character; each has its own distinct sources of support and popularity. The authority (and the pretensions) of the House derive from the frequency with which its members must face the people. For this reason, the House can claim to represent most closely the will of the people. Publius assumed that frequent elections would guarantee that representatives would be impressed with "an habitual recollection of their dependence on the people."[12] By contrast, the president is not, strictly speaking, a popular representative. Although he is elected indirectly by the people, the length of his term of office and his peculiar capacity to act alone create a certain distance between a president and the people. This distance breaks down that "habitual recollection" of the people characteristic of representatives. Over time, however, a president may earn the "respect and attachment of his fellow-citizens" by furnishing "proofs" of his "wisdom and integrity."[13] Above all, a president engenders public support for his administration through his actions or, to use Publius's term, his "energy." As Publius explains matters, the Senate stands somewhere in between the presidency and the House in terms of its sources of support and popularity.[14] The system of government as a whole will have the support and confidence of the people if, over time, it can provide for a sound "administration" of the basic purposes of government.[15]

The effectiveness argument for the separation of powers resembles that for the division of labor in economics. Specialization, as Adam Smith explained, is everywhere productive of efficiency. Yet this view, which is very close to the Whig view of the presidency, is too simple. In the first place, it overlooks the measures, such as the veto power, the framers took to arm the executive branch against encroachments by the legislative branch or, in other words, against a part (Congress) trying to act for the whole (the people). More than this, the president, Publius suggested, may at times represent the people by going against their very wishes. His charge is to represent the "deliberate sense of the community," not its passing whims, however strong.[16]

What of more positive forms of presidential leadership? The Constitution makes presidential leadership possible, but it does not make it inevitable, or even necessary, for the day-to-day functioning of the legislative branch. The president's formal powers in the areas of domestic policy and legislation are few: there is a certain amount of discretion inherent in the power to execute the laws; there is the veto, which can be used to shape legislation; and there are the powers to recommend and to provide information and advice. The president does, however, possess certain advantages over Congress that might be useful in shaping legislation. First, a president will have a certain advantage in terms of knowledge, expertise, and information because of his control of the executive branch. Second, a president can act quickly, decisively, and to some extent secretly, which Congress is almost always incapable of doing. In the right hands and at the right time, the possibilities for presidential leadership are considerable, as Washington (and his Treasury Secretary and Congressional liaison Hamilton) proved from the outset. Despite these advantages and potential advantages, the president's powers are limited. Congress can just say no or it can simply ignore a president. Only when there is some sort of crisis is Congress likely to be moved to act quickly. Even the great Washington was unable to get Congress to follow up on his proposal to establish a national university.

What could be the advantages of such an arrangement? First, it allows for a certain degree of presidential leadership. Second, the scope for such leadership increases in times of crisis, that is, when it is most necessary. Third, the formal powers of the president and his term of office provide him with an institutional base of support that is somewhat independent of public opinion and of Congress. This independence allows him to carry out his clear and unambiguous duties without interference. Where his responsibilities are not so clear, he should act with caution. A president whose reputation is bloodied in a domestic controversy might be reluctant to take warranted risks in foreign policy matters. Fourth, one function of the constitutional scheme was to help check the character defects of officeholders. In the case of the president, the design of the office was intended to make potentially bad presidents better by supporting their virtues and curbing their vices. Outside of the structure of the Constitution, the virtues and vices of a particular president would have free reign. In sum, rather than making government incapable of dealing with change, as Wilson thought, one purpose of the separation of powers was to equip government to deal with the variability of men and circumstances.

Partisanship

Parties and partisanship were clearly frowned upon by the *Federalist*. The violence of party disputes was said to have been the chief cause behind the continual failure of the republican form of government to deliver *good* government.[17] When political parties emerged in the 1790s, the leaders of those parties seem to have sincerely believed that their party's existence would be temporary. Once the fundamental differences of opinion that separated the parties were settled, *these* parties would no longer be necessary and would disappear.[18] But this did not mean that parties would disappear. Indeed, free and republican government meant that parties in some form or another would always be around. As Publius explained in the famous *Federalist* Number 10, there necessarily arises in civilized societies a variety of interests, and furthermore, the "regulation of these various and interfering interests forms the principal task of modern legislation, and involves the spirit of party and faction in the ordinary and necessary operations of government."[19]

Given the distrust of parties, it is not surprising that the Constitution deploys numerous powerful devices designed to break down the influence of parties: representation, bicameralism, federalism, and the separation of powers. The effectiveness of these measures might be judged from the notorious looseness of the American party system. By encouraging delay, reflection, and bargaining, the Constitution aims at insuring that constitutionally formed majorities will be reasonable and moderate. The separation of powers undercuts the influence of parties in two ways. First, it makes it difficult for one part of the government to speak with authority for the whole of the government. If one part is captured by a party that claims it speaks for the whole, the other parts of government need simply to speak up in order to deflate the pretensions of the usurper. The separation of powers plays a second and more subtle role in defeating the influence of party by channeling the ambition of public officials. It is likely that parties will be vehicles for the ambitious. In some situations, however, partisanship is likely to come into conflict with individual ambition. In the case of the president, in particular, the independence guaranteed by his office allows him the option of substantially freeing himself from the ties of party. Mention of the role of ambition is not out of place here. The last four years have been dominated by two very ambitious men who have set as their goal changing the nature of the American political debate: Bill Clinton and Newt Gingrich.

President Clinton: Paradox or Confusion?

Although President Clinton won just 43 percent of the popular vote, hopes were high that he could bring an end to the drift of the Bush era. A large majority of voters (62 percent) had voted against Bush. When Clinton took office, his approval rating was 58 percent.[20] Two features of the new Clinton presidency were cause for optimism. First, he was a self-proclaimed "New Democrat." The New Democrat policy agenda was designed, not only to regain the White House for the Democrats after a long exile, but to address certain long-standing and significant policy problems. Clinton promised to do this by transcending the liberal-conservative dichotomy. It was not that he was going to cease being a Democrat. But as a New Democrat, he was going to correct for the failures of the Old Democrat agenda—chiefly the tax-

and-spend policies associated with big government and the fraying of the social fabric which to some extent he attributed to Old Democrat policies. The paradox involved in the Clinton project was that the problems caused by government were to be attacked with new government programs. Government would be "reinvented" so as to make it both cheaper and more effective.

The paradoxical nature of the New Democrat approach gave rise to another cause for optimism. Since Clinton remained a Democrat, the pairing of a Democratic Congress and a Democratic White House aroused hopes among the public and among partisans that unified government would break gridlock. Clinton fed these hopes. He constantly invoked the images of activist and progressive presidents such as John Kennedy and Franklin Roosevelt. His inaugural address stressed again and again the need for "change," even "dramatic change." Indeed, during the campaign he had promised to have a "100 day" burst of change in the manner of Franklin Roosevelt's first term. These hopes have been disappointed. It was not that Clinton and the 103rd Congress accomplished nothing. Significant legislation, such as the Family and Medical Leave Act, that was left over from previous Democratic congresses was passed. Parts of the president's own agenda, including a deficit reduction package and a national service program, were also passed. Despite these achievements, Clinton's New Democrat project foundered in the earthquake congressional election of 1994. This setback hardly dooms his political chances for the future, but it is does mean that an opportunity to experiment with a new approach to real problems was lost or, perhaps, even frittered away.

The troubles of the Clinton administration were partly the product of the circumstances in which the president found himself when he took office. They were also partly the result of the president's strategic and tactical responses to these circumstances.[21] With regard to the former, two circumstances deserve mention: first, the wake of Ross Perot's antideficit campaign in 1992 and, second, the Old Democrat domination of the 103rd Congress. Ross Perot's 19 percent of the vote in 1992 was an indicator of the large number of voters who were disaffected with the major parties and for whom the deficit was a critical issue. If Clinton was to win reelection, he would somehow have to make sure he had their vote in 1996. The second circumstance was that Clinton took charge of a congressional Democratic Party that for two decades had subscribed to the Whig view of the presidency. And while the congressional Democrats had no desire to repeat the embarrassments of the Carter era, it was to a significant degree opposed in principle to presidential leadership. Furthermore, with regard to ideology, Clinton took office with no clear governing majority in either house of Congress. The congressional Democratic Party was lopsidedly Old Democrat in its leanings. The election did make Congress keenly aware of the deficit problem, but Congress was still wedded to old spending priorities. Thus, Clinton was presented with a choice of siding with the more powerful Old Democrats and forsaking his New Democrat agenda or taking the more risky course of staying with his New Democrat agenda despite its limited power base in Congress. That the Republican minority, especially in the Senate, was in a position to cause problems for the new administration only compounded this more fundamental problem.

The reasons behind the Clinton administration's inability to deal with these difficult circumstances were numerous. Many have been dealt with at length by scholars and journalists.[22] Simple ineptitude played a role. As did a very sloppy White House organization. For present purposes, three causes deserve extended attention: first, the policy paradox involved in the New Democrat agenda revealed itself to be policy incoherence; second, Clinton acted on the basis of a self-defeating understanding of the role of the president; and third, Clinton's "character" played a role in his fortunes. Of the three, Clinton's understanding of the role of the president was most critical because it exacerbated the other two.

Perhaps the New Democrat agenda might be revived in the future, but as it was practiced by the Clinton administration, it was more an unstable alloy than a pure metal: it was so many parts Old Democrat and so many parts moderate Republican. Lurking in the background here is the difficult question of what were the president's core beliefs. Was he really a New Democrat? Or an Old Democrat in disguise? Or simply confused? Whatever the answers to these questions, the administration proved to have great difficulty getting the mix right to satisfy a majority in Congress and in the public. The deficit situation turned out to be critical for revealing the administration's policy incoherence. Between the election and the inauguration, the deficit outlook worsened, which made it even more difficult both to fulfill Clinton's campaign promises and to meet deficit reduction targets. A campaign promise for a middle-class tax cut was quickly dropped. Other campaign promises had to be scaled down in order to put together a viable economic plan. Partly by choice and partly by necessity, the president relied solely on congressional Democrats to squeak out a victory for his first year's economic program. In the process, however, he suffered severely, not only at the hands of the Republican minority in the Senate, but also at the hands of his ostensible ideological allies, conservative congressional Democrats. His short-term economic stimulus package was killed, as were new broad-based energy taxes, and Congress cut expenditures to a point that deeply compromised the president's key campaign promise of increasing public investment.

Rather than scale down expectations about his presidency, Clinton forged ahead, redoubling his efforts to prove that government could work. In what was possibly the critical decision of his first two years, he made health care reform, rather than welfare reform, his first priority.[23] There seem to have been two reasons behind the decision. First and most clearly, welfare reform as Clinton envisaged it would cost, rather than save, money. That made it a problem for the deficit. Second, Clinton seems to have felt that the budget process had pushed him too far to the right. *Washington Post* reporter Bob Woodward relates that at one meeting, Clinton exploded at the thought of his agenda slipping away. "We're all Eisenhower Republicans," he remarked with bitter sarcasm.[24] To reestablish his reformist principles and the public legitimacy of governmental activism, he needed a big score. Perhaps welfare reform seemed just too Republican an issue.

Creating an entitlement to health care was a decidedly Old Democrat idea. Health care reform would continue the process, begun by Roosevelt, of tying society to government through entitlements. Furthermore, Clinton ruled out an incrementalist approach because it would not regain the policy initiative. Only a big and bold victory that guaranteed universal health care coverage would remove the taint of Eisenhowerism. The New Democrat dimension to the health care reform was to be the means for guaranteeing universal coverage. The starting point of the administration's health care reform plan was the notion of "managed competition," which used market incentives and mechanisms to expand coverage and reduce costs. The administration would guarantee *private* health insurance. That was the starting point anyway. The end result was something quite different. The final plan was a bewildering concoction of regulations and government programs. A bizarre process of secret meetings, in addition to technocratic hubris, contributed to the shape of the final plan, but perhaps no other outcome was possible given the goal of universal coverage.

The health care reform effort put on display many of the pathologies of the modern presidency.[25] A health care crisis was declared. A plan was conceived for dealing with the crisis. The president (and the first lady) went to Congress and the people to build public support for the plan. Congress balked.[26] The public's expectations were disappointed. The health care debacle was, however, a symptom of a larger problem. Indeed, for much of his first two years in office, Clinton appeared to be a parody of a modern president. It is often said that Clinton governed as he campaigned, but it must be added that the perpetual campaign is a natural outgrowth of the modern idea of the president as a national popular leader. He made many public appearances, traveled widely (within the United States), and held economic summits, "spotted owl" summits, Oval Office broadcasts, town meetings, and even jogging summits with critical members of Congress. As his aides finally came to realize, the president was "over-exposed"—the problem that frequently besets Hollywood celebrities. The president's hyperactivity did not translate into public or congressional support for his agenda. Consequently, he was forced to fall back on congressional Democrats. As I have noted, they were not inclined to let him suffer Jimmy Carter's fate, but the price of cooperation was high. The many "near death" experiences of the president's legislative agenda highlighted for the general public his utter dependence on Congress.[27] As a result, his enlistment of Republicans to support passage of the North American Free Trade Agreement seemed to be an act of desperation rather than bipartisanship.

A third problem for the Clinton administration was the president's character. During the campaign, many questions had been raised about Clinton's character both as a private man and as a leader. The surprise has been that what were thought to be his character strengths turned out to be mixed blessings.[28] Clinton's undeniable ability to think and talk at will about policy issues did not translate into an ability to make policy. He tended to think out loud and to talk more in the manner of a college professor than a chief executive. Furthermore, the hope that, unlike Carter, he would be sensitive to the nuances of the political process also proved to have a downside. In particular, Clinton turned out to be hypersensitive to public opinion. One symptom of this was that even as president, he continued to spend extraordinary sums on polling.[29] Clinton's understanding of the presidency put these private uncertainties on public display. His frequent position shifts and constant chatter undermined the public's confidence in him as a leader.

What alternative strategies were available? One surprising feature of the Clinton administration has been that for all its grand ambition, at times it has shown a remarkable lack of daring. On the critical issue of the budget deficit, it allowed itself to be hemmed in by Wall Street and Ross Perot when the underlying premises of Clinton's public investment program suggested quite clearly that the deficit was not the most important economic indicator. The first lady and Clinton's political advisors saw the deficit reduction package as a kind of gesture to appease a nervous Wall Street. But in retrospect, it turned out to be a gesture that cost them their agenda.[30]

Another approach would have involved distancing himself from Congress and pursuing a limited agenda more in keeping with the political resources he had available to him and with his designated constitutional role. This "less is more" approach might have been the more prudent course given the limited power base he had in Congress and in the public. Clinton could then have used the distance that the Constitution creates for the office of the president to begin gradually to build support for *his* agenda. As it was, he collapsed the distance between himself and both Congress and the American people. A concomitant of his approach to the presidency was a lamentable neglect of foreign policy. One sign of this was that while Clinton traveled constantly, he seldom ventured abroad. It is worth observing that Clinton's rise in the polls in late 1995 and early 1996 seems to have been due to two developments. First, the president began to take a higher profile in foreign affairs. It is paradoxical but hardly unintelligible that he seems to have benefited politically from taking the unpopular stand of dispatching troops to Bosnia. The second source of his new-found success seems to have been his deft usage of the veto in the budget battle with the Republican Congress, placing himself on the side of the people against their representatives. Both these actions have relied, for the most part, on the formal powers of the presidency.[31]

Speaker Gingrich: Clarity or Delusion?

Speaker Gingrich could not be accused of lacking either ambition or daring. He labored for more than a decade, in the face of opposition from both Democrats and moderate Republicans, to bring the Republican Party within striking distance of gaining control of Congress. As the 1994 midterm elections approached, only he and a few close confidants saw the opportunity presented by an unpopular president, the appearance of gridlock, and a scandal-ridden Congress. The Republicans stormed to power, taking the Senate and the House, the latter for the first time in forty years. It was a stunning victory. The Republicans were able to nationalize the elections in a way that defied the "all politics is local"/"pork barrel" electoral logic of recent decades. They won by making Washington liberalism and Bill Clinton the issues and now claimed that they had the mandate for change.[32]

Gingrich explained the mandate in terms of the Contract with America.[33] On September 27, 1994, some 367 Republican candidates for the House signed the contract (61 percent of signatories were successful).[34] It spelled out an agenda that the signatories promised to bring up for a vote in the House. There was not much in the contract that was novel. Even the idea of a contract was an old one. Gingrich had considered it during the 1992 campaign. The contract contained measures aimed at making government smaller, devolving power to the states, increasing personal responsibility, and restoring public confidence in government. It also proposed a balanced budget amendment. Republicans could be certain that there would be wide public support for most of these measures. Perot voters were a special target. To maximize its appeal, the contract avoided unnecessary controversy. Although it contained a proposal for a balanced budget amendment, it did not say just how the budget would be balanced and thereby avoided the controversial issue of the entitlement spending that lies behind the deficit. Just as significantly, the contract avoided completely the more controversial social issues such as abortion. While studies have shown that most voters were unaware of the contract, they probably understate its impact.[35] The contract provided a framework of ideas that Republican candidates used whether or not they explicitly mentioned the contract. The large number of signatories to the contract was an indication of the extent to which the Republican Party had become the ideological and disciplined party that Gingrich had been working to create. It was also a measure of Gingrich's personal influence over what would become the first Republican House in forty years.

Gingrich and the Republicans claimed that the election result was a mandate to implement the contract. There was nothing new about claiming a large electoral victory as a mandate for change. Thomas Jefferson perhaps began the practice by describing the election of 1800 as a "revolution."[36] Nevertheless, the Republican response to their victory was unprecedented. The so-called Republican revolution of 1994 presumed congressional government of a new sort. First, the House of Representatives would take the lead. Second, the Speaker would lead the House. Finally, all would be conducted with the kind of order and system associated with the executive branch. Like the

Clinton administration, the contract set a hundred-day FDR-style time frame for bringing the contract items up for a vote in the House.

By early 1996, the Republican revolution was faltering and its future uncertain. It and, in particular, Speaker Gingrich stumbled for three reasons: overreading their mandate, following a flawed strategy for restoring confidence in Congress, and exaggerating the power of the House. The Republicans overread their mandate by mixing talk of the contract with talk of a "Republican revolution." In addition, the social issues that the contract avoided quickly entered the congressional agenda. Indeed, Speaker Gingrich identified the Republican revolution with his own very broad cause of "renewing American civilization." Talk of a revolution came very naturally to the Speaker, who for years had practiced a kind of politics that shunned congressional pieties about comity and compromise. It also served a valuable partisan purpose of galvanizing Republicans into a formidable political force. This was of critical importance for Gingrich in view of the slim majorities the Republicans held in both houses.

But proclaiming a revolution was risky. The limited nature of the contract's commitment—bringing up the items for a vote in the House—was forgotten. House Republicans engaged in the kind of overpromising that had previously been reserved for presidential campaigns. Furthermore, there was always something a little strained about claiming an off-year election, however dramatic and surprising the result, as a mandate for a revolution. Hence, the Republicans placed themselves in a very vulnerable position. They created unrealistic expectations of change, and at the same time, they unsettled the public with their talk of a congressionally led revolution. One further consequence of replacing the contract with the revolution was that the 1996 presidential election did not seem to figure in Republican strategy. That a Republican realignment had taken place seemed to be taken for granted. (In this regard, however, it is possible that the Speaker's own presidential ambitions may have entered into his strategy of leading the Republican revolution from the Speaker's chair.) By way of contrast, Jefferson's approach to his own large and unquestionable electoral mandate is worth noting. In public, he downplayed the nature of the revolution. His words were reassuring: "We are all republicans—we are all federalists."[37] But in his capacity as president, as well as behind the scenes, he set about systematically reshaping American politics.

The second difficulty with the Republican revolution was the approach taken to the obviously laudable objective of restoring trust in government. The contract strategy in this regard was twofold: first, the

House would reform itself, and second, it would get government moving again. The contract contained, and the House quickly passed, measures to make Congress cheaper, more open, and more accountable. These measures gained considerable bipartisan support, and the initial public reaction was also positive. There was, however, one significant exception. The term limits item of the contract, which was the most visible and popular measure designed to restore confidence in government, garnered a bare majority, well short of the two-thirds vote needed to move a constitutional amendment.

The second element of the strategy for restoring confidence was to get government moving again. Here, too, there were problems. To begin with, although the House completed work on the contract in just ninety-seven days, the reforms contained measures that will make getting things done more difficult in the future. Opening up floor debate and ending proxy voting, for example, were two measures that made government more open and accountable, but they will necessarily slow the business of government. Perhaps more importantly, an unstated premise of the contract was that the business of Congress could be made attractive and respectable in the eyes of the public. Congress's approval ratings did double in the first hundred days. But this was from a very low base, and furthermore, Congress's approval rating began to slide back towards its 1994 low.[38] The problem is that no amount of reform will make Congress or, more precisely, what Congress does pretty. Lawmaking is a difficult, noisy, time-consuming, and messy process. Congress is neither an elegant debating society nor an institution designed for decisive action. It is a deliberative institution that establishes a process for lawmaking. Shining a bright light on this process is surely in the public interest; keeping members honest, even more so. But it is simply unrealistic to think that the public will find it attractive. This became clear as Congress began to deal with the more difficult and controversial measures implied by, rather than stated in, the contract, such as just how to balance the budget.

A third and fundamental difficulty was that the Republican revolution attempted to substitute a part of government for the whole. Put simply, it exaggerated the power of the House. It was well known that Senate Republicans were lukewarm about the contract. The Democratic minority, to say nothing of the Democrat in the White House, had little interest in expediting passage of even popular contract items. The role Speaker Gingrich assumed in this process deserves special mention. The office of Speaker is mentioned in the Constitution: he is to be chosen by members, but his powers are not specified. By tradition, the Speaker is a partisan quasi-executive who, while entrusted with seeing that the rules of the House are followed, is also charged with getting things done. As a rule, however, the Speaker has proved to be a very weak executive. The reason for the Speaker's weakness is clear and is the same as that which led the framers to reject an executive chosen by Congress. Such an executive would simply be too dependent on the legislature to execute his office and, when necessary, provide leadership.[39] The Speaker, whatever powers the House might from time to time give him, always remains a creature of the House.[40]

By late 1995, the intrinsic limitations of the Speaker's powers were beginning to show. This was particularly the case with the Speaker's strategy of "going public." Gingrich acted as though he were an alternative president or, perhaps, a prime minister. Like many recent presidents, he invoked the rhetoric of crisis to build public support: "No civilization can survive with 12-year-olds having babies, with 15-year-olds killing each other, with 17-year-olds dying of AIDS, with 18-year-olds getting diplomas they can't read."[41] At the conclusion of the contract period, he took the unprecedented step of addressing the nation—Oval Office-style. In general, he was constantly available to the press, sharing his ideas, his whimsies, and his personal turmoil. Gingrich, like Clinton—both are former college professors and both are baby boomers—displayed a tendency to talk to anybody who would listen, and especially about himself.[42] The Speakership, however, has little of the inherent or accumulated dignity of the presidency. What it has is, therefore, more quickly spent. Worse still, because the Speaker has few opportunities to capture the national stage, he has few opportunities to recover from missteps. When Gingrich complained that he had been confined to the back of the plane on the way to the funeral of slain Israeli Prime Minister Yitzhak Rabin, he looked childish. Much worse for Gingrich, however, was that his quip was juxtaposed with the president's moving speech at the funeral in which he spoke for the American people.

Conclusion: Less Is More

The experience of the last four years has shown the limitations of gridlock both as a partisan issue and as an intellectual concept. It has also shown the dangers of overpromising. Overpromising is a danger at any time, but it is a particular danger now because the public mood is so unsettled. To an important degree, the epidemic of overpromising and the widespread frustration with gridlock both grow out of a failure to recognize that the separation of powers places limits on what each part of government can accomplish by itself.

The unified government that Clinton took charge of was only nominally so. Beneath the surface were deep divisions within his own party and within society at large. Clinton failed to use the independence from the people and the Congress that the Constitution provides to make the best of his situation. As result, his agenda for confronting the problems that have bedeviled liberals and conservatives was discredited. Speaker Gingrich and the Republicans have also been guilty of overpromising. Their project of a Republican revolution was based on the impossibility that the House could speak and act for the whole government. Gingrich acted as a prime minister or president. His goal of beginning to restore confidence in government by following the simple "promises made promises kept" strategy of the contract was obscured in the excitement of the moment.

Both Clinton and Gingrich seem to have been tempted to stray from their constitutional roles by the plebiscitarian tendencies of the times. A plebiscitary democracy is completely open to change, in any direction and at any time. It has been the Constitution that has so far held these tendencies in check. One suspects that the sound of gridlock breaking would, in effect, be the sound of the Constitution breaking. The Constitution was designed, not to prevent change, but to provide a structure in which debate about the *proper* direction of change could take place. The Constitution, while acknowledging that it is human nature to seek to acquire power, begs public officials to do their constitutionally assigned jobs. It does this by connecting their interest with their duty. Whether government is divided or unified, this structure of incentives will remain in place. The fortunes of Clinton and Gingrich suggest that the constitutional structure of rewards and punishments is still relevant.

The strategy of doing one's job is open to the charge that it will lead to "lowballing," that is, understating what one ought to be held responsible for. This is possible, but in assessing the danger, one must bear in mind the present situation. The public's expectations of government are very low. This state of affairs is, to a large extent, the result of government having established expectations it cannot meet.[43] Ironically, lowering expectations might be necessary to begin to restore confidence in government.

Notes

1. Walter Bagehot, *The English Constitution* (Ithaca: Cornell University Press, 1966); Woodrow Wilson, *Congressional Government: A Study in American Politics* (Baltimore: Johns Hopkins University Press, 1981); idem, *Constitutional Government in the United States* (1908; reprint, New York: Columbia University Press, 1917).

2. See, for example, Daniel Lazare, *The Frozen Republic: How the Constitution Is Paralyzing Democracy* (New York: Harcourt Brace, 1996). Two influential statements about the need for reform are found in Lloyd N. Cutler, "To Form a Government," *Foreign Affairs* 59 (fall 1980): 126–43; and James L. Sundquist, *Constitutional Reform and Effective Government* (Washington, D.C.: Brookings Institution, 1986).

3. See especially Michael J. Malbin, "Was Divided Government Really Such a Big Problem?" in *Separation of Powers and Good Government*, ed. Peter W. Schramm and Bradford P. Wilson (Lanham, Md.: Rowman & Littlefield, 1994), 219–40.

4. For a defense of the separation of powers along these lines, see James Ceaser, "In Defense of the Separation of Powers," in *Separation of Powers: Does it Still Work?* ed. Robert A. Goldwin and Art Kaufman (Washington, D.C.: American Enterprise Institute, 1986), 168–93; and James Q. Wilson, "Does the Separation of Powers Still Work?" *Public Interest* 86 (winter 1987): 35–62.

5. Alexander Hamilton, John Jay, and James Madison, *The Federalist Papers*, ed. Clinton Rossiter (New York: Mentor, 1961), *Federalist* No. 72, p. 437.

6. Wilson, *Constitutional Government*, 59.

7. For an account of the modern presidency that stresses Wilson's role in establishing the president as a national and popular leader, see Jeffrey K. Tulis, *The Rhetorical Presidency* (Princeton: Princeton University Press, 1987).

8. *Federalist* Nos. 47–51.

9. Ibid. No. 70, p. 427.

10. According to Herbert J. Storing, "[t]his division is not aimed primarily at mutual checking but at the efficient performance of certain kinds of tasks." *What the Anti-Federalists Were For* (Chicago: University of Chicago Press, 1981), 60. In general, see David F. Epstein, *The Political Theory of The Federalist* (Chicago: University of Chicago Press, 1984), 126–46, 162–92. For an extended discussion of Hamilton's view of how a separation of powers might contribute to efficiency, see Harvey Flaumenhaft, *The Effective Republic: Administration and Constitution in the Thought of Alexander Hamilton* (Durham, N.C.: Duke University Press, 1992).

11. *Federalist* No. 70, p. 424.

12. Ibid. No. 57, p. 352.

13. Ibid. No. 71, pp. 434–35.

14. Ibid. Nos. 62–63.

15. Ibid. No. 17, p. 27.

16. Ibid. No. 71, p. 432.

17. Ibid. Nos. 9–10.

18. See James Roger Sharp, *American Politics in the Early Republic: The New Nation in Crisis* (New Haven: Yale University Press, 1993). The bitterness of these early party disputes should not be understated as we consider today's party squabbles.

19. *Federalist* No. 10, p. 79.

20. The many ups and downs of Clinton's approval ratings are charted by George C. Edwards, III, "Frustration and Folly: Bill Clinton and the Public Presidency," in *The Clinton Presidency: First Appraisals*, ed. Colin Campbell and Bert A. Rockman (Chatham, N.J.: Chatham House, 1996), 235–39.

21. Charles O. Jones attributes the misfortunes of the Clinton presidency to a mismatch between its agenda and the "status and resources" it began with. "Campaigning to Govern: The Clinton Style," in *Clinton Presidency*, ed. Campbell and Rockman, 15–50. The framework for his insightful analysis is contained in his *The Presidency in a Separated System* (Washington, D.C.: Brookings Institution, 1994).

22. Two engaging and often humorous accounts by journalists are found in Elizabeth Drew, *On the Edge: The Clinton Presidency* (New York: Simon & Schuster, 1994); and Bob Woodward, *The Agenda: Inside the Clinton White House* (New York: Simon & Schuster, 1994). For scholarly accounts, see the essays in *Clinton Presidency*, ed. Campbell and Rockman.

23. Mickey Kaus, "They Blew It," *New Republic*, 5 December 1994, 14–19.

24. Woodward, *The Agenda*, 185.

25. On this general subject, see Tulis, *Rhetorical Presidency*, and Jones, *Presidency in a Separated System*.

26. It was *Democratic* Senator Daniel Patrick Moynihan of New York who was one of the first to burst the crisis bubble. Not only did he do it on national television; he drew attention to what he thought was the real crisis—welfare—which the president was neglecting. Paul J. Quirk and Joseph Hinchcliffe, "Domestic Policy: The Trials of a Centrist Democrat," in *The Clinton Presidency*, ed. Campbell and Rockman, 276.

27. Democratic Senator John Kerrey of Nebraska cast the critical vote for Clinton's 1993 economic plan. But before doing so, he delivered a bitter speech in which he said that although he disagreed with the plan, he would not cast the vote that would "bring down" the Clinton presidency. The speech and the events surrounding it are recounted by Woodward, *The Agenda*, 362–64.

28. Cf. Bert A. Rockman, "Leadership Style and the Clinton Presidency," in *Clinton Presidency*, ed. Campbell and Rockman, 347.

29. "George Bush spent $216, 000 for public opinion polls in 1989 and 1990, while Clinton spent $1,986,410 in 1993 alone." Edwards, "Frustration and Folly," 234.

30. Woodward, *The Agenda*, 187.

31. For the advantages of using the formal powers of the presidency, see Terry Eastland, *Energy in the Executive: The Case for a Strong Presidency* (New York: Free Press, 1992).

32. For the background to the Republican victory, see Dan Balz and Ronald Brownstein, *Storming the Gates: Protest Politics and the Republican Revival* (Boston: Little, Brown & Co, 1996).

33. The background to the contract and an account of its passage through the House may be found in James G. Gimpel, *Fulfilling the Contract: The First 100 Days* (Boston: Allyn & Bacon, 1996).

34. Ibid., 8.

35. Cf. Gary C. Jacobson, "The 1994 Elections in Perspective," in *Midterm: The Elections of 1994 in Context*, ed. Philip A. Klinkner (Boulder, Colo.: Westview, 1996), 6–7.

36. Thomas Jefferson to Spencer Roane, 6 September 1819, *The Portable Jefferson*, ed. Merrill D. Peterson (New York: Viking Press, 1975), 562. See also Jefferson to Joseph Priestly, 21 March 1801, ibid., 483–85.

37. Thomas Jefferson, "First Inaugural Address," 4 March 1801, *The Portable Jefferson*, ed. Peterson, 292.

38. Gimpel, *Fulfilling the Contract*, 126–27; CNN/*USA Today*/Gallup Poll, 9–10 April 1996.

39. See especially the remarks of Gouveneur Morris and James Wilson, 17 and 24 July 1787, at the Federal Convention found in James Madison, *Notes of the Debates in the Federal Convention of 1787 Reported by James Madison* (New York: W. W. Norton, 1969), 288–97, 356–53.

40. Gingrich took a number of steps that enhanced the power of the Speaker, especially in relation to committee chairs. The powers of committee chairs were limited. Freshman members, beholden to the Speaker, were given plum committee assignments. A kind of cabinet (the Speaker's Advisory Group) was established to coordinate the House's business and offset the power of committee chairs. See Gimpel, *Fulfilling the Contract*, 31–41; and David Rogers, "General Newt," *Wall Street Journal*, 18 December 1995, 1.

41. Newt Gingrich, "Address to the Nation," 7 April 1995.

42. After a bruising budget battle with the president, during which the Republicans suffered badly, Gingrich gave an extraordinary interview to the *Washington Post* in which he revealed that the ordeal, especially the ethical questions raised about him, had reduced him to tears. *Washington Post National Weekly Edition*, 29 January–4 February 1996, 6–13.

43. The problem of lowering expectations is intimately bound up with the question of how to curtail what Sidney M. Milkis has called the "administrative state." See his essay in this volume and his *The President and the Parties: The Transformation of the American Party System since the New Deal* (New York: Oxford University Press, 1993). See also Robert Samuelson, *The Good Life and Its Discontents: The American Dream in the Age of Entitlements, 1945–1995* (New York: Times Books, 1995).

Bibliography

Abramowitz, Alan, and Jeffrey Segal. *Senate Elections*. Ann Arbor: University of Michigan Press, 1995.

Abramson, Paul R., John H. Aldrich, and David W. Rohde. *Change and Continuity in the 1992 Elections*. Washington, D.C.: Congressional Quarterly Press, 1994.

Alesina, Alberto, and Howard Rosenthal. "Partisan Cycles in Congressional Elections and the Macroeconomy." *American Political Science Review* 83 (1989): 373–98.

Alt, James E., and Robert C. Lowry. "Divided Government, Fiscal Institutions, and Budget Deficits: Evidence from the States." *American Political Science Review* 88 (1994): 811–28.

Alvarez, R. Michael, and Matthew M. Schousen. "Policy Moderation or Conflicting Expectations? Testing Intentional Models of Split-Ticket Voting." *American Politics Quarterly* 21 (1993): 410–38.

Arnold, R. Douglas. *The Logic of Congressional Action*. New Haven: Yale University Press, 1990.

Bagehot, Walter. *The English Constitution*. Ithaca: Cornell University Press, 1966.

Balz, Dan, and Ronald Brownstein. *Storming the Gates: Protest Politics and the Republican Revival*. Boston: Little, Brown & Co., 1996.

Barone, Michael, and Grant Ujifusa. *The Almanac of American Politics, 1994*. Washington, D.C.: National Journal, 1993.

Beer, Samuel. "In Search of a New Public Philosophy." In *The New American Political System*, edited by Anthony King. Washington, D.C.: American Enterprise Institute, 1979.

Bendiner, Robert. *Obstacle Course on Capitol Hill*. New York: McGraw Hill, 1964.

Benenson, Bob. "GATT Pact Lurches Off Course as Hollings Hits the Brake." *Congressional Quarterly Weekly Report*, 1 October 1994, 2761–64.

———. "Free Trade Carries the Day as GATT Easily Passes." *Congressional Quarterly Weekly Report*, 3 December 1994, 3446–50.

213

Bergeron, Paul. *The Presidency of James K. Polk.* Lawrence: University Press of Kansas, 1987.

Berke, Richard L. "Epic Political Realignments Often Aren't." *New York Times*, 1 January 1995, sec. 4, p. 3.

Black, Duncan. *The Theory of Committees and Elections.* Cambridge: Cambridge University Press, 1958.

Black, Gordon, and Benjamin Black. *The Politics of American Discontent: How a New Party Can Make Democracy Work.* New York: Wiley, 1994.

Blumenthal, Sidney. "Bob Dole's First Strike." *New Yorker*, 3 May 1993, 40–46.

Bond, Jon R., and Richard A. Fleisher. *The President in the Legislative Arena.* Chicago: University of Chicago Press, 1990.

Born, Richard. "Split-Ticket Voters, Divided Government, and Fiorina's Policy-Balancing Model." *Legislative Studies Quarterly* 19 (1994): 95–115 ("Rejoinder" at 126–29).

Bowman, Karlyn. "Public Attitudes on Health Care Reform: Are the Polls Misleading the Policy Makers?" Washington, D.C.: American Enterprise Institute, 1994.

Brinkley, Alan. "Roots." *New Republic*, 27 July 1992.

———. "The 43 Percent President." *New York Times Magazine*, 4 July 1993, 22.

Broder, David. *Boston Globe*, 20 December 1995, 15.

Burnham, Walter Dean. *Critical Elections and the Mainsprings of American Politics.* New York: W. W. Norton, 1970.

———. *The Current Crisis in American Politics.* New York: Oxford University Press, 1982.

———. "Critical Realignment: Dead or Alive?" In *The End of Realignment?: Interpreting American Electoral Eras,* edited by Bryon Shafer. Madison: University of Wisconsin Press, 1991.

Burtless, Gary. "Worsening American Income Inequality." *The Brookings Review* 14 (spring 1996), 29.

Campbell, Angus, et al. *The American Voter.* New York: Wiley, 1960.

———. *Elections and the Political Order.* New York: Wiley, 1966.

Campbell, Colin, and Bert A. Rockman, eds. *The Clinton Presidency: First Appraisals.* Chatham, N.J.: Chatham House, 1996.

Ceaser, James. "The Theory of Governance of the Reagan Administration." In *The Reagan Presidency and the Governing of America,* edited by Lester M. Salamon and Michael S. Lund. Washington, D.C.: Urban Institute, 1981.

———. "In Defense of the Separation of Powers." In *Separation of Powers: Does It Still Work?,* edited by Robert A. Goldwin and Art Kaufman. Washington, D.C.: American Enterprise Institute, 1986.

Chambers, William N., and Walter D. Burnham, eds. *The American Party Systems; Stages of Political Development.* 2d ed. New York: Oxford University Press, 1975.

Clinton, William. "The New Covenant: Responsibility and Rebuilding the American Community." Washington, D.C., 23 October 1991.

———. "Address before a Joint Session of Congress on Administration Goals." *Weekly Compilation of Presidential Documents*, 17 February 1993, 215–24.

———. "Address before a Joint Session of Congress on Health Care Reform." Printed in *Congressional Quarterly Weekly Report*, 25 September 1993, 2582–86.

———. "Address before a Joint Session of Congress on the State of the Union." Printed in *Congressional Quarterly Weekly Report*, 25 January 1994, 194–98.

———. "Address before a Joint Session of Congress on the State of the Union." Printed in *Congressional Quarterly Weekly Report*, 27 January 1996, 258–62.

Cloud, David S. "The Final Hours." *Congressional Quarterly Weekly Report*, 29 May 1993, 1343.

———. "As NAFTA Countdown Begins, Wheeling, Dealing Intensifies." *Congressional Quarterly Weekly Report*, 13 November 1993, 3104–7.

———. "Decisive Vote Brings Down Trade Walls with Mexico." *Congressional Quarterly Weekly Report*, 20 November 1993, 3174–78.

———. "Routine Approval in Senate Wraps Up NAFTA Fight." *Congressional Quarterly Weekly Report*, 27 November 1993, 3257.

———. "Leaders Turn To Arm-Twisting to Pass Gift Ban in House." *Congressional Quarterly Weekly Report*, 1 October 1994, 2756.

———. "End of Session Marked by Partisan Stalemate." *Congressional Quarterly Weekly Report*, 8 October 1994, 2847–49.

———. "GOP and Interest Groups Dig In To Dump Gift Ban in Senate." *Congressional Quarterly Weekly Report*, 8 October 1994, 2854–55.

———. "Health Care's Painful Demise Cast Pall on Clinton Agenda." *Congressional Quarterly Weekly Report*, 5 November 1994, 3142–45.

Clymer, Adam, Robert Pear, and Robin Toner. "For Health Care, Time Was a Killer." *New York Times*, 29 August 1994, A1, A8.

Clymer, Adam. "National Health Program, President's Greatest Goal, Declared Dead in Congress." *New York Times*, 27 September 1994, A1, B10.

———. "Politics and the Dead Arts of Compromise." *New York Times, News of The Week in Review*, 22 October 1995, 1.

Cohen, Richard E. "The Transformers." *National Journal*, 4 March 1995, 528–29, 531.

Cohen, Richard E., and William Schneider. "Voting in Unison." *National Journal*, 27 January 1996, 179–85.

Cole, Donald B. *The Presidency of Andrew Jackson*. Lawrence: University Press of Kansas, 1993.

Coletta, Paolo E. *The Presidency of William Howard Taft*. Lawrence: University Press of Kansas, 1973.

Congressional Record. 75th Congress, 3d Session. 8 April 1938.

Congressional Quarterly Weekly Report. "Assessing the 103rd Congress . . . What Passed and What Didn't." 5 November 1994, 3146–47.

———. "Guide to CQ's Voting Analyses."31 December 1994, 3651–78.

———. "Congressional Departures." 13 April 1996, 1005.

Cook, Rhodes. "DNC Under Wilhelm Seeking A New Role." *Congressional Quarterly Weekly Report,* 13 March 1993, 634.

Council of State Governments. *The Book of the States, 1990 and 1992.* Lexington, Ky.: The Council of State Governments.

Cox, Gary W., and Samuel Kernell, eds. *The Politics of Divided Government.* Boulder, Colo.: Westview, 1991.

Cox, Gary W., and Mathew D. McCubbins. "Divided Control of Fiscal Policy." In *The Politics of Divided Government,* edited by Gary W. Cox and Samuel Kernell. Boulder, Colo.: Westview, 1991.

———. *Legislative Leviathan: Party Government in the House.* Berkeley: University of California Press, 1993.

Croly, Herbert. *Progressive Democracy.* New York: Macmillan, 1914.

———. *The Promise of American Life.* New York: Macmillan, 1909; New York: Dutton, 1963.

Cushman, John H., Jr. "How New Congress Limits Administration." *New York Times,* 14 November 1994, B8.

Cutler, Lloyd N. "To Form a Government." *Foreign Affairs* 59 (fall 1980): 126–43.

———. "Some Reflections About Divided Government." *Presidential Studies Quarterly* 18 (1988): 387–402.

"Democratic Platform of 1936." In *National Party Platforms,* edited by Donald Bruce Johnson. Urbana: University of Illinois Press, 1978.

Derthick, Martha. *Policymaking for Social Security.* Washington, D.C.: Brookings Institution, 1983, quoting Franklin D. Roosevelt.

Dilulio, John J., and Donald Kettl. *The Contract with America, Devolution, and the Administrative Realities of American Federalism.* Washington, D.C.: Brookings Institution, 1995.

Doenecke, Justus D. *The Presidencies of James A. Garfield And Chester Alan Arthur.* Lawrence: University Press of Kansas, 1981.

Dole, Robert. "Republican Response to President Clinton's State of the Union Message." Printed in *Congressional Quarterly Weekly Report,* 29 January 1996, 262–63.

Donovan, Beth. "Republicans Plan Filibusters, Imperiling Senate Schedule." *Congressional Quarterly Weekly Report,* 24 September 1994, 2655.

———. "Democrats' Overhaul Bill Dies on Senate Procedural Votes." *Congressional Quarterly Weekly Report,* 1 October 1994, 2757–58.

Downs, Anthony. *An Economic Theory of Democracy.* New Haven: Yale University Press, 1957.

Drew, Elizabeth. *On the Edge: The Clinton Presidency.* New York: Simon & Schuster, 1994.

Duncan, Phil, and Steve Langdon. "When Congress Had to Choose, It Voted to Back Clinton." *Congressional Quarterly Weekly Report*, 18 December 1993, 3427–34.

Eastland, Terry. *Energy in the Executive: The Case for a Strong Presidency*. New York: Free Press, 1992.

Edwards, George C., III. *At the Margins: Presidential Leadership of Congress*. New Haven: Yale University Press, 1989.

———. "Frustration and Folly: Bill Clinton and the Public Presidency." In *The Clinton Presidency: First Appraisals*, edited by Colin Campbell and Bert A. Rockman. Chatham, N.J.: Chatham House, 1996.

Ehrenhalt, Alan. *The United States of Ambition: Politicians, Power and the Pursuit of Office*. New York: Random House, 1991.

Epstein, David F. *The Political Theory of the Federalist*. Chicago: University of Chicago Press, 1984.

Epstein, David F., and Sharyn O'Halloran. "Divided Government and the Design of Administrative Procedures." Paper presented to the annual meeting of the American Political Science Association, New York, 1994.

Erikson, Robert S. "The Puzzle of Midterm Loss." *Journal of Politics* 50 (1988): 1011–29.

———. "Why the Democrats Lose Presidential Elections." *PS: Political Science & Politics* 22 (1989): 30–34.

Fausold, Martin L. *The Presidency of Herbert C. Hoover*. Lawrence: University Press of Kansas, 1985.

Fiorina, Morris. *Divided Government*. New York: Macmillan, 1992.

———. *Divided Government*. 2d ed. Boston: Allyn & Bacon, 1996.

Fiorina, Morris P. "Response." *Legislative Studies Quarterly* 19 (1994): 117–25.

Flaumenhaft, Harvey. *The Effective Republic: Administration and Constitution in the Thought of Alexander Hamilton*. Durham, N.C.: Duke University Press, 1992.

Formisano, Ronald P. "Deferential-Participant Politics: The Early Republic's Political Culture." *American Political Science Review* 68 (June 1974): 473–87.

———. *The Transformation of American Political Culture: Massachusetts Parties, 1790s–1840s*. New York: Oxford University Press, 1983.

Frisch, Morton J. *Franklin D. Roosevelt: The Contribution of the New Deal to American Political Thought and Practice*. Boston: St. Wayne, 1975.

From, Al. "More than a Good Speech: The State of the Union Address Could Have Marked a Turning Point in History." *The New Democrat* (March–April 1996): 35–36.

From, Al, and Will Marshall. *The Road to Realignment: Democrats and the Perot Voters*. 1 July 1993. Washington, D.C.: Democratic Leadership Council: section 1, p. 3–5.

Frymar, Paul. "Ideological Consensus within Divided Party Government." *Political Science Quarterly* 109 (summer 1994): 310–11.

Gara, Larry. *The Presidency of Franklin Pierce.* Lawrence: University Press of Kansas, 1991.

Gelman, Andrew, and Gary King. "Estimating the Incumbency Advantage without Bias." *American Journal of Political Science* 34 (1994): 1142–64.

Gettinger, Stephen. "View from the Ivory Tower More Rosy than Media's." *Congressional Quarterly Weekly Report,* 8 October 1994, 2850–51.

———. " '94 Elections: Real Revolution or Blip on Political Radar?" *Congressional Quarterly Weekly Report,* 5 November 1994, 3127–32.

Gibson, Martha L. "Politics and Divided Government." Paper presented to the annual meeting of the American Political Science Association, New York, 1994.

Gienapp, William E. *The Origins of the Republican Party, 1852–1856.* New York: Oxford University Press, 1987.

Gimpel, James G. *Fulfilling the Contract: The First 100 Days.* Boston: Allyn & Bacon, 1996.

Gingrich, Newt. "Address to the Nation." 7 April 1995.

Ginsberg, Benjamin, Walter R. Mebane, Jr. and Martin Shefter. "The Presidency and Interest Groups: Why Presidents Cannot Govern." In *The Presidency and the Political System,* edited by Michael Nelson, 4th ed. Washington, D.C.: Congressional Quarterly, 1995.

Ginsberg, Benjamin, and Martin Shefter. *Politics By Other Means: The Declining Importance of Elections in America.* New York: Basic Books, 1990.

Goodman, John, and Gerald L. Musgrave, *Patient Power.* Washington, D.C.: Cato Institute, 1992.

Greenstein, Fred. *The Hidden-Hand Presidency: Eisenhower as Leader.* Baltimore: Johns Hopkins University Press, 1982.

Greve, Frank. "GOP Pollster Gauged Appeal of Slogans, Not of 'Contract.' " *San Diego Union,* 12 November 1995, A33.

Gulick, Luther. "Politics, Administration, and the New Deal." *Annals* 169 (September 1933).

Hager, George, and David S. Cloud. "Democrats Pull Off Squeaker In Approving Clinton Plan." *Congressional Quarterly Weekly Report,* 29 May 1993, 1340–45.

———. "Test For Divided Democrats: Forge a Budget Deal." *Congressional Quarterly Weekly Report,* 26 June 1993, 1631–35.

———. "Democrats Tie Their Fate To Clinton's Budget Bill." *Congressional Quarterly Weekly Report,* 7 August 1993, 2123–29.

Hamilton, Alexander, John Jay, and James Madison. *The Federalist Papers.* Edited by Clinton Rossiter. New York: Mentor, 1961.

Hamilton, Holman. *Prologue to Conflict: the Crisis and Compromise of 1850.* Lexington, Ky.: University Press of Kentucky, 1964.

Hansen, John Mark. "Public Constituencies for Deficit Financing." Paper presented at the annual meeting of the American Political Science Association, New York, 1993.

Hargreaves, Mary W. M. *The Presidency of John Quincy Adams.* Lawrence: University Press of Kansas, 1985.

Harris, Joseph P. "Outline for a New York Conference." *Papers of the Presidents Committee on Administrative Management.* Hyde Park, New York: Franklin D. Roosevelt Library, 1936.

Harris, Richard A., and Sidney M. Milkis. *The Politics of Regulatory Change: A Tale of Two Agencies,* 2d ed. New York: Oxford University Press, 1996.

Healey, Jon. "Democrats Look to Salvage Part of Stimulus Package." *Congressional Quarterly Weekly Report,* 24 April 1993, 1001–4.

———. "Saga of a Supplemental." *Congressional Quarterly Weekly Report,* 24 April 1993, 1002.

Healey, Jon, and Chuck Alston. "Stimulus Bill Prevails in House, but Senate Battle Awaits." *Congressional Quarterly Weekly Report,* 20 March 1993, 649–52.

Healey, Jon, and Thomas H. Moore. "Clinton Forms New Coalition to Win NAFTA Fight." *Congressional Quarterly Weekly Report,* 20 November 1993, 3181–83.

Herzberg, Roberta. "Blocking Coalitions and Institutional Equilibrium." Ph.D. diss., Washington University in St. Louis, 1985.

———. "Blocking Coalitions and Policy Change." In *Congress and Policy Change,* edited by Gerald C. Wright, Jr., Leroy Rieselbach, and Lawrence Dodd. New York: Agathon Press, 1986.

Hibbing, John R., and Elizabeth Theiss-Morse. *Congress as Public Enemy: Political Attitudes toward American Political Institutions.* New York: Cambridge University Press, 1995.

Hill, Kevin A. "Does the Creation of Majority Black Districts Aid Republicans? An Analysis of the 1992 Congressional Elections in Eight Southern States." *Journal of Politics* 57 (1995): 394–401.

Hofstadter, Richard. *The Idea of a Party System: The Rise of Legitimate Opposition in the United States, 1780–1840.* Berkeley: University of California Press, 1969.

Holt, Michael. *The Political Crisis of the 1850s.* New York: Norton, 1978.

Hoogenboom, Ari. *The Presidency of Rutherford B. Hayes.* Lawrence: University Press of Kansas, 1988.

Hopper, John Edward. "The Purge: Franklin D. Roosevelt and the 1938 Nominations." Ph.D. diss., University of Chicago, 1966.

Hotline, 26 September–15 November 1995.

Idelson, Holly. "More Cops, Jails: House Takes a $28 Billion Aim at Crime." *Congressional Quarterly Weekly Report,* 23 April 1994, 1001–5.

———. "In Surprising Turnaround, House OKs Weapons Ban." *Congressional Quarterly Weekly Report,* 7 May 1994, 1119–23.

———. "Clinton, Democrats Scramble To Save Anti-Crime Bill." *Congressional Quarterly Weekly Report,* 13 August 1994, 2340–43.

Idelson, Holly, and Richard Sammon. "Marathon Talks Produce New Anti-

Crime Bill." *Congressional Quarterly Weekly Report*, 20 August 1994, 2449–54.

Ifill, Gwen. "Fifty-Six Long Days of Coordinated Persuasion." *New York Times*, 19 November 1993, A27.

Ingberman, Daniel, and John Villani. "An Institutional Theory of Divided Government and Party Polarization." *American Journal of Political Science* 37 (1993): 429–71.

Jackson, Carlton. *Presidential Vetoes, 1792–1945*. Athens: University of Georgia Press, 1967.

Jacobson, Gary C. *The Electoral Origins of Divided Government: Competition in U.S. House Elections, 1946–1988*. Boulder, Colo.: Westview, 1990.

———. "The Persistence of Democratic House Majorities." In *The Politics of Divided Government*, edited by Gary Cox and Samuel Kernell. Boulder, Colo.: Westview, 1991.

———. *The Politics of Congressional Elections*, 3d ed. New York: Harper Collins, 1992.

———. "Deficit Cutting Politics and Congressional Elections." *Political Science Quarterly* 108 (1993): 375–402.

———. "Congress: Unusual Year, Unusual Election." In *The Elections of 1992*, edited by Michael Nelson. Washington, D.C.: Congressional Quarterly Press, 1993.

———. "The 1994 House Elections in Perspective." In *Midterm: The Elections of 1994 in Context*, edited by Philip A. Klinkner. Boulder, Colo.: Westview, 1996.

———. *The Politics of Congressional Elections*, 4th ed. New York: Harper Collins, 1997.

———. "Strategic Politicians and the Dynamics of U.S. House Elections, 1946–1986." *American Political Science Review* 83 (1989): 773–93.

Jacobson, Gary C., and Michael Dimock. "Checking Out: The Effects of Bank Overdrafts on the 1992 House Elections." *American Journal of Political Science* 38 (1994): 601–24.

Jacobson, Gary C. and Samuel Kernell. *Strategy and Choice in Congressional Elections*, 2d ed. New Haven: Yale University Press, 1983.

Jefferson, Thomas. *The Portable Jefferson*. Edited by Merrill D. Peterson. New York: Viking Press, 1975.

Jehl, Douglas. "Rejoicing Is Muted for the President in Budget Victory." *New York Times*, 8 August 1993, 1, 23.

Jillson, Calvin. "Patterns and Periodicity in American National Politics." In *The Dynamics of American Politics; Approaches and Interpretations*, edited by Lawrence C. Dodd and Calvin Jillson. Boulder, Colo.: Westview, 1994.

Jones, Charles O. *The Presidency in a Separated System*. Washington, D.C.: Brookings Institution, 1994.

———. "Campaigning to Govern: The Clinton Style." In *The Clinton Presidency: First Appraisals*, edited by Colin Campbell and Bert A. Rockman. Chatham, N.J.: Chatham House, 1996.

Kaus, Mickey. "They Blew It." *New Republic*, 5 December 1994, 14–19.

Keller, Morton. *Affairs of State: Public Life in Late Nineteenth Century America*. Cambridge: Belknap Press of Harvard University Press, 1977.

Kelly, Alfred H., Winfred A. Harbison, and Herman Belz. *The American Constitution: Its Origins and Development*, 7th ed. New York: Norton, 1991.

Kelly, Sean Q. "Divided We Govern? A Reassessment." *Polity* 25 (1993): 475–88.

———. "The Institutional Foundations of Inter-Branch Conflict in the Era of Divided Government." *Southeastern Political Review*. Forthcoming.

Kernell, Samuel. *Going Public: New Strategies of Presidential Leadership*, 2d ed. Washington, D.C.: Congressional Quarterly Press, 1992.

Key, V. O., Jr. "A Theory of Critical Elections." *Journal of Politics* 17 (February 1955): 3–18.

———. "Secular Realignment and the Party System." *Journal of Politics* 21 (May 1959): 198–210.

Kiewiet, D. Roderick, and Mathew D. McCubbins. *The Logic of Delegation: Congressional Parties and the Appropriations Process*. Chicago: University of Chicago Press, 1991.

Klements, Kendrick A. *The Presidency of Woodrow Wilson*. Lawrence: University Press of Kansas, 1992.

Kooper, Richard T. "GOP Changes Held in Check by Earlier Revolutionaries." *Los Angeles Times*, 31 December 1995, A13.

Koszczuk, Jackie. "Freshmen: New, Powerful Voice." *Congressional Quarterly Weekly Report*, 28 October 1995, 3251, quoting Steve Largent.

Krehbiel, Keith. *Information and Legislative Organization*. Ann Arbor: University of Michigan Press, 1991.

———. "A Theory of Divided and Unified Government." Graduate School of Business, Stanford University, 1994. Photocopy.

———. "Institutional and Partisan Sources of Gridlock: A Theory of Divided and Unified Government." *Journal of Theoretical Politics*. Forthcoming.

Kristol, William. Lecture at Harvard University, 2 December 1994.

Krock, Arthur, "New Deal Victory Laid to Federal Money Lure." *New York Times*, 28 May 1938, Sec. 4, p. 2.

Kuntz, Phil. "Tough-Minded Senate Adopts Crime Crackdown Package." *Congressional Quarterly Weekly Report*, 20 November 1993, 3199–201.

———. "Hard-Fought Crime Bill Battle Spoils Field for Health Care." *Congressional Quarterly Weekly Report*, 27 August 1994, 2485.

Kurtz, Karl. Personal communication, 18 March 1993.

———. "The Tide's In for Southern Republicans." *APSA Legislative Studies Section Newsletter* 18 (1994): 9–11.

Kuttner, Robert. "Up From 1994." *The American Prospect* 20 (winter 1995): 7–13.

Labaton, Stephen. "Senate Reports on Whitewater Offer Glimpse of Partisan Battling Still in Store." *New York Times*, 4 January 1995, A14.

Ladd, Everett Carll, "Public Opinion and the 'Congress Problem.' " *Public Interest* 100 (summer 1990): 57–67.

———. ed. *America at the Polls: 1994*. Storrs, Conn.: The Roper Institute, 1995.

LaFollette, Philip, Elmer Bensen, and Frank Murphy. "Why We Lost." *The Nation*, 3 December 1938, 586–7.

Langdon, Steve. "Clinton's High Victory Rate Conceals Disappointments." *Congressional Quarterly Weekly Report*, 31 December 1994, 3619–23.

Lazare, Daniel. *The Frozen Republic: How the Constitution Is Paralyzing Democracy*. New York: Harcourt Brace, 1996.

Levy, Frank S., and Richard C. Michel. *The Economic Future of American Families: Income and Wealth Trends*. Washington, D.C.: Urban Institute Press, 1991.

Lowi, Theodore J. *The Personal Presidency: Power Invested, Promise Unfulfilled*. Ithaca, NY: Cornell University Press, 1985.

———. "The Party Crasher." *New York Times Magazine*, 23 August 1992, 28, 33.

Lublin, David. "Gerrymander for Justice? Racial Redistricting and Black and Latino Representation." Ph.D. diss., Harvard University, 1994.

———. "Costs of Gerrymandering," *New York Times*, 13 December 1994.

Lynn, Alvin. "Party Formation and Operation in the House of Representatives, 1824–1837." Ph.D. diss., Rutgers University, 1972.

Maass, Arthur. *Congress and the Common Good*. New York: Basic Books, 1983.

Machiavelli. *Discourses*, XXV. New York: Modern Library, 1950.

Madison, James. *Notes of the Debates in the Federal Convention of 1787 Reported by James Madison*. New York: W. W. Norton, 1969.

Magleby, David, and Kelly Patterson. "The Polls—Poll Trends: Congressional Reform." *Public Opinion Quarterly* 58 (1994): 419–27.

Malbin, Michael J. "Was Divided Government Really Such a Big Problem?" In *Separation of Powers and Good Government*, edited by Bradford P. Wilson and Peter W. Schramm. Lanham, Md.: Rowman & Littlefield, 1994.

Marshall, Will, and Martin Schramm, eds. *Mandate for Change*. New York: Berkeley Books, 1993.

Martin, Cathie Jo. "Mandating Social Change within Corporate America." Paper presented at the annual meeting of the American Political Science Association, New York City, 1994.

Martis, Kenneth. *The Historical Atlas of Political Parties in the United States Congress, 1789–1989*. New York: Macmillan, 1989.

Masci, David. "$30 Billion Anti-Crime Bill Heads to Clinton's Desk." *Congressional Quarterly Weekly Report*, 27 August 1994, 2488–93.

Mayer, William G. "Changes in Elections and the Party System: 1992 in Historical Perspective." In *The New American Politics: Reflections on Political Change and the Clinton Administration*, edited by Bryan D. Jones. Boulder, Colo.: Westview, 1995.

Mayhew, David R. "Divided Party Control: Does It Make a Difference?" *PS: Political Science & Politics* 24 (1991): 637–40.

―――. *Divided We Govern: Party Control, Lawmaking, and Investigations, 1946–1990*. New Haven: Yale University Press, 1991.

―――. "The Return to Unified Party Control Under Clinton: How Much of a Difference in Lawmaking?" In *The New American Politics*, edited by Bryan D. Jones. Boulder, Colo.: Westview, 1995.

McCormick, Richard P. *The Presidential Game: The Origins of American Presidential Politics*. New York: Oxford University Press, 1982.

McCoy, Donald R. *The Presidency of Harry Truman*. Lawrence: University Press of Kansas, 1984.

McCubbins, Mathew D. "Government on Lay-Away: Federal Spending and Deficits Under Divided Party Control." In *The Politics of Divided Government*, edited by Gary W. Cox and Samuel Kernell. Boulder, Colo.: Westview, 1991.

―――. "Party Governance and U.S. Budget Deficits: Divided Government and Fiscal Stalemate." In *Politics and Economics in the 1980s*, edited by Alberto Alesina and Geoffrey Carliner. Chicago: University of Chicago Press, 1991.

McDonald, Forrest. *Novus Ordo Seclorum: The Intellectual Origins of the Constitution*. Lawrence: University Press of Kansas, 1985.

McGerr, Michael. *The Decline of Popular Politics: The American North, 1865–1928*. New York: Oxford University Press, 1986.

McWilliams, Wilson Carey. "Parties As Civic Associations." In *Party Renewal in America*, edited by Gerald Pomper. New York: Praeger, 1980.

Melnick, R. Shep. "The Courts, Congress, and Programmatic Rights." In *Remaking American Politics*, edited by Richard A. Harris and Sidney M. Milkis. Boulder, Colo.: Westview, 1989.

Milkis, Sidney M. *The President and the Parties: The Transformation of the American Party System since the New Deal*. New York: Oxford University Press, 1993.

Nathan, Richard. *The Administrative Presidency*. New York: Wiley, 1983.

National Center for Policy Analysis. *An Agenda for Solving America's Health Care Crisis*. Dallas: National Center for Policy Analysis, 1990.

Neustadt, Richard E. *Presidential Power and the Modern Presidents: Leadership from Roosevelt to Reagan*. New York: Wiley, 1990.

Newkirk, William. "Americans Crave Leadership, But What Is It? Candidates Cultivate Hard-To-Define Trait." *Chicago Tribune*, 24 December, 1995, 1.

New York Times. "The 103rd Congress: What Was Accomplished, and What Wasn't." 9 October 1994, 16.

Nie, Norman H., Sidney Verba, and John Petrocik. *The Changing American Voter*. Cambridge: Harvard University Press, 1976.

Ornstein, Norman, Thomas Mann, and Michael J. Malbin. *Vital Statistics on Congress, 1993–94*. Washington, D.C.: Congressional Quarterly Press, 1994.

Pach, Chester J., Jr., and Elmo Richardson. *The Presidency of Dwight D. Eisenhower.* Lawrence: University Press of Kansas, 1991.

Patterson, Kelly, and David Magleby. "Public Support for Congress." *Public Opinion Quarterly* 56 (1992): 539–51.

Pear, Robert. "Welfare Debate Will Re-Examine Core Assumptions." *New York Times,* 2 January 1995, 1, 9.

Peterson, Mark A. *Legislating Together: The White House and Capitol Hill from Eisenhower to Reagan.* Cambridge: Harvard University Press, 1990.

———. "Institutional Change and the Health Politics of the Nineties." In *Health Care Reform in the Nineties,* edited by Pauline Rosenau. Thousand Oaks, Calif.: Sage Publications, 1994.

Peterson, Norma L. *The Presidencies of William Henry Harrison and John Tyler.* Lawrence: University Press of Kansas, 1989.

Peterson, Paul E. "Vulnerable Politicians and Deficit Politics." Presented at the annual meeting of the American Political Science Association, Chicago, 1995.

Peterson, Paul E., and Jay P. Greene. "Why Executive-Legislative Conflict in the United States Is Dwindling." *British Journal of Political Science* 24 (1994): 33–55.

Petrocik, John R. "Divided Government: Is It All in the Campaigns?" In *The Politics of Divided Government,* edited by Gary W. Cox and Samuel Kernell. Boulder, Colo.: Westview, 1991.

———. "A Theory of Issue-Ownership and the 1980 Presidential Election." Presented at the annual meeting of the American Political Science Association, New York, 1994.

Pfiffner, James P. "Divided Government and the Problem of Governance." In *Divided Government: Cooperation and Conflict Between the President and Congress,* edited by James A. Thurber. Washington, D.C.: Congressional Quarterly Press, 1991.

Piereson, James. "Party Government." *Political Science Reviewer* 12 (fall 1982): 51–52.

Plesur, Milton. "The Republican Congressional Comeback of 1938." *Review of Politics* 24 (1962): 525–62.

Plott, Charles. "A Notion of Equilibrium and Its Possibility under Majority Rule." *American Economic Review* (1967): 787–806.

Poterba, James. "State Responses to Fiscal Crisis: The Effects of Budgetary Institutions and Politics." *Journal of Political Economy* 102 (1994): 799–821.

President's Committee on Administrative Management. "Outline for a New York Conference." 8 April 1936. Papers of the President's Committee on Administrative Management. Hyde Park, New York: Franklin D. Roosevelt Library.

President's Committee on Administrative Management. *Report of the President's Committee on Administrative Management.* Washington, D.C.: U.S. Government Printing Office, 1937.

Purdum, Todd S. "A Crippled President Seeks Not to Become a Lame Duck." *New York Times*, 8 December 1994, A1, B21.

Quirk, Paul J., and Joseph Hinchcliffe. "Domestic Policy: The Trials of a Centrist Democrat." In *The Clinton Presidency: First Appraisals*, edited by Colin Campbell and Bert A. Rockman. Chatham, N.J.: Chatham House, 1996.

Quirk, Paul J., and B. Nesmith. "Divided Government and Policy Making: Negotiating the Laws." In *The Presidency and the Political System*, edited by Michael Nelson. Washington, D.C.: Congressional Quarterly Press, 1995.

Rabkin, Jeremy. "The Judiciary in the Administrative State." *Public Interest* 71 (spring 1983): 662–84.

Reichley, A. James. "The Rise of National Parties." In *The New Direction in American Politics*, edited by John E. Chubb and Paul E. Peterson. Washington, D.C.: Brookings Institution, 1985.

———. *The Life of the Parties: A History of American Political Parties.* New York: Free Press, 1992.

Remini, Robert. *Martin Van Buren and the Making of the Democratic Party.* New York: Columbia University Press, 1959.

Riddle, Don. *Congressman Abraham Lincoln.* Urbana, Ill.: University of Illinois Press, 1987.

Riker, William H. "Rhetorical Interaction in the Ratification Campaign." In *Agenda Formation*, edited by William Riker. Ann Arbor: University of Michigan Press, 1993.

Rockman, Bert A. *The Leadership Question: The Presidency and the American System.* New York: Praeger, 1984.

———. "Leadership Style and the Clinton Presidency." In *The Clinton Presidency: First Appraisals*, edited by Colin Campbell and Bert A. Rockman. Chatham, N.J.: Chatham House, 1996.

Rogers, David. "General Newt." *Wall Street Journal*, 18 December 1995, 1.

Rohde, David W. *Parties and Leaders in the Postreform House.* Chicago: University of Chicago Press, 1991.

Roosevelt, Franklin D. *Public Papers and Addresses*, 13 vols., edited by Samuel J. Rosenman. New York: Random House, 1938–1950.

Rotunda, Ronald D. "The Liberal Label: Roosevelt's Capture of a Symbol." In *Public Policy*, vol. 17, edited by John D. Montgomery and Albert O. Hirschman. Cambridge: Harvard University Press, 1968.

Rubin, Alissa J. "Dole, Clinton Compromise Greases Wheels for GATT." *Congressional Quarterly Weekly Report*, 26 November 1994, 3405.

Samuelson, Robert. *The Good Life and Its Discontents: The American Dream in the Age of Entitlements, 1945–1995.* New York: Times Books, 1995.

San Diego Union. "GOP Says It Expects to Gain Up to 30 House Seats in '96." 4 November 1995, A12.

Sartori, Giovanni. *Parties and Party Systems: A Framework for Analysis.* New York: Cambridge University Press, 1976.

Schattschneider, E. E. "The Struggle For Party Government." In *The Party Battle*, edited by Leon Stein. New York: Arno, 1974.

Schick, Allen. "Congress and the 'Details of Administration.' " *Public Administration Review* 36 (September/October 1976): 516–28.

Schlesinger, Arthur M., ed. *History of American Presidential Elections, 1789–1968*. 4 vols. New York: Chelsea House, 1971.

Schneider, William. "A Loud Vote For Change." *National Journal*, 7 November 1992, 2544.

———. "Clinton: The Reason Why." *National Journal*, 12 November 1994, 2630–32.

Schroeder, John H. *Mr. Polk's War: American Opposition and Dissent, 1846–1848*. Madison: University of Wisconsin Press, 1973.

Shafer, Byron, ed. *The End of Realignment?: Interpreting American Electoral Eras*. Madison: University of Wisconsin Press, 1991.

Sharp, James Roger. *American Politics in the Early Republic: The New Nation in Crisis*. New Haven: Yale University Press, 1993.

Shear, Jeff. "United They Stand." *National Journal*, 28 October 1995, 2646–50.

Shogren, Elizabeth. "GOP Budget Plans Would Put Burden on the Poor." *Los Angeles Times*, 29 October 1995, A1.

Shribman, David M. "Budget Battle a Hollow One for President." *Boston Globe*, 8 August 1993, 1, 24.

———. "A New Brand of D.C. Politics." *Boston Globe*, 18 November 1993, 15.

———. "Helm's Jibe at Clinton Draws Fire." *Boston Globe*, 23 November 1994.

———. "Tsongas Suggests Third Party, Sees Powell as a Candidate." *Boston Globe*, 13 December 1994, 1, 28.

Silbey, Joel H. "Beyond Realignment and Realignment Theory: American Political Eras, 1789–1989." In *The End of Realignment?: Interpreting American Electoral Eras*, edited by Bryon Shafer. Madison: University of Wisconsin Press, 1991.

———. *The American Political Nation, 1838–1893*. Stanford: Stanford University Press, 1991.

Sinclair, Barbara. *The Transformation of the U.S. Senate*. Baltimore: Johns Hopkins University Press, 1989.

Skowronek, Stephen. *Building a New American State: The Expansion of National Administrative Capacities, 1877–1920*. Cambridge: Harvard University Press, 1982.

———. *The Politics Presidents Make: Leadership from John Adams to George Bush*. Cambridge: Harvard University Press, 1993.

Smith, Craig. Personal communication, 19 October 1993.

Smith, Elbert B. *The Presidency of James Buchanan*. Lawrence: University Press of Kansas, 1975.

———. *The Presidencies of Zachary Taylor and Millard Fillmore*. Lawrence: University Press of Kansas, 1988.

Socolofsky, Homer E., and Allan B. Spetter. *The Presidency of Benjamin Harrison*. Lawrence: University Press of Kansas, 1987.

Spitzer, Robert. *The Politics of Gun Control*. Chatham, N.J.: Chatham House, 1995.

Stewart, Richard B. "The Reformation of American Administrative Law." *Harvard Law Review*, vol. 88, no. 8 (June 1975): 1669–1813.

Stokes, Thomas. *Chip Off My Shoulder*. Princeton: Princeton University Press, 1940.

Storing, Herbert J. *What the Anti-Federalists Were For*. Chicago: University of Chicago Press, 1981.

Sundquist, James L. *Constitutional Reform and Effective Government*. Washington D.C.: Brookings Institution, 1986.

———. "Needed: A Political Theory for the New Era of Coalition Government in the United States." *Political Science Quarterly* 103 (winter 1988–89): 613–35.

Taylor, Andrew J. "Understanding Madison's Curse: Divided Government and Domestic Policy, 1955–1992." Paper presented at the annual meeting of the American Political Science Association, New York, 1994.

Thurber, James A. "Representation, Accountability, and Efficiency in Divided Party Control of Government." *PS: Political Science & Politics* 24 (1991): 653–657.

Tocqueville, Alexis de. *Democracy in America*. New York: Doubleday, 1969.

Toner, Robin. "Alliance to Buy Health Care: Bureaucrat or Public Servant?" *New York Times*, 5 December 1993, 1, 38.

Towell, Pat. "Months of Hope, Anger, Anguish Produce Policy Few Admire." *Congressional Quarterly Weekly Report*, 24 July 1993, 1966–70.

———. "Battle over Gay Ban Moves into the Courts." *Congressional Quarterly Weekly Report*, 31 July 1993, 2075.

———. "The Legislative Word on Gays." *Congressional Quarterly Weekly Report*, 31 July 1993, 2076.

Tulis, Jeffrey K. *The Rhetorical Presidency*. Princeton, N.J.: Princeton University Press, 1987.

U.S. Bureau of the Census. *Historical Statistics of the United States from Colonial Times to 1970*. Washington, D.C.: U. S. Government Printing Office, 1975.

U.S. Congress. *The Biographical Directory of the American Congress, 1774–1989*. Washington, D.C.: U. S. Government Printing Office, 1989.

Vallely, Richard M. "Divided They Govern." In *The American Prospect: Reader in American Politics*, edited by Walter Dean Burnham. Chatham, N.J.: Chatham House Publishers, 1995.

Van Dunk, Emily, and Thomas M. Holbrook. "The 1994 State Legislative Elections." *Extension of Remarks, APSA Legislative Studies Newsletter* 18 (1994): 8–11.

Van Riper, Paul. *History of the United States Civil Service*. Evanston, Ill.: Row, Peterson, 1958.

Wall Street Journal, 15 August 1994, A12.

Wall Street Journal, 4 January 1995, A12.

Washington Post. "The Record of the 103rd Congress." 9 October 1994, A21.

Washington Post National Weekly Edition. "Perhaps the Worst Congress." 17–23 October 1994, 27.

Wattenberg, Martin P. *The Rise of Candidate-Centered Politics*. Cambridge: Harvard University Press, 1991.

———. "The Republican Presidential Advantage in the Age of Party Disunity." In *The Politics of Divided Government*, edited by Gary Cox and Samuel Kernell. Boulder, Colo.: Westview, 1991.

Weatherford, M. Stephen. "Responsiveness and Deliberation in Divided Government: Presidential Leadership in Tax Policy Making." *British Journal of Political Science* 24 (1994): 1–31.

Weisberg, Herbert F., and David C. Kimball. "Attitudinal Correlates of the 1992 Presidential Vote: Party Identification and Beyond." In *Democracy's Feast: Elections in America*, edited by Herbert F. Weisberg. Chatham, N.J.: Chatham House, 1995.

Welch, Richard E., Jr. *The Presidencies of Grover Cleveland*. Lawrence: University Press of Kansas, 1988.

Wilhelm, David. Personal communication, 18 October 1993.

Wilson, James Q. "Does the Separation of Powers Still Work?" *Public Interest* 86 (winter 1987): 35–62.

Wilson, Woodrow. *Constitutional Government in the United States*. 1908. New York: Columbia University Press, 1917.

———. *Congressional Government: A Study in American Politics*. Baltimore: Johns Hopkins University Press, 1981.

Wines, Michael. "Republicans Seek Sweeping Changes in the House's Rules." *New York Times*, 8 December 1994, A1, B21.

———. "Moderate Republicans Seek an Identity for Gingrich Era." *New York Times*, 26 December 1994, 1, 22.

Woodward, Bob. *The Agenda: Inside the Clinton White House*. New York: Simon & Schuster, 1994.

Young, James Sterling, and Russell L. Riley. "Party Government and Political Culture." Paper presented at the annual meeting of the American Political Science Association, San Francisco, 1990.

Zuckman, Jill. "As Family Leave Is Enacted, Some See End to Logjam." *Congressional Quarterly Weekly Report*, 6 February 1993: 267–69.

———. "Pared Funding Speeds Passage of National Service." *Congressional Quarterly Weekly Report*, 7 August 1993: 2160–61.

Index

abortion, 160
accountability, 53–54, 206
activist government, 46
Adams, John Quincy, 11, 13, 14, 15, 31n15
"administrative presidency," 142, 151, 152
AFDC. *See* Aid to Families with Dependent Children
affirmative action, 70
agencies, administrative, 139, 184
Aid to Families with Dependent Children (AFDC), 155, 170n66
Alesina, Alberto, 86
Alt, James E., 52
anticrime bill, 47, 48, 113, 117, 120–22
Arthur, Chester A., 13
assault weapons ban, 121–22

Bagehot, Walter, 191
banking scandal (House). *See* House Bank scandal
behavioral balancers, 93
Bendiner, Robert, 174
bicameralism, 198
bipartisanship, 49, 67, 136, 192, 202; coalitions and, 158; health care reform and, 178, 181
Black, Benjamin, 28
Black, Duncan, 178

Black, Gordon, 28
Boehner, John, 80
Bonoir, David, 123
Boren, David, 120
Born, Richard, 92, 103
Bosnia, 111, 203
Brady bill (handgun control), 48, 126
Breaux, John, 125
Broder, David, 34n49
Brooks, Jack, 54, 58
Brown, Jerry, 35
Brownlow Committee Report, 147, 149
Buchanan, James, 11, 20
Buchanan, Patrick, 7n8
budget: balancing, 78, 161, 184, 192, 204; bill veto, 162; Clinton stimulus package, 52, 124, 136, 156; compromise, 66, 185; entitlement spending, 64–65; middle class entitlements, 78; as 1994 election issue, 62, 65, 66, 68, 71; pay as you go, 66; policy, 175
budget deficits, 5, 49, 200; Clinton policy re, 119–20, 199, 203; divided government and, 51–53; reduction, 51, 55, 68, 119–20, 199; voter dislike of, 55
Bureau of the Budget, 148
bureaucratic intrusion, 55

Burnham, Walter Dean, 25, 138
Bush, George, 163; administration, 62; administrative presidency and, 152; approval rating, 1, 35; conservatism, 136; deficit and, 80; election losses, 42, 61, 72, 73, 77, 198; health care plan, 177, 187n8; NAFTA and, 2; taxes and, 49, 51, 52, 66–68; vetoes, 51, 119
Byrd, Robert, 124

campaign finance reform, 124
campaigns: issues and, 90; nationalization of, 72–75, 159, 181
Campbell, Ben Nighthorse, 75, 134n30
career politicians, 74
Carter, Jimmy, 48, 54, 135, 136, 200, 202, 203; assault weapons ban and, 121; policy successes, 114; political isolation of, 157, 169n56
CBO. *See* Congressional Budget Office
Chafee, John, 125, 159
Chambers, William N., 25
checks and balances, 3, 129, 154, 182, 193. *See also* separation of powers
Christian activists, 72
civil rights, 20, 42, 63, 152
Civil War, 138, 154
Clay, Henry, 15, 16
Cleveland, Grover, 9, 13, 17, 20
Clinton, Hillary Rodham, 71, 125, 158, 203
Clinton, William (Bill), 198–200; as activist, 46; agenda, 113; alienation of constituents, 70–71; budget, 47, 52; campaign promises, 67–68, 113; character, 202; coalition building by, 119, 120–26, 136, 202; compromise and, 29, 46, 81; deficit reduction package, 68, 119, 203; Democratic Party and, 157–58, 169n56; economic poli-

cies, 136, 156, 200–201, 203; extremism and, 185; failures, 159; health care reform plan (*see* health care reform); liberal programs and, 155–57; losses, 124–26; NAFTA and, 158; 1992 elections, 2, 37, 67, 135, 154–55, 177, 180; 1994 elections and, 137, 159; as "old Democrat," 52; 103rd Congress and, 67–72; opposition by, 185; policy differences with Republicans, 28; policy making, 46–47; political future, 35; presidential role and, 200–201; Republican Congress and, 163; on role of government, 198–99; successes, 114, 119–23, 126, 174, 198–200; tax increases, 52; unified government and, 208; vetoes, 47, 50, 79, 128, 162, 203
coalition government, 46
coalitions, cross-party, 34n49, 46, 158; Clinton and, 119, 120–26, 136, 202; historical, 18, 20, 27; president's ability to build, 112, 119, 126. *See also* compromise; consensus
cognitive balancers, 93, 104–5
committees. *See* congressional committees; interest groups; subcommittees
Commonwealth Club address, 140, 155
compromise, 3, 16–17, 21; anticrime bill measures, 122; on budget, 66, 185; Clinton and, 47, 81; refusals, 4, 34n49, 47, 49, 120, 124, 205; Republican attitude toward, 47; voter attitudes toward, 64, 186n6. *See also* coalitions, cross-party; consensus
Congress: authority of, 20; legislative role, 88; New Deal and (*see* New Deal); 1992 elections (*see* 1992 elections); 1994 elections (*see* 1994

elections); opposition to president, 22, 179–80; organizational structure of, 111, 112, 126; pay raises, 69; public image of, 46, 69–70; restoring confidence in, 205–6; scandals in, 37, 67, 69, 203. *See also* House of Representatives; Senate
Congressional Black Caucus, 120, 121, 122
Congressional Budget Office (CBO), 65, 185
congressional committees, 51, 67, 78; health care and, 125, 180; opposition to policy from, 126; subcommittees, 5, 111; Ways and Means, 120, 123
congressional scandals, 37, 67, 69, 203
consensus, 3, 29, 56, 70. *See also* coalitions, cross-party; compromise
conservatives, 72, 136, 151
Constitution: allocation of governmental authority, 110–11; change and, 208; expansion of rights, 147, 150, 155, 166n22; governmental divisions under, 3, 11; gridlock and, 126–27, 191; political parties and, 198; reform of, 191; return to, 193
Contract with America, 77, 105, 127, 159, 162, 176, 204; on abortion, 160; balanced budget and, 161; effect of, 71; implementation of, 206; as Republican policy base, 128, 184; Senate view of, 206; support for, 80, 206
copartisanship, 49
"court-packing" plan, 148
crime, 69, 71, 109. *See also* anticrime bill
Croly, Herbert, 141, 143
crosspartisanship, 49, 52
cross-pressure, defined, 102–3

Deal, Nathan, 134n30
DeConcini, Dennis, 121
defense spending, 62, 161
Democratic Congressional Campaign Committee, 76
Democratic Leadership Council, 154, 157
Democratic Party: candidate development, 74, 88; constituency, 42, 63, 78, 158; election strategies, 88; extremism in, 88, 154; funding, 76; future, 75–76, 77; historical, 21, 25, 27; liberalism and, 144, 199–200; during New Deal, 143, 144–46, 148–49; 1992 elections, 42; 1994 elections, 42, 184; PAC contributions, 75–76; party switchers, 75, 134n30; policy orientation, 88; problem issues for, 42; programmatic interests, 86; Southern, 63; splits in, 63, 121, 179; strong issues, 63
Democratic-Republican Party, 142, 143
districts (voting), 40, 42, 77
divided government, 1, 2; academic view of, 1–2, 135; acceptance of, 85; attitudes toward, 92–94; as cause of gridlock, 192; causes of, 52, 86, 105, 129n8, 151, 182; under Constitution, 3, 11; context of, 23; continuation of, 43, 45; definitions of, 10–11; desirability of, 93; effect on policy, 135–36; effect on policy process, 110, 173–86; electoral politics and, 80–81; experiences associated with, 17, 24, 29, 30; government performance under, 50–51, 53, 109–10; gridlock and, 174; historical episodes of, 10–14, 23, 26; historical study of, 9–10, 23; history, 11–22, 85–86; issues and (*see* issues); negative effects of, 46, 53; as norm, 19–20, 21, 23,

135; patterns of, 45; political parties and (*see* political parties); unimportance of, 48–49, 50, 55. *See also* ticket-splitting; unified government
Divided Government, 9, 35, 46
Doherty, Joseph, 4
Dole, Robert (Bob), 70; anticrime bill and, 122; on Clinton, 163; on Clinton tax increases, 68; as conservative, 163; filibuster by, 136; on GATT, 132n23; health care and, 125; on telecommunications legislation, 133n26
Downs, Anthony, 178
Dukakis, Michael, 37

economic growth, 68
economic populism, 68
economic uncertainty, 69
economics, supply-side, 65
economy: Bush's handling of, 46; Clinton stimulus package, 52, 124, 136, 156; Constitution and, 141; federal government's role in, 16; growth of, 69; Hamilton proposals, 141, 142; Roosevelt and, 140–41
efficiency, 196
Ehrenhalt, Alan, 105
Eisenhower, Dwight D., 9, 10, 11, 13, 201; policy successes, 114, 131n14
elections: candidate-centered, 63; cycles, 4; of 1992 (*see* 1992 elections); of 1994 (*see* 1994 elections); off-year (*see* midterm elections); rules, 85
electoral college, 85
employer mandates, 179
entitlement programs, 64–65, 153, 155, 157; cuts, 120; health care, 201; Republicans and, 161–62
environmental issues, 47, 63, 123, 152, 162
Epstein, David F., 110

Erikson, Robert S., 81, 86, 91
Espy, Mike, 120
executive: authority, 110, 143, 147–48; role, 88, 148–49. *See also* president
Executive Reorganization Act of 1939, 147–48, 149
executive-legislative relations, 16, 49–50, 110–11, 161–63

factionalism, 11, 18, 22, 26, 27
Family and Medical Leave Act, 48, 113, 119, 199
farmers, 63, 122, 123
Federalists, 25, 26
filibusters, 126, 159; as opposition tactic, 124, 128, 133n26, 136–37
Fillmore, Millard, 11, 13, 18
Fiorina, Morris P., 4; on divided government, 1, 2, 9, 85; on voter behavior, 86, 92, 103, 104
fiscal policy, 65
Flake, Floyd, 123
Foley, Thomas, 54, 114
Ford, Gerald, 121
foreign relations, 49, 111, 203
fragmented government, 29–30
From, Al, 162
Frymar, Paul, 29

gag rule, 153, 168n49
GATT. *See* General Agreement on Tariffs and Trade
gays. *See* homosexuals in the military
gender, 70
General Agreement on Tariffs and Trade (GATT), 47, 48, 132n23
Gephardt, Richard, 123, 125
gerrymandering, 76
Gingrich, Newt, 23, 61, 71, 203–7; agenda, 162; budget and, 79; failures, 205; NAFTA support, 47; nationalization of campaign, 159, 181; 1994 elections and, 183; over-

promising by, 208; partisan division and, 161, 175; Republican revolution and, 183–85, 204–6; separation of powers and, 198; as Speaker of House, 206–7; as symbol, 80
Ginsberg, Benjamin, 135
Glickman, Dan, 58
Gordon, Bart, 123
Gore, Albert, 117, 120, 123, 158
government: activist, 141, 154; authority of, 151; branches, 3, 4, 11, 16; centralization of, 140–45, 154; divided (*see* divided government); effectiveness of, 56, 195 (*see also* gridlock); extension of role, 140, 142; fragmented (*see* fragmented government); limited, 154; New Deal realignment of, 147–48; party (*see* New Deal; political parties); responsibility in, 195; role of, 16, 158, 173; state (*see* state governments)
government inaction. *See* gridlock
government performance. *See* gridlock
government shutdown, 79
Grant, Ulysses S., 13, 20
grazing rights, 47
Great Society initiatives, 55
Greene, Jay P., 51
gridlock, 36, 164, 192, 207–8; causes of, 3, 5, 109, 126–27, 154, 191; under divided government, 22, 51, 53; explanations of, 112–13; in 1992 elections, 1, 46; under unified government, 70
Gulf War, 1, 66
Gulick, Luther, 147
gun control, 57n14, 71, 111

Hamilton, Alexander, 142, 143, 196
Harrison, Benjamin, 13
Hatch Act, 48, 131n17

Hayes, Rutherford B., 13
health care, 55, 113, 201
health care reform, 2, 5, 47, 125, 126, 176–80, 201–2; as 1992 election issue, 186n4; 1994 elections and, 180–82; public's attitude toward, 55; Republican opposition, 136; role of government in, 158–59
Herzberg, Roberta Q., 5
Hibbing, John R., 64
Hill, Anita, 67
historical perspective, 9–34
historical record, use of, 23–25
Hollings, Fritz, 47
homosexuals in the military, 46, 70–71; as Clinton policy issue, 2, 125–26, 155–56
Hoover, Herbert, 13, 22
House Bank scandal, 37, 67, 69
House of Representatives: membership, 1, 3; New Deal and (*see* New Deal); 1992 elections (*see* 1992 elections); 1994 elections (*see* 1994 elections); power of, 206; role of, 195; rule changes, 180–81. *See also* Congress

impeachment, 16
income inequality, 69
incumbents, 13, 54, 66, 92, 112
independent counsel, 131n14
Indian affairs, 15
individualism, 140, 143, 155
inflation, 62, 64–65, 185
Ingberman, Daniel, 88
interbranch conflict, 46, 50, 51, 56; history of, 10, 11, 14, 20, 26
interest groups, 5, 11, 27
interest rates, 65
Iran-Contra affair, 135, 151
issues: as cause of divided government, 105; cross-pressured voting and, 100; distributive, 88, 89

Jackson, Andrew, 11, 14–16, 18
Jacobson, Gary, 4, 88, 89, 91, 105; on Democratic majority, 183
Jefferson, Thomas, 142, 143, 166n24; on mandates, 204, 205
Jeffersonians, 138, 142, 143, 161
Jillson, Calvin, 29
job training programs, 78, 157
Johnson, Andrew, 20, 32n26
Johnson, Lyndon B., 10, 55, 152
Joint Economic Committee, 78
Jones, Charles O., 48, 49–50, 52
judges, 3
judiciary, 152, 153

Kaptur, Marcy, 120
Keating Five scandal, 37, 69
Kelly, Sean Q., 51, 109
Kennedy, John F., 48, 49, 199
Kennedy-Kassebaum reform bill, 181, 182
Kernell, Samuel, 91
Key, V. O., 25
King, Peter, 123
Krehbiel, Keith, 49, 50, 70
Kreidler, Mike, 123
Kristol, William, 159
Kuttner, Robert, 160

labor unions, 63, 158
Ladd, Everett Carll, 88
LaFollette, Philip, 145
Largent, Steve, 80
Laughlin, Greg, 134n30
leadership, 55; challenges to, 128; conditions for, 113; gridlock and, 112–13; by president, 194, 196
legislative output. *See* gridlock
legislatures: authority of, 110; split, 39–40, 44, 52
Lewis, Tom, 123
liberalism, 141–42; Clinton and, 155; in Democratic party, 144; programmatic (*see* programmatic liberalism)

Lincoln, Abraham, 18, 20
Lott, Trent, 68
Lowry, Robert C., 52
Lublin, David, 42
Lynn, Alvin, 15

Madison, James, 142, 166n24
Magaziner, Ira, 158
Margolies-Mezvinski, Marjorie, 115, 120
Marshall Plan, 49
Mayhew, David R., 49, 109, 110; on divided versus unified party control, 3, 164n1; on 103rd Congress, 48; on refusal to compromise, 34n49
McCubbins, Mathew D., 53
McDermott, Jim, 179
McGovern-Fraser reforms, 137
McNamara, Peter, 5
Medicaid, 68, 155, 182, 184
Medicare, 62, 68, 79, 141, 155, 162; cost reduction, 182; curtailment of, 161, 184, 185
Melnick, R. Shep, 166n22
Mexico, 17, 18, 123
Michel, Robert, 122
Michigan Survey Research Group, 25
middle class, 124, 200; entitlements, 78; incomes, 69; tax cuts, 113; values, 42
midterm elections, 13, 72–73, 90–91, 159, 180, 205. *See also* 1994 elections
Milkis, Sidney M., 5
mining law, 114
Mitchell, George, 122, 125, 159
moderate, defined, 96
"modern" presidency, 143–50
monetary policies, 20
"motor voter" registration, 48, 131n17

NAFTA. *See* North American Free Trade Agreement

National Republican Congressional (House) Committee, 76, 150
National Republican Senatorial Committee, 150
National Rifle Association (NRA), 63, 121
National Service Corps, 48, 115, 155, 157
national university, 197
NES. *See* 1992 National Election Study
Neustadt, Richard E., 110, 112
New Covenant, 155, 156, 157
New Deal, 21, 135–71, 194; challenges to, 150, 151; evolution of policies, 152; partisan realignment and, 137–39, 145; political parties under, 144–50; public philosophy of, 140–44
New Democrat, 198–200, 201
1992 elections, 36–41, 113; Clinton (*see* Clinton, William); gridlock issue, 45–46; pre-election situation, 35–36; in states, 38–41; third party's effect, 37; victory conditions, 37
1992 National Election Study (NES), 94
1994 Defense Authorization Bill, 126
1994 elections, 36, 41–45, 61–81; campaign nationalization, 72–75, 159, 181; health care reform issue in, 180–82; results, 127–28, 159, 203; in states, 44–45
Nixon, Richard M., 150, 151, 154
North American Free Trade Agreement (NAFTA), 2, 48, 71, 113; passage of, 47, 116, 117, 122–23, 158, 202
NRA. *See* National Rifle Association
NRCC. *See* National Republican Congressional Committee
Nunn, Sam, 156

O'Halloran, Sharyn, 110
O'Neill, Thomas P. ("Tip"), 63, 112
Office of Management and Budget, 65, 152
Old Democrats, 198–200
103rd Congress, 110, 113–19, 199
104th Congress, 77–81, 128
opinion polls, 192
opposition, legitimate, 16, 17, 21
overpromising, 207–8

PAC. *See* Political Action Committees
parliamentary government, 192
parties. *See* political parties
partisanship, 49, 52, 197–98; attacks on, 25; basis of, 192; as cause of divided government, 11; gridlock and, 112; historical, 18; modern, 24; under New Deal, 137, 145; policy coalitions and, 34n49; in Reagan-Bush era, 137, 159; role reversal, 77
party affiliation, 173
party identification, 14, 105
party loyalty, 23, 128, 137, 153–54, 183
party policy distance, 95
Paxon, Bill, 76
pensions, federal, 68
Perot, H. Ross, 163–64; attacks on Constitution, 191; budget deficit and, 203; as candidate, 35, 37, 67, 137; constituency, 70; effect of candidacy, 137, 199; Gore debate, 158
Peterson, Mark A., 177
Peterson, Paul E., 51
Petrocik, John R., 4, 183
Pierce, Franklin, 11, 20
Piereson, James, 143
policy process, 128. *See also* gridlock
policymaking, 179–80; Clinton and, 46–47; inefficient (*see* gridlock); Krehbiel model of, 50; unified government and, 113–27, 174, 176

Political Action Committees (PACs), 75–76, 78, 79
political eras, 26–29
political parties: Constitution and, 198; decline of, 27–28; defections by members, 49, 134n30; distinguishing, 95–96, 173; early, 14; effect on divided government, 26–27; effect on policymaking, 174; extremism in, 88, 94, 154; need for, 165n14, 197; New Deal and, 137–39, 142–46; opposing, 25; party identification, 14, 105; policy positions, 95; role of, 144, 146, 166n24, 197; strength of, 193; voters' view of, 136. *See also* two-party system
Polk, James K., 11, 17, 18, 20
pork-barrel legislation, 48, 204
post office scandal (House), 37, 69
Poterba, James, 52
Powell, Colin, 156
powers, separation of. *See* separation of powers
premodern era, 11, 14, 21
president: authority of, 21, 110–11, 156; party domination by, 145; as popular representative, 195–96; role of, 20, 110, 149, 194, 195–97, 200. *See also* executive; "modern" presidency
procurement, government, 48
programmatic liberalism, 138, 140–44, 150; Republican attacks on, 151–53, 162–63
Progressives, 21, 141, 142, 145, 146
Publius, 195–96, 197
purge campaign of 1938, 145, 146

quality of life, 69
Quayle, Dan, 152

Rabin, Yitzhak, 207
race, 70

racial gerrymandering. *See* redistricting
Ramspeck Act of 1940, 149
Rayburn, Sam, 10, 148
Reagan, Ronald, 6n2, 86, 135–36, 150, 163; administration, 62; administrative presidency and, 151–52; assault weapons ban and, 121; Congress and, 48; deficit and, 53, 80; House control by, 49; New Deal and, 150, 151; policy successes, 131n14; "revolution," 154
reapportionment. *See* redistricting
redistricting, 42, 76–77
reelection, presidential, 13
reform: campaign finance, 124; constitutional, 191; health care (*see* health care reform); procedural, 48; welfare (*see* welfare reform)
regulatory relief, 150, 151, 152
Reno, Janet, 121
Republican National Committee, 150
Republican Party: candidates, 74–75, 183; compromises by, 120; as conservative, 144; defections, 100; extremism in, 88, 154; funding, 76, 150; future risks, 75–76; health care reform (*see* health care reform); mandate overreading, 205; minority, 136; 1992 elections, 36, 38–41, 66; 1994 election strategy, 71–72, 183; 1994 elections, 36, 41–44, 54, 61, 72–81, 203–4; obstructionist tactics, 184; party building, 150; policy orientation, 88, 173; programmatic interests, 64, 86; reform policies, 170n66, 184 (*see also* Contract with America); in South, 42; strong issues, 63; unity, 28
Republican revolution (1994), 182–86, 204–6, 208
Rieselbach, Leroy, 5
Riker, William H., 88

Roosevelt, Franklin D., 46, 49, 137, 140, 199; as candidate, 145–46, 160; New Deal, 140–44; political parties and, 138–39, 143, 144–50; on separation of powers, 191; vetoes by, 4
Roosevelt, Theodore, 137, 141
Rosenthal, Howard, 86
Rostenkowski, Daniel, 37, 120, 123
Rules Committee, 180

Safe Drinking Water Act, 114
Sanders, Bernard, 116
Sartori, Giovanni, 106
Sasser, Jim, 54
Schattschneider, E. E., 146
Schneider, William, 159
Second World War. *See* World War II
sectionalism, 11, 18, 19, 26
Senate, 3, 196; elections (*see* elections). *See also* Congress
Senate Judiciary Committee, 67
separation of powers, 194–97; advantages of, 194–97; effect on change, 193–94; gridlock and, 129; New Deal and, 140, 142; reform of, 191; role of, 198. *See also* checks and balances
Shalala, Donna, 156
Shefter, Martin, 135
Shelby, Richard, 43, 75, 134n30
Silbey, Joel H., 5
Skowronek, Stephen, 143
slavery, 18, 19
Smith, Adam, 196
social programs, 78–79. *See also* entitlement programs
Social Security, 62, 155, 161
Social Security Act of 1935, 141
specialization, 196
spending cuts, 68
split-party control. *See* divided government
"Spot Resolutions" of 1847, 18

state governments, 36, 45, 52
Stokes, Thomas, 145
student loan legislation, 68, 79, 131n14, 157
subcommittees, 5, 111
Sundquist, James L., 46, 51
superconducting super collider, 48
Superfund, 47
Supreme Court, 15, 40

Taft, William Howard, 13, 22
tariff policies, 20
taxes: Bush and, 49, 51, 52, 66–68; cuts, 78, 113, 124, 159, 161, 184, 191, 192, 200; increases, 52, 64–65, 68, 79, 121, 156; voter dislike of, 55
Taylor, Andrew J., 110
Taylor, Zachary, 11, 13, 18
telecommunications legislation, 114, 126, 133n26
term limits, 38, 66, 71, 78, 128, 206
Theiss-Morse, Elizabeth, 64
third (minor) parties, 37, 85, 106n2, 192
Thurber, James A., 48
ticket-splitting: as balancing strategy, 86–88, 90–97; as cause of divided government, 86; causes of, 62–63, 89, 90, 100; cross-pressured voting, 97–103; incidence of, 86, 38, 40, 154; intentional model of, 96; issue ownership and, 88–90; 1992 elections, 36; policy orientation and, 88
Tocqueville, Alexis de, 165n14
trade relations, 111
Truman, Harry S., 9, 13, 22, 48, 77, 135; Marshall Plan and, 49
Tsongas, Paul, 35
Twelfth Amendment, 3
two-party system, 11, 24, 30, 193; basis of, 85; historical role, 25; nationalization of, 145; New Deal

and, 140; opposition to centralization, 143
two-thirds rule, 145
Tyler, John, 11, 14–17, 31n15, 32n26

unemployment, 62
unified government, 3, 9, 29; accountability under, 53–54; efficiency and effectiveness under, 46–50; majoritarian institutions in, 85; 1992 elections, 1–2; policymaking under, 113–27, 139, 174, 176. *See also* divided government

Van Buren, Martin, 15
Van Riper, Paul, 149
vetoes, presidential, 58n19, 184, 196; Bush, 51, 119; Clinton, 47, 50, 79, 128, 162, 203; effect of, 1; historical, 4, 15, 16, 20; overriding, 16, 19
Vietnam War, 152
Villani, John, 88
voters: African-American, 77; attitudes toward compromise, 64; attitudes toward divided government, 47, 92–94; behavior (under balancing theory), 95–96, 173; as behavioral Madisonians, 105; candidate choice by, 145; for Clinton, 100; contradictory policy preferences,

55, 56, 62, 63, 65, 79, 192; divided government restoration, 41; estrangement, 154, 199; intentions, 92; "investor," 86; issues and, 88–90; nature of choices by, 89, 173, 176; for Perot, 36, 38, 70, 158, 204; plan of, 105; preference for divided government, 4, 96, 136, 182; same-party, 86; satisfaction with government, 55–56; view of political parties, 136, 193

War Powers Act, 78
Washington, George, 196, 197
Wattenberg, Martin P., 183
Ways and Means Committee, 120, 123
welfare reform, 113, 124, 138, 201; party positions, 63, 185
Whigs, 16, 18, 25, 27; economic program, 15; view of presidency, 196, 199
White House Office, 148
Wilson, Woodrow, 13, 22, 141; on political parties, 138; separation of powers critique, 191, 193, 194, 197
Winthrop, Robert, 18
Woford, Harris, 176
women, 63
Woodward, Robert (Bob), 201
World Trade Organization, 132n23
World War II, 11, 28, 49, 135

About the Contributors

Joseph Doherty is a graduate student of political science and a senior research fellow at the Center for the Study of Society and Politics at the University of California, Los Angeles. He is currently working on a study of local party organizations.

Morris P. Fiorina is a professor of government at Harvard University. His works include *Retrospective Voting in American National Elections, The Personal Vote: Constituency Service and Electoral Independence* (winner of the 1988 Richard F. Fenno, Jr., Award), and *Divided Government*.

Peter F. Galderisi is an associate professor of political science at Utah State University. He is coeditor of *The Politics of Realignment: Party Change in the Mountain West*. He has written articles on partisanship and redistricting and is currently coauthoring, with John Petrocik, a text on political parties.

Roberta Q. Herzberg is an associate professor of political science at Utah State University. She has written extensively on health care reform, gender research, and public choice theory, and is coauthoring, with Rick Wilson, a book on institutional analysis.

Gary C. Jacobson is a professor and chair of the Department of Political Science at the University of California, San Diego. His works include *Money in Congressional Elections* (winner of the 1981 Gladys E. Kammerer Award), *The Electoral Origins of Divided Government*, and, with Samuel Kernell, *Strategy and Choice in Congressional Elections*.

239

Peter McNamara is an assistant professor of political science at Utah State University. His research and publications are in the areas of the American founding and the origins of political economy. He is the author of *Political Economy and Statesmanship* (forthcoming).

Sidney M. Milkis is an associate professor and chair of the department of politics at Brandeis University. His works include *The American Presidency: Origins and Development, 1776–1990; The President and the Parties: The Transformation of the American Party System Since the New Deal*; and, with Richard A. Harris, *The Politics of Regulatory Change: A Tale of Two Agencies.*

John R. Petrocik is a professor of political science and director of the Center for the Study of Society and Politics at the University of California, Los Angeles. His works include *Party Coalitions: Realignments and the Decline of the New Deal Party System* and, with Norman H. Nie and Sidney Verba, *The Changing American Voter* (winner of the 1977 Woodrow Wilson Award). He is currently authoring a book on issue ownership.

Leroy N. Rieselbach is a professor of political science at Indiana University. His works include *Congressional Reform: The Changing Modern Congress* and *Congressional Politics: The Evolving Legislative System.* He coedited, with Gerald C. Wright and Lawrence C. Dodd, *Congress and Policy Change.*

Joel H. Silbey is the President White Professor of History at Cornell University. His works include *The Partisan Imperative: The Dynamics of American Politics before the Civil War* and *The American Political Nation, 1838–1893.* He is the editor of *The Congress of the United States: Its Origins and Early Development.*